utah
camping

The essential handbook
for planning & enjoying
your next outdoors trip

guide

Senior writer
Gaylen W. Webb

Contributing writers
Brian Brinkerhoff
Dave Webb
Marcia C. Dibble

UTAHOUTDOORS.COM

Publisher:
Bryan Brandenburg
UtahOutdoors.com
6322 South 3000 East, Suite G-50
Salt Lake City, Utah 84121
801 858-3450
www.UtahOutdoors.com

Senior writer:
Gaylen W. Webb

Editors:
Marcia C. Dibble
Dave Webb

Contributing writers:
Brian Brinkerhoff
Dave Webb
Marcia C. Dibble

Editorial assistants
Benjamin Wagner
Stephen Duncan
Claire Jones

Design:
Cory Maylett,
UtahOutdoors.com

Maps:
Peter Strohmeyer,
MindMeld *works*

Cover photos:
Cheyenne Rouse
Ryan Poore
Collin Turner
Wendell Cheek

Contributing photographers:
Cheyenne Rouse
David Whitten
Wendell Cheek

Printer:
McNaughton & Gunn, Inc.
Saline, Michigan

©2000 UtahOutdoors.com

Printed in the USA.

Library of Congress Catalog Card Number: 00-191194
ISBN: 0-9671738-5-X

Dedication

The *Utah Camping Guide* is dedicated to outdoor enthusiasts of all ages and sizes, who share a common bond of love and appreciation for Utah's magnificent outdoor recreational opportunities.

Acknowledgments

The *Utah Camping Guide* would not be possible without the insight, support, and contributions of Utah Outdoors. Special thanks to Dave Webb and his staff, and publisher Bryan Brandenburg for making the book possible. We also thank the many contributing writers, with special thanks to Brian Brinkerhoff, whose years of camping experience, research, and insight have proven invaluable.

We appreciate the support of the Utah Travel Council, Forest Service, Bureau of Land Management, National Parks Service, Utah Division of Wildlife Resources, Utah State Parks, and other land management agencies; each has added insight to this text. Without their commitment and dedication to our many recreational areas there would be no need for this guide.

We also tip our hats to all who share a love for the Utah outdoors and desire to preserve our rich recreational heritage. It is for them this book was written.

TABLE OF CONTENTS

PREFACE

When I was a boy growing up in southern Utah, the state didn't offer year-round fishing. I used to lie awake at night, counting down the days to the opening of fishing season. Our "opening weekend" camping trip was an annual event, a tradition made sacred by years of excursions to the same hallowed ground — a little bend in the East Fork of the Sevier River, nestled in a canyon below the Boulder Mountains. We considered this our personal camping area. It was relatively undiscovered and we hoped to keep it that way. With no amenities like toilets and running water, there was little to encourage the masses — except nice scenery and great fishing.

We always camped along the stream near an abandoned flour mill. We were tight-lipped if a passerby inquired about the fishing, and offended if anyone encroached on our "camping territory." To discourage would-be "trespassers," we conjured up stories about giant rattlesnakes that could strike from 10 feet away.

It's been 21 years since I left home to start a family of my own. Our traditional camping trips have broadened to other destinations, but the smell of campfire smoke always takes me back in time. I still see my mother frying pancakes on a Coleman stove. I still feel the wooden flutes my dad made for me out of willows, and still hear my older brothers jawing over whose fish was the biggest. I can still hear my sisters complaining about no toilets or running water, and I doubt I'll ever see the Milky Way as bright as it was on those moonless nights when we were supposed to be sleeping, but instead searched the skies for shooting stars, flying saucers, and satellites.

Perhaps you have fond memories of camping trips when you were a youth and want to create some memories for your children. Perhaps you are new to the state and want to know some great places to go camping. Or maybe you are a veteran Utah camper and would prefer we didn't publish this guide because you don't want your secret destination discovered. Then again, maybe your traditional campsite has already been overrun by the masses, so you are looking for a different destination.

Whatever your level of interest, location, age, or size, Utah's camping opportunities beckon you 365 days a year. Whether you regularly head out to one of the state's natural wonders is entirely up to you. Every Utah dawn offers magical wonders to outdoor recreationists, whether in alpine snow, a carpet of wildflowers in spring or summer, or hillsides clothed in autumn's fall foliage. Adventures unfold daily in the backcountry. And if you don't mind spreading your wings a little farther, some great opportunities exist just outside the Utah borders. We couldn't resist including some notes about the Grand Canyon in Arizona, Great Basin National Park in Nevada, Yellowstone National Park in Wyoming, the Grand Tetons in Wyoming, and the beautiful wilderness of the Wind River Mountains in Wyoming.

While our camping opportunities are vast, our natural resources are not unlimited. We hope this guide will help expand your camping experiences, deepen your appreciation for the state's natural resources, and instill a desire to preserve them for future generations.

May all your days be filled with new adventures!

Gaylen W. Webb
Senior writer

INTRODUCTION

With over 7,000 improved campsites and virtually unlimited primitive camping in the state, it was a significant endeavor just to list the many camping opportunities within the state of Utah. However, we believe you deserve more than just a campground list. To be a real "guide," we've made this book functional, authoritative, and informative for both the novice and experienced camper alike.

The guide is organized into four parts. In Part One you will find a suggested camper's code of ethics and important information about selecting your camping destination, planning your adventure, camping with children, camping opportunities for seniors and the disabled, and the best sites for reunions.

Part Two highlights various camping opportunities according to the type of experience you are looking for (backpacking, boat camping, pack trips by horse, bicycling, pack trips by ATV, trailer camping, and winter camping).

In Part Three we discuss planning tips, the advantages and disadvantages of using global positioning systems (GPS) and topographical maps, cooking equipment, other useful camping gear, and safety issues, including treating water. It also includes our master list for first aid and our suggested camping list.

Part Four encompasses the Regional Campground Directory, Appendix and Index. Because there are numerous private campgrounds and RV parks, we have included many within the directory. However, inclusion or exclusion of a private campground or RV park does not constitute an endorsement or indicate disapproval by the authors or publisher. We have tried to make our listings as comprehensive as possible.

The state's campgrounds are listed alphabetically by region in the Regional Campground Directory, with state and federal sites listed first, followed by private sites. Each campground listing contains a complete list of facilities and accommodations available, but we have also used the following symbols in the directory to provide you information at a glance on what we considered the top six features of interest:

- ⚰ Drinking water
- ⌗ Group sites
- ♿ Handicap facilities
- 🚐 RV sites
- 🚿 Showers
- 🚻 Toilets

Maps. To make the *Utah Camping Guide* easier to use, we have divided the state into regions. Each section of the Campground Directory includes a map of its region, highlighting major areas (such as national and state parks). For greater detail, we have also included separate maps of each major area.

We have made every attempt to make this book as accurate as possible. If the *Utah Camping Guide* should still prove to be less than complete, or contain inaccuracies, any oversights brought to our attention will be gratefully received and acknowledged.

Camping can be a wonderful outdoor experience for people of all ages, but outdoor activities are, by their very nature, potentially dangerous. Although many hazards and difficulties have been addressed in this guide, the text does not cover all potential threats or hazards you might encounter. No text can substitute for common sense, intelligent decision-making, and respect for nature. Camp wisely, obey all laws, and follow the advice of local agencies, trail signs, and other resources. Watch for potential hazards and dangers that may exist — especially changing weather conditions, wild animals, and dangerous terrain.

PART ONE: A CAMPING OVERVIEW

A Camper's Code of Ethics

ONE OF THE BASIC TENETS of camping ideology is to escape the crowds and pressures of daily life and be "free from it all." Being told what to do while camping doesn't set well with most recreationists. However, as the camping populace increases, to preserve the resources we enjoy for future generations it is necessary that we all abide by some fundamental camping ethics. The following ethics we suggest are fairly benign, requiring little additional effort on the part of the camper, but if adopted would go a long way to preserve our resources and make camping pleasurable for those who follow after you.

Quiet Times

For many recreationists, camping is an opportunity to get away from the city noise, pollution, work pressure, etc. Since many developed camping areas have designated quiet times, noise during those times should be kept to a minimum. Generators and loud activities should be silenced at these times, allowing others to sleep in peace or enjoy the sounds of wind and wildlife, crickets, frogs, or a babbling brook. Be respectful of others at all times by keeping radios and other noise to a minimum.

Leave No Trace

We all lose when recreational areas are trashed. As the Utah population grows and larger numbers of new recreationists visit our natural resources, it is increasingly important to share the principles of preservation and instill in others a greater understanding of the critical role we play in our natural environment.

Each wildflower that is picked reduces the brilliance of the landscape and limits the number of seeds for next year's display. Vandalism is extremely difficult to erase from trees and rocks, thus reducing the pristine experience we all seek to enjoy. Wandering off designated paths increases erosion, scars the land, and increases sediment in the waterways, which reduces fishing opportunities.

The "Leave No Trace" ideology promotes seven principles to help us enjoy the outdoors while showing respect and appreciation for the wilds:

1. Plan Ahead and Prepare

Effective trip planning and preparation helps recreationists achieve trip goals safely and enjoyably while minimizing damage to natural and cultural resources. Poorly prepared campers, confronted with unexpected situations, often resort to high-impact solutions that degrade the outdoors or put themselves at risk. Poor planning often results in high-risk travel because the recreationist failed to obtain information about geography and weather. Poor planning encourages improperly located campsites, campfires, and needless trash removal problems.

2. Travel and Camp on Durable Surfaces

Damage to land occurs when surface vegetation or communities of organisms are trampled. The resulting barren area leads to soil erosion, decreased wildlife habitat, unusable trails and poor camping conditions.

Should you concentrate activity or spread your group out? In high-use areas, campers should gently concentrate activity. Use trails whenever possible and select campsites so heavily used that further damage is unlikely. In areas of very little or no use, campers should gently spread out. Take different paths when hiking off-trail to avoid creating new trails that cause erosion. When camping, disperse tents and cooking equipment and move camp regularly to avoid creating permanent-looking campsites.

Minimize alterations to the natural surroundings. Do not dig tent trenches or build lean-tos, tables or chairs. Avoid hammering nails into trees, hacking at them with hatchets or saws, or damaging bark and roots by tying horses to trees for extended periods. If you clear an area of rocks or twigs, replace these items before leaving. At high-impact sites it is appropriate to clean the site and dismantle user-built facilities, such as multiple fire rings and log seats or tables. Good campsites are found rather than made.

3. Dispose of Waste Properly

Avoid littering our magnificent landscape. Trash plagues all recreational areas, including streams, reservoirs, hiking trails, campgrounds, and vehicle pullout areas. "Pack It In, Pack It Out" is the slogan for all ethical campers. This common saying is an effective way to encourage visitors to take their trash home with them. Trash and litter detract from an area's natural beauty. The essentials of the "Pack It In, Pack It Out" mentality include:

a. Be responsible for your litter and the litter of those in your group. Bring enough garbage bags to pack out all the trash that will result from your trip.

b. Encourage, through your example, other outdoor users to accept responsibility for their refuse.

c. Bring an extra garbage bag and pack out trash left by others. Leave the area better than you found it.

d. When visiting an area with garbage cans, make sure the container's lid is tightly closed after depositing your trash. Your noble efforts to properly dispose of trash could be wasted because varmints or the wind can quickly unload your newly deposited garbage.

e. Properly dispose of what you can't pack out. Body waste, wastewater, food scraps, and anything that can't be packed out should be buried. Prevent the concentration of solid and liquid wastes near natural water sources. Use biodegradable soap. Dispose of dishwater far away from springs, streams, and lakes. Minimize the need to pack out food scraps by carefully planning meals. Proper disposal of human waste prevents the spread of disease and exposure to others, and speeds decomposition. Catholes dug 6 to 8 inches deep and 200 feet from water are often the most practical and environmentally sound ways to dispose of feces.

A couple set up their tent at an established camping area in a Utah forest.

4. Leave What You Find

Allow others a sense of discovery. Leave rocks, plants, archaeological artifacts and other natural objects undisturbed where you found them.

5. Minimize Campfire Impacts

Some people would not think of camping without a campfire. But the naturalness of many areas has been degraded by overuse of fires and an increasing demand for firewood. Lightweight camp stoves are essential for low-impact camping and are a better alternative to fires. Stoves are convenient and efficient, and reduce the requirement for firewood as a campsite selection concern. If the kids have to roast marshmallows on an open fire, when considering the location of a fire pit, choose an area with the least potential for damage to the environment. The best place to build a fire is within an existing fire ring in a well-placed campsite. Choose not to have a fire in areas with little wood, in heavily used areas, or in desert settings. True "Leave No Trace" fires show no evidence of having ever been constructed.

6. Respect Wildlife

Maintain respect for wildlife at all times to ensure all parties remain safe and happy. Remember that you are a guest in their home when you visit. Harassment of wildlife is dangerous and illegal.

7. Be Considerate of Other Visitors

Be courteous to others. Allow others to enjoy the outdoor experiences they seek in their limited recreational time. This includes respecting other's space, keeping noise to a minimum, and maintaining a friendly demeanor to passersby.

Let's Go Camping!

Utah's recreational opportunities are unsurpassed. Few other states can compare to the variety of camping opportunities within the Utah landscape: alpine camping in the Uinta highlands or one of the many other high mountain ranges; desert camping among the cacti and Manzanita brush of Utah's red rock country; boat camping on Lake Powell, Flaming Gorge, or one of the many other lakes and reservoirs; primitive camping in a wilderness area, or a more civilized put-in at one of the state's five national parks or six national forests.

SO MANY CHOICES

With so many camping opportunities available, one of the most difficult aspects of Utah camping can be deciding where to go. The *Utah Camping Guide* was written to help you get "there," wherever "there" is.

Utah features six national forests with over 194 campgrounds and more than 5,400 campsites within the U.S. Forest Service system. Our national recreation areas and several of our national monuments also offer outstanding camping possibilities. The state also boasts five national parks, each of which offers its own camping opportunities:

- Arches National Park
- Bryce Canyon National Park
- Canyonlands National Park
- Capitol Reef National Park
- Zion National Park

Utah State Parks offers more than 1,600 campsites in 29 of 45 recreational areas, with variety for almost every taste. From Bear Lake's cool, blue waters in the north to the warm sands of the Coral Pink Sand Dunes in the south, Utah State Parks offers unique camping experiences throughout the entire year.

CAMPGROUND SELECTION

The easiest way to narrow your campground selection is to first determine what you want to do there: fish, hike, mountain bike, boat, raft, etc. Some areas, like the national parks, lend themselves more to hiking than fishing. Other camping areas offer both. Many of the camping areas require that you make a reservation or buy a permit to camp there. Limits on length of stay may vary as well, so make sure you inquire when you look into reservations.

Next, determine what amenities you want in your preferred campsite. Amenities will vary from campground to campground. Do you want an improved campsite with barbecue grills, running water and toilets? Or would you prefer an unimproved campground with only a fire pit. (Beware: Some campgrounds don't allow open pit fires.) Some facilities may even include hot showers and full utility hookups. The Regional Campground Directory later in this book lists the amenities available at each campground.

Top 14 Camping Areas in the State

What are the top camping areas in the state? That all depends on your point of view. To some it might be a remote site in the wilderness of Zion National Park, with no amenities and few other campers. To another it might be a put-in with an RV hookup, or running water, showers, and flush toilets. At the risk of being called biased, blind, or outright wrong by those who read this guide, we put together the following list of what we consider the state's top 14 camping areas. Why 14? Well, we started out trying to list the top 10, but couldn't stop there. Our list was not determined by any scientific or statistical data, just the following criteria:

- Scenery
- Accessibility
- Things to do there
- Amenities

Some of the sites may meet all four criteria, some three or two, some just one. They were all included because they are exceptional in at least one of the criteria. Please note that many of the areas listed require an entrance fee or permit.

Boulder Mountain

One of the largest high-elevation plateaus in the United States, Boulder Mountain is dotted with numerous lakes, excellent scenery and unlimited primitive camping opportunities. Part of the Dixie National Forest, the Boulders are laced by thousands of miles of dirt roads that are excellent for four-wheel-drive and off-highway vehicles. The Boulders are also excellent for pack trips by horse or llama. Several outfitters and guides offer pack trips into the Boulder backcountry. Four improved campgrounds are located on the east side of the mountain range, south of Teasdale. However, the campground at Lower Bown Reservoir has no culinary water.

Mirror Lake/Hwy. 150

Hwy. 150 from Kamas to Evanston, Wyo., offers numerous camping opportunities along the west side of the Uinta Mountains. These campgrounds are very popular, so if you want to obtain a campsite, reserve it early. Mirror Lake Campground is one of the most popular along Hwy. 150. At an elevation of 10,000 feet, you have ample opportunity to breathe in some clear alfresco. Fish the lake by boat or from shore, or hike one of the nature trails. There is plenty to do in this beautiful alpine setting.

Coral Pink Sand Dunes State Park

Coral Pink Sand Dunes State Park offers spectacular contrasts of red rock cliffs, blue skies, juniper and pinyon pine trees, and a sweeping 3,000-acre expanse of sand dunes. The park is perfect for camping and off-highway vehicles. Facilities include 22 camping units, modern restrooms, showers, a sanitary disposal station, and a resident park ranger. The park is located about 22 miles northwest of Kanab in the southern part of the state.

Goblin Valley State Park

At one time Goblin Valley was recommended as a national monument. While it was never designated as such, it was designated as a state park by Utah Parks and Recreation. Located 35 miles northwest of Hanksville in the southeastern part of the state, Goblin Valley is a favorite because of its geological wonders — scores of intricately eroded creatures, haunting rocks and coves. Off-highway vehicle enthusiasts prefer the area because adjacent to the park there are hundreds of miles of dirt roads to explore. Facilities include a 21-unit campground, modern restrooms, hot showers, and a sanitary disposal station. Water is limited, however, so bring plenty.

PHOTO: CHEYENNE ROUSE

A site beneath sandstone castles in Goblin Valley.

Jordanelle State Park

The Rock Cliff campground at Jordanelle offers a wonderful variety of wildlife viewing and scenery for the visitor, along with a boardwalk trail system and plenty of fishing opportunities nearby. Located along the Provo River just before it enters Jordanelle Reservoir, this scenic camping area offers recreational opportunities to visitors year-round. Campsites are set back away from the parking areas. Carts are available to pack your camping gear to and from your vehicle. A gentle trail system was designed to help you reach your campsite with little effort. Ambitious beavers frequent the area, and considerable evidence of their handiwork abounds among the trees along the river. Be careful of high water in the Provo River during the spring as the snow melts in the upper drainage.

Lake Powell/Glen Canyon National Recreation Area

Lake Powell is a boating mecca for recreationists from all over the country. With thousands of miles of shoreline, the lake is unsurpassed for boat camping. There's plenty of opportunity to enjoy solitude on some lonely beach. However, the developed campgrounds and facilities are superb, albeit crowded on summer weekends. Opportunities abound for all kinds of water sports, including boating, skiing, jet skiing, and even kayaking. Fishing is exceptional from April through October. In wintertime, the temperament of the lake changes: it is moody, often stormy, even threatening... but always beautiful. Many consider the lonely winter scenery to be Powell's best.

Skyline Drive

This narrow roadway, mostly bumpy dirt, begins at Hwy. 6 in Spanish Fork Canyon and follows the ridgelines south to I-70 in Salina Canyon. It's a rough and tumble ride, requiring four-wheel-drive in places. Along the way it passes through beautiful forest and past scenic alpine lakes, and provides incredible views in every direction. There are marvelous primitive camping opportunities along the roadway on top of the mountains, and very nice developed campgrounds along streams or adjacent to lakes in many area canyons.

American Fork Canyon

Called the "Alpine Loop," American Fork Canyon offers extraordinary mountain vistas reminiscent of the Swiss Alps. In the fall, the autumn foliage is spectacular. However, because it is so popular, the canyon has been turned into a fee area. Even to drive the loop requires a fee — unless you don't plan to stop for sightseeing. There are many campgrounds available. Opportunities for scenic viewing and photography are abundant: waterfalls, rugged terrain, glacial snow, and wildflowers. Timpanogos Cave National Monument is located in the canyon, offering a great hike and an interesting tour through the cave. Cascade Springs Scenic Highway, a 7.5-mile paved road off of the Alpine Loop, offers additional camping opportunities and great sightseeing. At the Cascade Springs Interpretive Site, large springs of water cascade down the mountain in a series of limestone terraces and pools. Boardwalks wind through the area allowing for wildlife viewing.

Zion National Park

Towering canyon walls and sculpted monolithic mountains await you at Zion National Park. However, the Zion Canyon scenic drive has become so popular the National Park Service has restricted private vehicle access severely, instead offering mass transit into the area. Cars must be parked in Springdale or at the park Visitor Center, with a shuttle providing transportation into the canyon. There are two campgrounds in the park; both are open all year. South Campground is open on a first-come, first-served basis. Watchman Campground is available by reservation from April 15 through October. Both offer tent and trailer sites, RV hookups and flush toilets. If you want to camp in the backcountry you must obtain a backcountry permit and pay the fee at the visitor center. The park also features a lodge and restaurant. Zion National Park is located east of St. George in the southwest corner of the state.

Currant Creek Reservoir and Recreation Area

Located 40 miles southeast of Heber City, Currant Creek offers a beautiful campground with 103 units. The campground is surrounded by pines and aspen. Facilities include culinary water and modern restrooms. Currant Creek Reservoir offers great fishing, and there are numerous hiking and horseback riding trails. The Forest Service has provided special campground facilities to keep riding stock.

Bear Lake State Park

One of the deepest lakes in the state, Bear Lake is nestled in the Rocky Mountains on the border of Utah and Idaho. Its deep blue waters are loved by outdoor enthusiasts of all types. The lake offers waterskiing, swimming, scuba diving, sailing, and fishing for record cutthroat, mackinaw, and whitefish. Bear Lake's Rendezvous Beach on the south shore offers 136 campsites — 46 with utility hookups, modern restrooms, and hot showers. The wide, sandy beach provides excellent camping, picnicking and watercraft activity, and is a popular area for family reunions. Bear Lake Marina also has 13 campsites, a group pavilion, disposal station, modern restrooms, hot showers, and a visitor center. Six primitive campgrounds are available on the east side of the lake (bring your own drinking water).

Snow Canyon State Park

Because of southern Utah's moderate winter climate, Snow Canyon is a popular spring and fall destination. Red and white sandstone cliffs capped by black lava rock offer excellent hiking, camping and photographic opportunities. Facilities include a 35-unit campground, modern restrooms, hot showers, electric hookups, a sewage disposal station and a covered group-use pavilion. Snow Canyon State Park is located 11 miles northwest of St. George, in the southwest corner of the state.

Bryce Canyon National Park

The result of monumental interplay between earth, water and time, Bryce Canyon is an enchanting destination with uncommon beauty. Unfortunately, millions have discovered that beauty. Spring, summer and fall are the most popular times to visit the park. You can hike or horseback ride the many trails. Cross-country skiing and snowshoeing are popular in the winter at the park. Bryce offers two campgrounds and a lodge. The campgrounds have more than 200 campsites, but do not offer RV hookups. Campsites are available on a first-come, first-served basis. Weekends and holidays are generally the most difficult time to find an open campsite. No firewood gathering is allowed, so bring your own wood for campfires.

Smith and Morehouse Reservoir

For alpine camping in close proximity to the Wasatch Front, you won't find anything prettier than the campsites at Smith and Morehouse Reservoir. It's just far enough away to be "away," yet it doesn't take "forever" to get there. The campground features 34 units, culinary water, toilets, and handicapped facilities. The reservoir offers great fishing, while the surrounding mountains offer plenty of hiking opportunities. Smith and Morehouse Reservoir and campground are located east of Kamas.

Top 12 Spots for Family Reunions

Utah offers some excellent put-ins for family reunions and group camping. Be aware that weekends and holidays are most popular among recreationists. If your preferred destination requires a reservation, make it early. If no reservation is required, send a few people to your destination early to stake your claim. Otherwise, there might not be a site available when you arrive.

- Kodachrome Basin State Park
- Jordanelle Reservoir and State Park
- Flaming Gorge/Green River
- Lake Powell/Glen Canyon National Recreation Area
- Mirror Lake/Hwy. 150
- Bryce Canyon National Park
- Fish Lake
- Payson Lakes
- Moon Lake
- Currant Creek Reservoir
- Bear Lake State Park
- Zion National Park

PHOTO: CHEYENNE ROUSE

A group camping site in Zion National Park.

Top 5 Spots for Senior Citizens or the Disabled

- Currant Creek
- Jordanelle State Park
- American Fork Canyon (Little Mill Campground has units reserved for individuals with disabilities)
- Zion National Park

Utah resources for more information on recreation for elders and individuals with disabilities include:

■ The Salt Lake City-area SPLORE (Special Populations Learning Outdoor Recreation and Education), which plans trips for special populations into the outdoors, including cross-country ski/sledding lessons, half-day tours and overnight adventures to individuals with disabilities and special needs. (801) 484-4128, or www.xmission.com/~splore/splore.htm

■ The National Ability Center in Park City, which provides sports and recreational programs including water skiing, horseback riding, fishing, outdoor education trips, cycling and swimming for individuals with disabilities and their families (435) 649-3991, or www.utahrec.com/nac/

■ Salt Lake County sponsors an adaptive recreation program. (801) 561-0075.

■ Out of Orem, SPORT Tours specializes in recreational tours and trips for people with disabilities. (801) 225-8540.

■ The Great Outdoor Recreation Pages site www.gorp.com/gorp/eclectic/disabled.htm allows users to review trails and read others' reviews, and features an excellent article on specific facilities at Zion National Park.

■ For more information on southwestern Utah (Zion, Cedar Breaks, Bryce Canyon, etc.) the St. George area independent-living center, Red Rock Center for Independents, has more details on area facilities. (800) 649-2340.

■ The DRM Regional Resource Directory offers a plethora of other links for seniors and people with disabilities: www.disabilityresources.org/UTAH.html

■ For other numbers and some specifics on facilities throughout the state, the Access Utah Network is the statewide information and referral contact for disability-related issues. (800) 333-8824, or www.accessut.state.ut.us/csd.html

Camping with Children

The magic of camping with children comes to those who forget the destination and focus on the journey. Meander with your children along a trail through a solitary grove of quaking aspen, noticing the birds, bugs, and berries. It will awaken your own senses to the incredible beauty around you, and help your children discover nature. Your youngsters will learn that the woods are alive as they catch their first fish, see a deer, hike through a field of breathtaking wildflowers, or listen to the night sounds of frogs, crickets, owls, and coyotes.

Many of the following tips are provided for families taking youngsters on their first camping experience, although some tips are appropriate for family campers of all skill levels.

Plan together. To motivate and excite everyone, you will need to plan your excursion together, from pulling out the maps, guides, and brochures, to making campground reservations, determining activities, and checking gear. Part of the fun is simply deciding where to go and the anticipation that builds as the trip draws near.Allow your children to participate at a level they can handle, giving them a sense of accomplishment and being part of the decision-making group. Initially, it may not lessen your load, but as you educate them, eventually they will be able to take on much of the preparation burden, providing them with additional self-respect. Let them help decide where to go, what to eat, and what to do when you arrive at camp. Allowing each member to contribute will help the family function better as a team.

Prepare them before heading out. Backyard camping is a great way to teach your children how to set up their own tents, use camp gear properly, and avoid accidents. Setting up camp behind your house will allow them to become familiar with sleeping in a tent, while sparking an interest in the fun activities camping can offer. Bring plenty of snacks and games for the nighttime activities. Spend time as a family to give them an idea of what to expect for the real outing.

Familiarize them with the outdoors. Youth that have trouble with camping are sometimes intimidated by the unfamiliar surroundings and unprepared for the uniqueness of the experience. Try an after-work hike, a marshmallow roast, or an evening fishing trip in a day-use area of a nearby canyon. Short day excursions are also great opportunities where your children can learn about the dangers of fire, swift water, and steep drop-offs. Teach them which plants to avoid, and what to do if they get lost. Mini adventures after work will help your youngsters develop a feeling for the outdoors and eliminate many fears they might have about their first camping adventure.

Bring extra gear. Always remember that with children, clothing will get wet and dirty. Bring plenty of extra clothing to help them stay warm, dry, and comfortable. Once children become uncomfortable, everyone will know it. Don't forget warmer clothing to ward off the night chill and warm sleeping bags for comfortable rest.

Gear designed for children is also important to consider. Bring gear that specifically meets their needs, including time-release insect repellents. DEET, the most effective insect repellent available, can be a significant concern for parents of younger users. To address this concern, many manufacturers are now offering time-release products that minimize overall exposure yet provide an effective repellent to mosquitoes and other pesky insects. Other natural formulations are available on the market, with varying degrees of effectiveness. Look for sunscreen with a high level of protection from the sun's harmful rays. Don't forget medicines in appropriate strengths, bandages, hats, and additional protective clothing for inclement weather.

Allow younger children to bring a few select toys, teddy bears or games. Avoid the temptation to bring too many or you can guarantee that parts will be lost and clutter will become a problem. A small daypack for each child may be the answer for some families. Inside the pack, youngsters should include a personal stash of snacks, safety gear, and extra clothing.

The night can be frightening for some little ones, but when empowered with their own personal flashlight, they will have some control of the darkness that surrounds camp. Coleman has also recently released a remote controlled nightlight for late night "nature calls" and visiting critters.

Bring plenty of snacks. Trail mix, jerky, apples, and cookies are certainly part of the experience for many campers. Take food your family likes to eat. Just because you are camping, you don't have to eat bird food. If your children like trail mix and the assorted dried foods that go along with it, great. If not, let them acquire a taste for it as they grow. Your family will be happier if they are fed well.

Bring a camera. Collect the memories as you make them. Photograph the first fish, the family campsite, a water fight, or the day hike destination. Your family will savor these moments when they are grown. Bringing a camera will also help keep the fondest memories fresh when it comes time to plan your next camping excursion.

Keep first trips short. Keep your first campout short. It is always better to bring them home before they are ready to go, leaving them hungry for more. Spending too much time on a first trip may make them a little tired and cranky, ending the vacation on a less than happy moment. By keeping trips short, it is easier to plan, keep everyone's energy up, and leave on a good note. In addition, less food and gear is required, reducing the possibility of leaving something home. Make travel brief. Try to break up the monotony of the travel with frequent stops. Play car games to keep the children entertained. Plan some games in advance so you will not be stymied when they get bored.

Have backup plans. If fishing is slow and attention spans are short, have a backup plan to keep your children interested. Whether you plan a short nature hike or a game of cards, stay a step ahead of your children and prevent boredom for younger family members. In addition, remind them of planned future activities, to build anticipation and excitement. Many youth are more than willing to help prepare upcoming campfire programs or marshmallow roasts. Allow them to be part of the action.

Teach them respect. Respect for Mother Nature may help save a child's life. Skills acquired in the outdoors will last a lifetime. These skills include what to do if you get lost, how to start a fire, catching and cleaning fish, and identifying wildlife.

In addition, respect for the outdoors will help preserve the beauty that you enjoy for other generations to follow. When teaching youth about the outdoors, we also learn more about ourselves. Outdoor ethics are easy to teach when they are young, when they look to role models, like yourself, in this unknown beautiful world.

PHOTO: CHEYENNE ROUSE

A young hiker watches a llama graze in the Wind River area of Wyoming.

24 great destinations to take children

The destinations listed below were selected for their scenery, available activities, and facilities:

Northern Utah
- Jordanelle Reservoir and State Park (Hailstone campground)
- American Fork Canyon
- Tony Grove Lake
- Mirror Lake
- Bear Lake State Park
- Antelope Island State Park
- Nebo Loop
- Smith and Morehouse Reservoir
- Currant Creek Reservoir
- Hobble Creek Canyon
- Mill Hollow

Eastern Utah
- Flaming Gorge/Green River

Central Utah
- Fish Lake
- Skyline Drive

Southeastern Utah
- Canyonlands National Park
- Glen Canyon National Recreation Area

Southwestern Utah
- Capitol Reef National Park
- Yankee Meadow Reservoir (up Parowan Canyon near Vermillion Castle)
- Red Cliff
- Zion National Park
- Navajo Lake
- Bryce Canyon National Park
- Snow Canyon State Park

PHOTO: WENDELL CHEEK

A moose drinks in Yellowstone National Park.

Over-the-Border Destinations

If you have had your fill of Utah camping destinations and want to cross some borders, Wyoming, Idaho, Arizona and Nevada offer great camping opportunities within a reasonable drive from Utah's Wasatch Front.

Destinations to consider include: Yellowstone National Park, the Wind River Mountains, Grand Canyon National Park, Grand Teton National Park, and Great Basin National Park. Interstate sites such as Flaming Gorge and Glen Canyon are listed in the Utah regional campground directory. Specific campground information on these out-of-state sites are in the Over-the-Border Destinations section after the Utah regions.

Grand Canyon National Park. This is a must-see destination, whether you just want to stand on the rim and take in the incredible views or put on your hiking boots and make an extended trek into the backcountry. The south rim has the largest number of developed facilities, with three nice campgrounds. It also attracts the most people. The north rim offers one developed campground, and perhaps the most spectacular vistas on earth.

Grand Teton National Park. On the way to or from Yellowstone, take some time to enjoy the scenery of Grand Teton National Park. In 1929 Congress created the park to preserve its spectacular values. This area was originally considered for an expansion of Yellowstone. All five campgrounds of Grand Teton National Park are first-come, first-served. Jenny Lake campground is for tents only and usually fills by 8 a.m. The four other campgrounds will accommodate tents, trailers and RVs, but there are no utility hookups; Signal Mountain usually fills by 10 a.m. Reservations are available for groups of 10 or more by mail. Park concessionaires also host trailer villages at Colter Bay and Flagg Ranch. Reservations for the village at Colter Bay can be made at (800) 628-9928; for Flagg Ranch, at (800) 443-2311. Camping in the backcountry requires a permit and you may camp only in designated campsites. The maximum stay at Jenny Lake campground is seven days. The maximum stay at any National Park Service campground is14 days.

Great Basin National Park. The youngest of our nation's national parks, Great Basin National Park is located in Nevada near the Utah/Nevada border west from Delta. The national park was set aside by President Reagan in 1986. The park has six campgrounds. Amenities include water (in summer), restrooms, fire rings, and picnic tables. There are primitive campgrounds along Shoshone Creek and Snake Creek that have tables and pit toilets, but no water. Only Lower Lehman Campground is open year-round. The other campgrounds and primitive sites open as snow levels permit.

Seminoe State Park. This large reservoir, located in southern Wyoming, is a popular destination for camping, fishing, and water sports. The state park campgrounds are very nice, and there are several other camping opportunities in the area.

Wind River Mountains. This Wyoming area offers world-class opportunities for backpacking and fishing. It is similar to Utah's High Uintas, with miles of trails probing into the wilderness, and countless lakes and streams teeming with fish. Developed campgrounds are located at several access points.

Yellowstone. The first national park to be created, Yellowstone offers remarkable diversity in geology, birds, mammals, and fish. With more than two million acres of steaming geysers, crystalline lakes, towering waterfalls, and majestic vistas, it's no wonder people come from around the world to visit the park. Yellowstone has 12 park campgrounds, seven of which are open on a first-come, first-served basis. Five campgrounds, with 1,750 RV and tent sites, may be reserved in advance by calling AmFac Parks and Resorts, (307) 344-7311. Fishing Bridge has 341 RV sites with full hookups.

Most of the campgrounds have tables, fire grills, drinking water, garbage cans, and flush or pit toilets. Lewis Lake, Slough Creek and the reservable campgrounds offer accessible campsites and restrooms for persons with disabilities.

Because of bears, food should be stored in vehicles or the bear-proof lockers provided at some campsites.

PART TWO: A PLETHORA OF CAMPING OPPORTUNITIES

WHATEVER YOUR MODE OF LOCOMOTION, a camping destination awaits you. Primitive camp in an undeveloped campground, camp along a ridge in a backcountry location, backpack into a remote location and pitch your tent, or try some exotic camping by boat, ATV, 4x4, ski, or mountain bike.

BACKPACKING

There is something inherently satisfying about backpacking, about challenging nature face to face, depending solely on supplies and equipment carried on your own back. When backpacking, you revert to a primeval, basic existence, living on simple foods, carrying your shelter with you, depending on fire for your safety and comfort. It is a refreshing step back from our modern society.

Pack animals can make a trip more comfortable and enjoyable able by allowing you to bring more and heavier gear — more of the comforts of home. They can also make longer trips possible, by carrying enough supplies to support an extended stay. For more details, see the section in the book on horse and llama packing.

Popular destinations

High Uintas Wilderness: This is a beautiful, high mountain area with heavy forest and hundreds of lakes full of feisty trout. The spectacular scenery is a major draw, along with the excellent fishing. Treks can range from a few miles to 50 miles or more. King's Peak, the highest point in Utah, is a major destination.

Boulder Mountain: Another high mountain area with heavy forest and numerous lakes that offer good fishing. In addition to the mountain scenery, many trails provide views of Capitol Reef National Park or the Escalante Canyons areas.

Zion Park backcountry: Many people consider Zion Park to be one of the most scenic areas on earth. Zion Canyon attracts thousands of visitors every week during warm weather months, but far fewer people visit the backcountry. Still, backpacking is becoming very popular here. Permits are required to control visitation and reduce impact on the land. The Virgin River Narrows and Kolob Arch are popular destinations.

Capitol Reef backcountry: This is desert country cut by rugged canyons. Arches, slot canyons, pinnacles, and other rocky monuments are abundant here. This is a great place to get away from the crowds.

San Rafael Swell: Similar to Capitol Reef, with spectacular canyons, including some of the tightest slots around. Some destinations feature relics from Native American, cowboy, outlaw and mining history. Wild horses still roam in some areas. Open mines here can be dangerous.

Wasatch Mountains: The canyons in these mountains are close to our largest cities, yet a world apart. Drive for a few minutes, hike for a few more, and you can leave the crowds behind and find peace and solitude in scenic surroundings. The mountain peaks offer unparalleled vistas and numerous small lakes provide fishing opportunities.

Escalante Canyons: These are extremely scenic but very rugged canyons along the Escalante River, between Boulder Mountain and Lake Powell. These canyons are most appropriate for experienced backpackers.

Common mistakes

Carrying a pack that is too heavy. Pack weight should be proportional to body size and strength, starting at about 20 pounds for younger children and ranging up to about 60 pounds for strong adults.

Trying to go too far in a day. Adults who are not in great shape, or groups with children, should plan to hike only five to eight miles a day. Strong backpackers can go 12 miles or more, depending on the terrain and the weight of their packs.

Getting lost. It's easy to get lost in the backcountry. Even experienced backpackers can get turned around, if they aren't careful. Take a few precautions to avoid trouble. Carry a detailed map that shows your destination and the surrounding area. Study the map so you know the lay of the land and major landmarks. Don't move from one drainage to another unless you really know what you are doing. Tell someone where you are going and when you expect to be back.

Using poor-quality gear. When backpacking, every ounce counts. Good sleeping bags and tents are essential. They must be small and lightweight, yet fully functional. Boots must fit properly and be broken in. Problems with gear can make your stay uncomfortable and even dangerous.

BICYCLE CAMPING

Without a doubt, one of the fastest growing sports of the last decade is cycling. More people are enjoying Utah's diverse cycling opportunities than in any other state. It is a natural to create new camping opportunities by combining the best of Utah's exploding biking with the peace and serenity of Utah's spectacular scenery. Whether you prefer your tires fat and knobby or slick and skinny, you can find exciting camping options from Bear Lake to the Grand Staircase; from Dinosaur National Monument to Great Basin National Park.

Popular destinations

When you think of biking in Utah, the first place that comes to mind is Moab. Moab is at the hub of many biking adventures. Stay in any of the numerous accommodations and do day trips to such famed locales as the 10-mile Slickrock Trail, Klondike Bluffs, Bull Canyon, Porcupine Rim, and Poison Spider Mesa. Moab is also the preferred jumping-off point for Canyonlands and Arches national parks. Arches does not allow off-road biking but does have spectacular opportunities along its surface road system. More dedicated biker/campers should investigate the White Rim Trail in Canyonlands. This challenging route covers 100 miles of red rock scenery climbing from 1,500 feet below Island In The Sky Mesa to 1,000 feet above the Green and Colorado rivers — a two- to four-day trip. Trail of the Ancients, kicking off from Blanding, provides road riders a 150-mile ride and the beauty of scenery as diverse as Natural Bridges National Monument and the San Juan River. Henderson Lake Loop and Twisted Forest are among the popular trails near Brian Head (north of Cedar Breaks and south of Parowan), which hosts a winter ski resort that also opens up to mountain biking in the summer. Remember, there are specific regulations regarding national parks, forests, and monuments — understand them. Also, red rock biking means carrying your own water — lots of it.

PHOTO: CHEYENNE ROUSE

A group of mountain bikers prepares to set out in Canyonlands National Park.

Southern Utah isn't the only location for worthwhile riding. Sections of the Great Western Trail and Skyline Drive provide unequaled alpine bike camping in northern Utah and can be accessed from Ogden, Bountiful, and several points in Salt Lake City. A lesser-known but beautiful ride can be found starting at Pineview Reservoir and heading east on Hwy. 39 up the South Fork of the Ogden River to Causey Reservoir. The 60-mile ride offers camping and fishing, and could be augmented by a trip to the famed Trappist Monastery for some wonderful honey. Don't pass up a chance to cycle Utah's desert isle — Antelope Island. Divide your day between biking, bison, and bird watching at one of the most important migratory bird habitats in the world. So while you're staring at your bike and your backpack trying to make a choice, throw the saddlebags on the bike and do both!

Resources
• Bicycle Utah: Publishes a state bicycle vacation guide as well as more detailed regional guides. (435) 649-5806, web site: www.bicycleutah.com

- Cycling Utah: (801) 268-2652, web site: www.cyclingutah.com
- San Juan County Travel Council: (435) 587-3235, (800) 574-4FUN, web site: www.canyonlands-utah.com
- Grand County Travel Council: (435) 259-8825, (800) 635--MOAB, web site: www.canyonlands-utah.com
- Golden Spike Empire: Info about Great Western Trail and Skyline Trail plus\ other northern Utah destinations. (801) 627-8288, (800) 255-8824, web site: www.ogdencvb.org
- Davis County Tourism: Info about Antelope Island. (801) 451-3286, web site: www.co.davis.ut.us/discoverdavis/

BOAT CAMPING

Load your camping gear into your boat, shove out from the dock and let the waterway serve as your highway to adventure — away from automobiles and asphalt and crowds of screaming people. Several Utah waters provide the opportunity to camp at spots accessible only by boat. The experience can be remarkably serene.

Popular destinations

Lake Powell: This is our premier destination for boat camping, offering more shoreline than America's Pacific coast and countless canyons to explore. On a clear night, away from the marinas, moonlight dances on the water and silhouettes the canyon walls, creating a scene of remarkable beauty. This lake's sandy beaches make ideal playgrounds.

Houseboats are popular here. Rental boats are available at the marinas and provide all the conveniences of a well-equipped RV — soft beds, flush toilets, running water, lights, a stove, etc. However, there are drawbacks to houseboats: they are expensive, you have to reserve them a year or more in advance, they move slowly on the big lake, and they can't navigate some of the narrow canyons. For more details, or to reserve a boat, contact Lake Powell Resorts and Marinas: (800) 528-6154, www.visitlakepowell.com/

Runabout, ski or fishing boats are often used by people beach-camping on the lake's shoreline. They can also be rented from Lake Powell Resorts and Marinas, at the number above. They are much less expensive than houseboats, and may be available with just a few weeks advance notice.

Most of the shoreline at Powell is open for camping. However, campers must bring their own marine toilet or port-a-potty system.

Flaming Gorge: Houseboats are also popular on this large, scenic reservoir. However, the experience is completely different from that offered by Lake Powell. With rocky shorelines, and brush and trees coming down to the water's edge, this reservoir doesn't offer the sandy beaches that make Powell popular. Still, there are plenty of coves where you can tie up a houseboat and enjoy the spectacular scenery and wonderful fishing.

Most people using powerboats or fishing boats prefer to camp in developed campgrounds. There are campgrounds near every marina, and four campgrounds

PHOTO: DAVID WHITTEN

Boaters take in the sights on Lake Powell.

that are accessible only by boat (Kingfisher Island, Hideout, Gooseneck, and Jarvies). All campgrounds are administered by the National Forest Service. For reservations, call (877) 444-6777 (TDD 877-833-6777), or visit: www.reserveusa.com/

Yuba State Park: Sandy beaches and relatively warm water attract campers and boaters to this reservoir. The Oasis campground offers modern facilities at the water's edge. There is a designated primitive camping area at Painted Rocks; primitive camping is also allowed at North, West and East beaches. Reservations can be made by calling the State Parks reservation system: (800) 322-3770.

Starvation State Park: This reservoir is reminiscent of Lake Powell, with sheer cliffs and sandy beaches. The state park campground near the boat ramp is very nice, with modern facilities adjacent to a wonderful beach area. Primitive camping is allowed at designated areas around the reservoir.

Colorado River: Many kinds of boats can operate on the Colorado River in the Moab area, including jet boats, airboats, kayaks, and rafts. Multi-day flat-water floats are possible. Tex's Riverways, (435) 259-5101, will shuttle floaters or paddlers back to town from the lower reaches of the calm-water stretch.

Permits are required to float the famous whitewater stretches (like Cataract and Grand Canyon). Novice rafters are encouraged to schedule a trip with a licensed guide service.

Green River: Desolation Canyon is suitable for multi-day do-it-yourself float trips, with moderate whitewater. Recreation in the canyon is managed by the BLM, and a permit is required to float the river. Call the BLM river office at (435) 636-3622, or visit them on the web: www.blm.gov/utah/price/riverinf.htm

HORSE OR LLAMA PACK TRIPS

Horses and camping have been a part of Utah's outdoor tradition since the first explorers and trappers moved west. Pack trails to the Uinta and Boulder Mountains are well established and can be easily accessed. These trips wind through classic alpine terrain with spectacular mountain vistas and high altitude fishing that typify the best of our state's outdoor opportunities.

Red rock horse camping in the south and southeast are rapidly gaining in popularity and offer experiences for adults as well as children and families. Also gaining in popularity are working ranch trips where participants live the life of a cowboy on the range. Sleeping in canvas tents, eating from a chuck wagon, and living in the saddle are partnered with other western and outdoor activities to provide an unforgettable camping trip.

In an effort to create assisted camping experiences that are less stressful on the environment, llamas are becoming a common sight in backcountry statewide. Llamas, though not capable of carrying the same loads as horses or mules because of soft footpads, are less damaging to sensitive terrain. Children are drawn to the animals and they tend to have pleasant dispositions, creating one more option for an unforgettable camping vacation.

Perhaps the most unique camping experience in the state is a camel trek through Utah's desert backcountry. Park City Camel Ventures uses camels on pack trips into the San Rafael Swell. Call them at (435) 649-0710, or write to Park City Camel Ventures, 1950 Woodbine, WY, Park City, UT 84060.

Contact the Utah Travel Council and have them send you the latest "Utah Accommodations Guide" for a compilation of horse outfitters and guides: (801) 538-1030, (800) 200-1160, web site: www.Utah.com. The guide is published in partnership with the Utah Hotel & Lodging Association, (801) 359-0104, e-mail: uhla@lodgingutah.com

OFF-ROAD VEHICLE CAMPING

One of the discouraging factors about trying to get away from it all is that you have to carry everything. Camping with an ATV, motorcycle, or 4x4 can bring a whole new perspective to the experience. "Farther, faster" is the theme for camping with off-road vehicles. Utah has thousands of miles of state-maintained ATV trails that are world class.

Popular destinations

The Paiute ATV Trail was rated one of the best 15 trails in the country by Dirt Wheels magazine. Two-hundred-and-seventy miles long, from Fillmore and Salina at the north edge of the loop to Circleville at the south, over 800 miles of marked side trails and 1,000-plus miles of side forest roads await you. It would take at least 25 hours of nonstop riding to see just the main trail. That's why camping was created!

The Uinta Basin has a new addition — the Forest Service's two new 30-mile loop trails in the Uintas. Well-marked, they can be conquered in one day or made to last by stopping to fish for hungry trout, taking a hike to a lonely peak, or stop-

A llama packed and ready to go.

ping to admire meadows full of wildflowers. ATVs are available to rent across the state for self-guided tours or you can take an expert to show you the way.

Southern Utah has become a mecca for 4x4s as well as bikers. Canyonlands, Capitol Reef, Grand Staircase and the San Rafael Swell offer challenges as easy as improved gravel roads to frame-wrenching, cage-rolling trails over rocky ledges. A most rewarding trip reaches from St. George south into Arizona to Grand Canyon National Park at Toroweap Point, where a 3,000-foot drop to the Colorado awaits you. More technical trails with names like Cliff Hanger, Hell's Revenge, and Metal Masher can be found that require modified rigs and guides who know what they're doing. A little practice can be a good thing and there are clubs and associations with rides and trips scheduled on a monthly basis. Many of these clubs also associate service with the hobby, providing clothing for needy villages in Mexico or back-country trail cleanup projects.

When using ORVs or 4x4s to carry you to your campsite, remember to tread lightly. Several thousand pounds of steel and rubber can undo in a few seconds what it has taken nature millennia to build.

Resources
- Paiute ATV Trail: 26 pages of material on this unique trail. Web site: www.marysvale.org/contents.html
- Trail map Silver Sage Enterprises: (801) 261-5340
- Southern Utah off-road links: Web site: MOAB-OffRoad.Com (no "www")
- Utah Four Wheel Drive Association, P.O. Box 20310, Salt Lake City, UT 84120
- Utah Trail Machine Association: Web site: www.utma.net

- NOHVCC Representative, Mary Ricks; fax: (801) 756-1760, e-mail: starassoc@aol.com
- Utah ATV Association: Web site: home.att.net/~utahatv/ (no "www")
- United Four Wheel Drive Associations: Web site: www.ufwda.org

TRAILER/RV CAMPING

Trailer camping has been described by some as bringing your own portable cabin with you. A trailer or RV allows you to enjoy the best of the outdoors with some of the comforts of home. Depending on the size of your trailer or RV, you can bring your whole wardrobe, the contents of your refrigerator, the dog, cat, the neighbors — and you don't have to haul anything out to set up camp! You have access to almost all of the put-ins of the campsites at improved campgrounds, and all the conveniences when you camp at an unimproved campground.

Trailer/RV camping is great for small children, older adults or those with disabilities. It's also just the ticket for those who believe "roughing it" still includes flush toilets, showers, and TV.

Even with all of the benefits, trailer/RV camping can be frustrating without proper preparation. Checking the following items can help avoid breakdowns during your camping trips.

Check reservation status. Before heading to a designated private or public campground, especially during holiday weekends, confirm reservations before leaving to avoid being turned away at a full campground. Some areas are first-come, first-served, and an early start is required to ensure you obtain a site. Other areas take reservations up to a year in advance. Plan early and make appropriate reservations, if possible, and have a backup plan ready.

Renew registration early. Avoid long lines by renewing your trailer registration early. Renewing through the mail is most convenient. Avoid procrastinating until the end of the month or before a holiday weekend, when lines are the longest. Many trailer and boat registrations are renewed just before Memorial Day or Easter. Especially long lines await these unfortunate campers. Again, avoid this by planning ahead.

Check insurance. Some insurance policies do not provide coverage when towing a trailer. Check your policy or call your insurance agent to see if you are fully covered. AAA also offers special service packages for trailer and RV owners. Call (801) 364-5615 for more information or check AAA's web site: www.aaa.com.

Prepare towing vehicle. Prepare your towing vehicle for the additional rigors of hauling a trailer by inspecting engine, hoses, belts, electrical systems, tires, brakes, etc. Check fluid levels or change as necessary, including coolants, windshield washing fluids, oil, brake and transmission fluids. Examine brake pads, since these will endure extra stress during your journey. Replace worn or damaged tires to avoid blowouts on the road. Check your spare tires (at least one for the towing vehicle and one for the trailer), jack, lug wrench, tool kits, and spare parts, which may be required along the way.

We know a guy who had a flat tire on an excursion to Utah's desert west of Delta. He thought he was in good shape because he had two spare tires (a lesson learned from previous excursions when he was faced with two flat tires on the same trip). Unfortunately, while he was changing the tire, his lug wrench broke!

Appliances and trailer systems. Check all appliances, including internal lighting, refrigerators, microwaves, and stoves to ensure that all function properly. Check all systems, including gas, heating, water, sewer, etc. for wear or damage. Replace worn or damaged parts to minimize unsafe operation. If your trailer was properly winterized, drain all antifreeze solution from the lines and flush potable water lines before filling with fresh water. If your systems were not properly winterized, you may have some additional repair work ahead. Dump grey and blackwater tanks, charge and reconnect your storage batteries, check your generator, and fill all necessary fluids, including propane tanks. Install new batteries in your smoke, liquid propane gas, and carbon monoxide detectors. Check fire extinguishers for proper charge, and restock extra fuses, repair kits, first aid kits, cookware, maps, and information for emergency situations.

Wheels and hubs. Before each trip, check for loose or missing lug nuts to avoid wobble, improper tire wear, or wheel loss during your journey. Check to ensure that your lug wrench is the right size and replace missing nuts promptly. The jack and lug wrench from your tow vehicle may not work with your trailer. Replacement nuts should be an exact match to the original and should hold the wheel securely against the hub when fully tightened. Check for proper thread match, and keep wheel bearings properly lubricated to avoid possible bearing loss. In addition, avoid submerging your trailer hubs in water, unless equipped with water-protected hubs. It is wise to check wheel hubs at every gas stop to see if they are unusually hot before continuing.

Tires. Check tires for proper inflation and adequate tread. Under-inflated tires can result in tire failure, so check for proper pressure, while the tires are cold, to avoid problems down the road. Replace worn or damaged tires promptly with the same type tire. For example, radial tires are not designed for some trailers and it is recommended to avoid these if the original tires were not radials. Also check your spare for proper inflation and size, and that it matches remaining trailer tires.

Brakes. If your trailer is equipped with brakes, check them when you inspect the bearings. Examine brake linings and replace damaged and worn parts. Remember that wet brakes will not hold well, but applying the brakes several times at slow speeds will help dry them for when they are really needed. Trailer brakes are particularly useful whenever heading down any hill or canyon. Also check your vehicles brakes, since they tend to take additional abuse when pulling a trailer.

Lights. Electrical systems are subject to corrosion, wearing insulation, and rusted terminals. State and federal regulations require all trailers to be equipped with tail, stop, turn, and side marker lights. When connecting trailer lights to the towing vehicle, use a special wiring harness for ease and attach the white ground wire from the connector to the trailer frame, avoiding use of the hitch ball as an electrical connection. At least once a year, trace the wiring system from the tow vehicle to the trailer, inspecting for bare wires, cracked or chafed insulation, or corroded terminals. Replace worn parts. Place a small amount of waterproof grease on plug contacts and bulb bases to prevent rust and corrosion. Before each trip, check for burned out or broken bulbs, cracked or broken lenses, etc.

Couplers. Check the coupler and latch assembly for damage. The coupling socket should not be set on the ground where sand and dirt can cause jamming or excessive wear to the locking mechanism. Clean and oil the latch mechanism regularly to ensure that it closes firmly when placed on the ball.

Trailer jacks. Maintaining the trailer jack is easy. Grease the drive gear, rack and pinion, and oil the wheel bearings and caster frequently to make sure all function properly. To avoid damage, make sure that the jack is fully retracted before moving the trailer.

Trailer hitch. Check the hitch ball to see that it fits perfectly to your trailer coupler. Your trailer coupler should be marked with the correct ball diameter to ensure the proper size is used. Even a 1/8-inch difference in size can cause a trailer to become unhitched while towing. Have a professional install the correct hitch that matches your trailer and vehicle.

Safety chains. Safety chains provide additional insurance that your trailer does not become detached while towing. Chains should be checked to see that they are properly attached between the towing vehicle and the trailer before each trip. Your trailer hitch should provide a place for attaching safety chains, including holes or rings on both sides of the hitch ball. We recommend (and most states require) that you crisscross the chains under the trailer tongue (the chain on the trailer's left side attaches to the hole or ring on the hitch ball's right side and the right chain attaches to the hole or ring on the hitch ball's left side. This prevents the trailer tongue from dropping to the road if the trailer coupler separates from the hitch ball. Chains should be rigged as tight as possible with just enough slack to permit tight turns. If you find it necessary to replace a safety chain, never use a lighter weight chain.

Weight distribution. To avoid fishtailing and loss of control, proper tongue weight and weight distribution will save you considerable problems. The trailer coupling ball should feel approximately 5-10% of the total trailer weight when the tongue is parallel to the ground. Use a bathroom scale (on smaller trailers) to determine if you are close. Weight information is often provided by the trailer manufacturer for each model. Approximately 100-200 pounds would be expected for a gross vehicle weight of 2,000 lbs. Shifting equipment in the trailer can help adjust the tongue weight if it falls outside the parameters set by the manufacturer. Remember that all weight placed in the trailer must be pulled by your vehicle's engine. Find out how much your vehicle can tow and avoid exceeding its capabilities. Water, gear, propane tanks, etc. can easily add up in excess weight. Check to ensure that trailer and gear do not exceed the maximum load-carrying capacity of the trailer. This information is usually found on the metal or plastic certification label attached by the manufacturer. Also check that the total weight of your loaded trailer does not exceed the hitch's load capacity. A weight-carrying hitch is usually adequate for cars towing lighter rigs, but a weight-distributing hitch may be recom-

A group RV camps at Willard Bay, north of Ogden.

mended for heavier rigs. Consult the manufacturer's recommendations before deciding which to use.

Check with local retailers. Local trailer retailers can offer additional help in preparing your trailer for the warmer weather. Many offer great professional service in winterizing and de-winterizing trailers and RVs. Make appointments far in advance of scheduled adventures to ensure service technicians can fit your trailer into their busy schedules. Some businesses also offer camper rental programs to help you avoid much of the required maintenance. Check with several for competitive pricing and services.

Hitching up reminders:
- Back your tow vehicle to the trailer as close as possible
- Check the coupler locking device to ensure it is released
- Raise trailer front end. Position coupler directly over hitch ball and lower all the way down
- Check under coupling to ensure that the ball clamp is below the ball and not riding on top
- Lock coupler to ball hitch. Lift up the trailer tongue to see that it is in the locked position. If it comes loose from the ball, unlock and start over
- Make sure trailer jack is fully retracted
- If equipped with a weight-distribution hitch and spring bars, follow the above steps, then attach the spring bar chain or cable to the trailer and tighten until the trailer and vehicle are in normal level position
- If equipped with a break-away cable or chain, attach it to the tow vehicle with enough slack for tight turns

- Attach safety chains
- Connect trailer wiring harness to tow vehicle and inspect for proper operation

Road rules:

Remember that towing a trailer will change the way you can maneuver on the road. Your rig suddenly becomes longer, wider, and taller, and you will need to compensate for these changes. Keep dimensions and weights in mind for bridge, road, and canopy restrictions, and consider these tips:

- It is always wise to take a short ride to familiarize yourself with the new handling characteristics and check to ensure that all systems are functioning properly. Practice backing up in an empty parking lot to avoid embarrassment or crisis in a full campground.
- Slow down to reduce strain on your vehicle and trailer. Slower speeds will also help conserve fuel. Wind resistance can hurt your gas mileage, especially at faster speeds.
- Allow extra time for passing and stopping, especially if the trailer is not equipped with its own brake system. Sudden stops can cause potential jackknifing, skids, and slides. Avoid the necessity to stop quickly while turning. Smooth starts and stops will reduce strain on your tie downs and improve fuel mileage. Also remember that it is much more difficult to accelerate and stop properly. Allow additional space between yourself and the vehicle ahead of you. Allow at least one car and trailer length between you and the vehicle ahead for every 10 miles of speed.
- Make sure that side view mirrors are out far enough to see beyond the trailer and adjusted for optimal viewing. Check both side and rear-view mirrors often to ensure that the trailer is riding properly behind you.
- Swing wider at turns, since the trailer wheels are closer to the inside of turns than those on your towing vehicle.
- Watch for wind and buffeting when larger vehicles pass from either direction. Maintain slower speeds and hold tightly to the wheel for additional control.
- Use signals long before you make lane changes, turns, etc. to help others be aware of your intentions and avoid potential hazards.
- Shift to lower gears when going up steep hills or on dirt roads to ease the load on your engine and transmission. Overdrive gears will also help you achieve better fuel mileage in the lower gears.
- Be courteous to faster moving vehicles, allowing them to pass and avoid heated tempers. Keep to the right side of the road and slow down if they need extra time to return to their proper lane.
- Stay cool for potential problems. Don't panic, and avoid sudden driving tactics. A sudden bump or fishtailing may simply be a flat tire. Avoid stomping on the brakes or on the gas to drive out of it. Stop slowly and in as straight a line as possible. Allow your rig to coast to a slow speed, if conditions permit, to avoid braking. Brake only when your wheels are straight ahead and both sections of your rig are in line.

WINTER CAMPING

Camping in winter can be as varied as the weather. If it's mild conditions you seek, head for southern Utah's Dixie or red rock country. If you are a hardy hedonist, a snow cave beats a tent. Just remember winter's special risks — be prepared, check weather reports, and pay attention to avalanche warnings. Below, some top choices for the snow-bound.

Popular destinations

Take the thousands of miles of Utah trails maintained for off-road vehicles and cover them with snow. Add a snow machine or cross-country skis and now you can enjoy those same areas with a different perspective in winter. Rapidly, Utah is becoming a magnet for snowmobilers wanting a world class winter camping experience.

PHOTO: CHEYENNE ROUSE

A camper begins to settle in after snowshoeing to her campsite.

The Monte Cristo Mountains are accessed by Hwy. 101 up Blacksmith Fork Canyon or from Hwy. 39 east of Huntsville. Consider mile after mile of groomed trails to Franklin Basin; open play areas on U.S. Forest Service, state and private land; the famous Sinks area; or the Hardware Ranch Groomed Trail — a 63-mile loop groomed by Utah State Parks and Recreation from Hardware Ranch to Ant Flat, Monte Cristo, and Curtis Creek.

Daniels Summit, with access to 200 miles of groomed trails and acres of open play areas, features deluxe accommodations if your idea of roughing it includes a Jacuzzi. Rentals are available that include helmets and all the gear you'll need for a safe, fun winter camping experience near Strawberry Reservoir that could include some ice fishing on one of the state's best fishing destinations.

If, however, solitude and quiet are on your winter camping agenda, then strap on your skinny skis or your snowshoes and head for the miles of trails — groomed and ungroomed — that can be accessed from every metropolitan area in the state. Or, load up your snow cave gear and head into the wilderness. One of the most critical aspects of backcountry winter travel is avalanche danger. Do not attempt to challenge the backcountry without a basic understanding of snow conditions and avalanche safety.

An unusual opportunity for winter campers that is gaining popularity is yurt camping. Utah offers everything from luxury accommodations with gourmet meals to ski-in and do-it-yourself. Originating in Mongolia centuries ago, yurts are large, framed, circular tents traditionally made of heavy felt. Several organizations operate yurts year-round in the Uinta, Wasatch, and Tushar mountains and provide environmentally sound shelters without the difficulties of carrying heavy gear.

Resources
- Utah Avalanche Forecast Center: (801) 364-1581, web site: www.wasatch.com/~uafc
- Bear River Avalanche Information Center: Web site: www.wasatch.usu.edu/~uafclogn
- Westwide Avalanche Network: Worldwide avalanche info. Web site: www.avalanche.org
- Daniels Summit Lodge: (800) 519-9969, web site: www.danielssummit.com
- Park City Yurts: (435) 615-YURT, web site: www.parkcityyurts.com
- Norwegian School: (800) 649-5322, web site: www.utahnordic.com
- Bear River Outdoor Recreation Alliance: (307) 789-1770, web site: www.evanstonwy.com/brora
- Vernal Ranger District: (435) 789-1181
- Tushar Mountains: (435) 438-6191
- For specific snowmobile, cross-country ski and snowshoe trail information, contact the local Forest Service Ranger Stations or state parks and recreation.

PART THREE: GEAR & OTHER PREPARATIONS

Planning Your Adventure

AN IS THE ONLY SPECIES that can create his own environment and haul it with him. Personal camping requirements are as unique as your fingerprint. While one camper may be inclined to haul an entire grocery store, kitchen, wardrobe and full-length mirror into the backcountry, another may find it fulfilling to exist with the most rudimentary essentials. Whatever your requirements are, planning your camping trip requires answers to some simple questions, each of which begs other questions:

• Where to go?

If you are the typical camper, for the past thirty years you've had one or two favorite spots that you visit yearly, and that's your repertoire of camping destinations. Will this be another trip to the usual haunt, or a new destination? With so many choices, this can be the toughest decision you make.

• When to go?

What is the season of the year? Will it be an overnighter, a weekend getaway, or a midweek adventure? Work, family responsibilities, holidays, weather, and campsite availability all play a part in determining your escape to the backcountry. However, if you wait for the most convenient or perfect time, you might never make the trip.

• Who will go?

Will this be a solo experience, a group of friends, a trip with young children, or a family reunion? Different numbers have different requirements. There is something magical about camping with young children. The bonds you build and the memories you make while camping will last a lifetime. Excursions with friends or family reunions can also provide bonding experiences. But if it is solitude you seek, camping in larger groups is unadvisable. Going solo, on the other hand, can be fun if you have the inner resources and mental strength to control emotions, which become more intense when you are alone: phobias, worries, highs, and lows may make you jittery. We don't want you bouncing off of pine trees with no one around to rescue you.

• How far/long will you go?

If this is a pack trip, determine your drive time, pack in and pack out time.

• What to bring?

The answer to this question will vary widely depending on how far/long you go, the season of the year, who will go (young children), what you plan to do on the trip (fishing, hunting, hiking), and your mode/s of locomotion:

- Car, camper, RV/trailer
- Mountain bike
- Canoe
- ATV
- Horse
- Cross-country ski/snowmobile
- By foot

Car camping — meaning car, camper, or trailer/RV — is great for small children, the disabled, or seniors. You don't have to haul anything but out of your trunk (if you have a camper/trailer/motor home, you don't have to haul anything out!), you can sleep in your camper or in the back seat of your car, or you can pitch a tent.

10 Keys to a Great Camping Adventure

1. Plan for the worst weather.
2. Plan sharing loads and responsibilities beforehand.
3. Keep things simple.
4. Check your gear in advance. Replace the worn-out or inoperative. Bring extra gear.
5. Play on the way and when you get there — isn't that what you're there for?
6. Let kids participate — let them light the fire, help pitch the tent, mix the pancake batter, or paddle the canoe.
7. Take food you like to eat.
8. Make reservations well in advance.
9. If this is a new destination, read as much as you can about it beforehand.
10. Use a checklist before you go. Don't leave anything to chance.

Camping Checklists and Tips

There are many different camping checklists you could use. Your list will vary according to the type of camping you expect to do. Our list is a generic master list, to cover most of the items you might need and a few you might not. Since camping is an individual experience, you will have different or additional items to add to the list. We suggest you create additional lists pertaining to the specific type of camping you plan to do: canoeing, backpacking, rafting, mountain biking, cross-country skiing. We are assuming you will shut the garage door and turn off the lights, but maybe you should add them to your list. Your car is another issue, and may require a pre-trip checklist. Using a checklist will help you avoid leaving an item behind. But if you do leave something behind, and life can go on without it, then improvise!

MASTER CHECKLIST

❑ Make campground reservations early

❑ Do you have your permit or reservation information?

❑ Do you have your map(s)?

❑ Tell someone you trust — family, neighbor, friend — where you are going and when you expect to return. Leave detailed information so they can track you down if you don't return or there's an emergency at home

❑ Stop the newspaper and ask the Post Office to hold your mail — or ask a friend to collect them for you on a daily basis while you are away

❑ If you are not taking your pets, make special arrangements for someone to feed them, or for them to stay with a relative or friend. Leave plenty of food, the name and phone number of your vet, and instructions for special needs

❑ Make arrangements for plant care so your houseplants will still be alive when you return

❑ Plan special medications so you will have an ample supply on the trip and extra for when you return. Store in a waterproof container

❑ Label all medications as to what they are and for whom. In an emergency, medical workers may need this information to administer a dose

❑ Tent — Keep in mind where you will be camping. Not all campsites are created equal. Your tent size may require a bigger campsite

❑ Ground cloth

❑ Tarp(s) — use tarps as ground cloths to protect against moistue, or over your tent to protect it from dripping sap, bird droppings, sparks, the sun, or for extra rain protection. If using the tarp over your tent, try to get one bigger than your tent so you'll have an overhang by your tent door. This keeps the inside of your tent drier in the rain! Some people have been known to buy an inexpensive dining canopy just for the poles to use for the tarp over their tent

❑ First aid kit — refer to the chapter on first aid kits for our master list of contents

❑ Wood cover — if you plan to chop wood for the campfire

❑ Lantern(s) — Depending on your lantern, don't forget the re-charger or propane fuel. For propane lanterns, invest in a bulk propane tank, which also requires a pipe and hose. The bulk tank provides significant savings over 1 pound cylinders. For weekend camping the bulk tank may be extreme, but for anything longer than a weekend it's worth it

❑ Coleman fuel and funnel

❑ Mantles — there are even "clip-on" style mantles out now

❑ Fire extinguisher

❑ Matches — keep matches in a square Tupperware container to keep them dry. This also makes it a little harder for the little kids to get at them. Keep them out of sight in another container

❑ Dependable flashlight -— with Mag Lights, make sure you lube up those o-rings on a regular basis. This helps seal out moisture and dirt

❑ Snake lights — they hang around your neck, freeing both hands for whatever task you're doing. They also can be coiled so they stand up like a desk lamp for reading etc.

❑ Lantern tree hanger — long chain (with a big stable hook) that wraps around a tree. Here you can hang your lantern out of reach from your little ones. No worries about a child tipping the lantern over or burning themselves. This added height also increases the light your lantern will give off

❑ Small hatchet — but please don't let the kids chop trees

❑ Stake hammering mallet or hammer — the best are rubber with a hook on the other end for pulling up stakes

❑ Whisk broom to sweep out your tent

❑ Small rug for outside your tent door — this is important because it really cuts down on the dirt that would otherwise end up in your tent! Some campers don't wear shoes in their tents (saves on tent wear and tear). They use a small rug inside the tent to keep the shoes on

❑ Clothesline and clothespins

❑ Cooler(s) — Take two, both different colors – one for beverages, the other for food

❑ Ice — Some handy campers reuse 2-liter soda bottles. Fill them with water and freeze. Put them in your cooler before you go and they will stay frozen a long time. When they melt, you have fresh 'home' water and it isn't all over the bottom of your cooler!

❑ 5-gallon water container — one with a spigot for drinking is nice. A square shaped one will pack easier in your car than a round one

❑ Sleeping bags

❑ Pillows and pillowcases

❑ Sleeping mat/pad or cot -— the combination of foam and air makes for a great insulator in all types of temperatures. Air mattresses can deflate during the night and will fill up with cold air on cold nights

❑ Large size utility bags — to store sleeping bags, pads, and pillows

❑ Pack all clothes in duffel bags or Rubbermaid containers, or roll them up inside the sleeping bags

❑ Fanny packs — the ones that hold a water bottle or two

Some of the gear for a well-equipped campsite.

PHOTO: CHEYENNE ROUSE

❑ Camp cooking gear — Gas stove, Dutch ovens, etc.
❑ Chuck box where you can keep can and bottle openers, scissors, measuring
   spoons/cups, spatulas, pot scrubbers, vegetable peelers, wooden spoon,
   ladle, medicine spoons, BBQ fork
❑ Eating utensils — knives, forks, spoons
❑ Dishes — enamel ware or paper plates, mugs and bowls
❑ Coffee/tea/hot chocolate
❑ Thermal mugs
❑ Cooking timer
❑ Sandwich-size zip bags
❑ Bungee cords/straps — you know, those rubber cords covered with fabric
   that have metal hooks at each end
❑ Paper towels
❑ Tablecloth
❑ Gallon-size zip bags
❑ Plastic grocery bags
❑ Garbage bags — use the large size. If you forget your rain gear you can cut a
   hole in them for your face. They should cover you and your backpack
❑ Sugar or other sweetener
❑ Salt and pepper
❑ Garlic or seasoning salt
❑ Small "ditty bag" with tablecloth clips — buy the metal tablecloth clips in
   the camping section of your sporting goods store (the springs on the fancy
   plastic clips break too easy). Buy two packs — more than you would need

for just the tablecloth. Clip two of these tablecloth clips to the end of the table about a foot apart. Take one of the bungee cords/straps you brought along and hang it on one of these clips. Take a roll of paper towels and put the bungee cord/strap through it and hang the other end of the cord by the other clip to produce a convenient paper towel holder. Clip another tablecloth clip on the end of your table to a plastic grocery bag attached to it. Now you have a convenient garbage sack. Hang two — one for garbage and one for recycleables. This way you don't have so much garbage hanging around attracting animals throughout the day. If it rains, these sacks don't fall apart. Hang your extra sacks from another clip on the table

❏ Pot holders
❏ Pots with lids — the thin enamelware pans heat water very quickly, saving on fuel
❏ Popcorn pan or over the campfire popcorn popper
❏ 10″ cast iron skillet — cast iron is heavy, but it distributes the heat evenly and a well-seasoned pan cleans easily
❏ Cast iron griddle
❏ Funnel
❏ Stainless steel bowl
❏ Camping toaster
❏ Ladle
❏ Heavy-duty aluminum foil
❏ Wooden cutting board
❏ Clothing
❏ Footwear
❏ Rain Gear
❏ Insect repellents/sunscreen
❏ Caladryl Clear for poison oak
❏ Bug/tick repellent — Avon's Skin-So-Soft is a good bug repellent for very young children. Repel Insect Block - Sportsmen Formula is a good product. For those who don't like smelling like bug repellent, the Sportsmen Formula isn't as fragrant as some insect repellents. To get the repellent on your face, spray the repellent on the back of your hand and then dab it on the for head and cheeks. Do not get any in the eyes
❏ Bottle of rubbing alcohol — great for getting the pitch (pine tar) off of hands or clothing
❏ Dish soap (antibacterial) — use it for hand soap, too
❏ Suntan lotion/sun screen
❏ Towels/hand towels
❏ Dish cloth
❏ Sanitary items
❏ Folding chairs or chaise lounge

Additional items you might want to take:

- ❏ Wool blankets — nothing beats a wool blanket as an insulator on cool/cold nights
- ❏ Backpack(s)
- ❏ Canoe/raft
- ❏ Fishing gear
- ❏ Bait
- ❏ Waders, float tubes, etc.
- ❏ Swim suits
- ❏ Water filter, bleach, or other purifier — depending on your water source. Also put a small amount (a tablespoon or so) of bleach in your rinse water for sanitizing dishes. Wiping down your table with the "bleach rinse water" helps to keep your table more sanitary
- ❏ Life jackets/inflatable water toys and sand toys for children — a mesh bag is great to keep these toys in. This can be dunked in the lake to rinse off the sand before it goes back in the car

For babies and young children:

- ❏ Extra clothes
- ❏ Diapers
- ❏ Wipes
- ❏ Diaper rash ointments
- ❏ Infant seat — hang a camping mirror from the handle of baby's infant seat. Great entertainment for baby
- ❏ Chaise lounge
- ❏ Playpen
- ❏ "Johnny Jump-Up" type seat if your campsite has trees
- ❏ Front/sling type baby carrier or backpack carrier, depending on your preferred method of "wearing" your baby
- ❏ Folding, "clip-on" style highchair
- ❏ Stroller
- ❏ Mosquito netting, depending on where you are camping
- ❏ Oblong tub to use as baby's/toddler's bathtub
- ❏ If you have a toddler you are potty training, bring the "little white potty chair" along (and tissue)
- ❏ A medicine spoon
- ❏ Whistle — in case they get lost. Put it on a cord or chain they can wear around their necks
- ❏ Rain suit
- ❏ Tie-on hat
- ❏ Biodegradable soap
- ❏ Ipecac — in case you need to induce vomiting
- ❏ Pedialyte — for diarrhea

Basic weekend packing guide for children ages 3 and up:

- ❏ Sleeping bag
- ❏ Pillow
- ❏ Pad
- ❏ Flashlight
- ❏ Glow sticks for when it gets dark. They last all night and are very bright
- ❏ Underwear
- ❏ Socks
- ❏ Long underwear for sleeping
- ❏ Jeans (2 pair)
- ❏ Shorts
- ❏ Shirts (at least one long-sleeve)
- ❏ Sweatpants and hooded sweatshirt
- ❏ Jacket (rain poncho/rain jacket)
- ❏ Shoes/sandals (2 pair)
- ❏ Toothbrush

Outdoor Cooking

Nothing compares to the smell of a hot breakfast in the backcountry or joys of roasting marshmallows around a campfire. No matter how you prepare your vittles in the outdoors, simplicity, the right gear, and safety are key to enjoying delicious outdoor cooking.

Keep it Simple

In general, outdoor chefs require simplicity and efficiency. Bringing too much gear can be cumbersome, difficult, and oftentimes confusing. Preparation space is limited and campers usually want to maximize fishing, hiking, or relaxing, while minimizing preparation and clean-up.

Whenever possible, bring foods that are easily prepared or begin your more complicated meals at home. Using Ziploc bags or other sealable containers, many camp meals can be planned to require only heating and eating.

When weight and cook times become a priority, dehydrated products become very appealing. Several local companies produce dehydrated gourmet camping food, including Bear Creek Country Kitchens, who recently received 10 national awards for their newly emerging dry soup mixes. Bear Creek Country Kitchens offers a wide range of food products, requiring only water and a 10-minute cook time for a delicious warm meal. Available at almost all grocery chains, cost savings is significant when compared to specialty foods sold in outdoor stores.

Great Gear

Family campers will want to check out the products offered by Camp Chef, a local company with a national reputation. Camp Chef offers quality propane cookers to prepare fast hot meals and maximize your recreation time. Cookstoves range from the basic setup to items that will make any outdoor chef drool. Reasonably priced, their stoves offer more bang for the buck than any other cookstove on the market. They generate enough heat to compensate for adverse weather conditions, which usually steal your warmth and extend cook times. They are also built solid to prepare large volumes of food, whether it be a big pot of chili or a kettle of crawdads.

Camp Chef recently came out with a Professional Series doubleburner cooker, featuring two all-purpose 30,000 BTU/hour burners and a windscreen. The cooker holds in temperatures and protects the flames in breezy conditions. New side shelves offer a convenient preparation area and fold up to serve as a portable lid. Built with Camp Chef's famous sturdy folding leg design, this unit weighs less than 50 lbs. and offers hot food in minutes to hungry outdoor enthusiasts. Camp Chef offers additional accessories, including a griddle, barbecue box, wok ring, and a 34-quart pot with basket for deep frying that turkey or cooking crawdads at Strawberry Reservoir.

Also new to Camp Chef's lineup is the Ultimate Dutch Oven, also known as the "outdoor microwave. "This ingenious 9.5-quart pot (available in both iron and case aluminum) has been manufactured with a design that promotes convection cooking, eliminating cold spots and speeding cooking — culinary artists can prepare a roast, complete with vegetables and sauce, in less than 30 minutes. Designed to work effectively with Camp Chef's universal output propane burner, it also works with traditional Dutch oven cooking methods, like charcoal. The lid doubles as a deep dish skillet for frying pancakes or scones, and the oven comes with two racks for a greater variety of cooking applications.

Camp Chef also offers the king of barbecue accessory kits, which comes with its own individual carrying case. Available at most sporting goods stores, their line has a reputation for quality and value. Their web site is found at www.campchef.com

Another good brand is GSI Outdoors. GSI produces stainless steel cookware, nonstick Teflon cookware, and enamelware for durable outdoor food preparations, and is becoming known for its Lexan goblets, flasks, cutlery, and Java Press. Lexan is a durable plastic, designed to be almost indestructible, and offers an elegant gourmet touch to outdoor dining. GSI also manufactures lightweight stainless steel mess kits, percolators, and even an outdoor pressure cooker. Their quality products can be found almost everywhere along the Wasatch Front. For more information about GSI Outdoors, call (800) 704-4474., or see their web site, www.gsioutdoors.com. To purchase GSI products online, see the web site: www.globe-mart.com/outdoors/kitchen/cookware/gsi/index.htm

If you have ever roasted hot dogs on a stick and lost your lunch to the fire, another useful item has recently emerged to help family recreationists. Cowboy Hank's Hot Dog Holders offer stability and ease when roasting these popular treats over the campfire. Made in the United States of durable stainless steel, they attach to almost any stick for convenience and are a much smarter solution than coat hangers. They are inexpensive, sanitary and reusable, and are also great for roasting marshmallows. These items come three per package and can be found in many major sporting goods stores in the state. For locations, their web address is www.cowboyhank.com

Another great cooking item is the Adjust A Grill, distributed by Panacea, Inc. From grilling burgers over the open fire to warming a kettle of water, this item is simple to use and is great for campers, anglers, and hunters. The grill swings away from the heat to prevent roasting your knuckles, and can be raised or lowered to adjust for required heat. It is durable and built to last for many years of use over the campfire.

Dutch Oven Cooking

Cast iron cookware has certainly become popular in recent years, with the Dutch oven dominating outdoor cooking. The Camp Chef Dutch oven (see above) is excellent. Lodge also produces some of the finest ovens on the market and is fast becoming the leader in ironware. Many a Dutch oven enthusiast will be found with at least one in their arsenal. The Lodge company is over 100 years old, and quality has always been their first priority. For more information check out www.lodgemfg.com.

If you are looking for a different look, however, you may want to try the potjie, a cast iron pot that looks like a cauldron. Imported from Africa, these are designed

A cook prepares pancakes on a solid, well-used cast iron griddle.

with a round bottom to minimize burning, by allowing food and liquids to settle to the lowest point. Because of the tall legs, the potjie is ideal for setting over the coals and also works well over a gas range. Many stores do carry the potjie, but due to its popularity, quantities disappear quickly. Check out www.actionafrica.com for more information.

Educational opportunities abound if you want to learn more about the magic of Dutch oven cooking. The International Dutch Oven Society offers instruction, cooking competitions and support to individuals interested in learning more about this fascinating cooking art. Almost anything can be prepared with a Dutch oven, using the right techniques and information. These folks can explain how to care for and season your oven properly or how to calculate the number of charcoal briquettes required to heat your meal. Headquartered in Logan, numerous events are scheduled throughout the year and more information can always be obtained from their web site, www.idos.com. They may also be contacted by calling their president, Kent Mayberry, at (801) 363-3624.

Safety

Even with all the greatest gear on the market, one of the most important items to remember for safe food preparation is to keep a clean camp. This keeps you safe from scavenging critters and limits food spoilage. Remember that without refrigeration, spoilage is a major concern and planning ahead is crucial. Plan your meals to use the most sensitive items first and then less susceptible foods later in the trip. Refrain from eating questionable food items and keep everything in the cooler when it is not actually being eaten.

In addition, avoid leaving food where it can attract insects and other less desirable guests. Wash all cookware thoroughly with biodegradable soap and clean, hot water to reduce the chance of illness. Some even recommend placing a few drops of bleach in the rinse water to kill anything that may be in the rinse water itself. Wash hands properly before preparing food and wash equipment that comes in contact with raw food, especially meats, before it comes in contact with finished food.

Teach children to respect fire and to avoid playing in it. When used properly, fire is a great cooking tool, but it can also be a hazard when misused, improperly cared for, or left unattended. Be careful when around propane cylinders, any gas-powered appliance, or anything that can be potentially hot. Treat all cookware as if it were hot to avoid painful burns. Also avoid using gas-powered stoves in enclosed areas to prevent carbon monoxide poisoning. Remember that safety should always be your first priority to ensure many more great outdoor meals in the future.

Ultimate Camping Gear

Roughing it has never been easier. Developments in technology offer new and unique comforts for camping enthusiasts. Camping gear is now warmer, more comfortable, and more durable than ever before. Through the new gadgetry we highlight in this section you may enjoy the comforts of home at your campsite!

Solar generators

For those who want to bring along a source of electrical power for their camp, but don't like noisy generators, Intermountain Solar offers portable power systems that charge silently during the day and light your camp by night. With one charging, even their smallest units can light your trailer up to seven nights, using high efficiency lighting. A built-in inverter powers your 120-volt radios, televisions, or appliances. Packaged in a convenient cooler box, the safety-sealed deep cycle batteries offer a great alternative for campers who want to listen to the campfire and crickets before retiring. To speak to a salesperson or get a referral to an RV dealer, call (801) 501-9353. For general information, product comparison and online ordering, see their web site at www.intermountainsolar.com

Camp furniture

Coleman is about to release a new line of durable inflatable camp furniture, including a sleeper sofa and chair. An excellent alternative to stumps and rocks, this line of rugged furniture is built from the same thick grade of PVC used for inflatable boats, and can inflate in less than 3 minutes using the new Coleman Rechargeable Quick Pump. The furniture can also deflate in less than two minutes, using the same pump. Used as a sofa by day, it doubles as a luxurious bed by night, keeping you off the cold, rocky ground. This new furniture can give your camping experience the semblance of home.

Remote-controlled lanterns

For those late night nature calls or times when animals wander into camp, Coleman has introduced a line of portable remote-controlled fluorescent lanterns. Powered by eight D-cell batteries, the brightness of the lanterns can be adjusted by handy remote controls from up to 50 feet away. On its nightlight setting, the lanterns can operate continuously for more than 100 hours, offering additional security for younger campers who might be fearful of the dark. Convenience of the remote control minimizes fumbling in the dark and allows the lantern to be placed where the entire campsite can be lit. Priced at $34.99, these units are great for family camping. Check them out at Coleman's web site: www.colemanoutdoors.com/products.htm

Night vision

ITT Industries offers a wide selection of night vision products and accessories to extend your outdoor adventures beyond the twilight hours. More effective than a flashlight, night vision allows users to see well beyond the limited range of a flashlight beam. Generation-three technology improves visibility significantly more than earlier generation models on the market today. Used for night fishing, setting up camp, security, wildlife viewing or photography, ITT night vision products include a wide range of tools to improve your vision after dark. Night hikes have never been safer with the new selection of vision products. For more information, check out their web site at: www.ittind.com/prd/index.html

Hot showers

Hot showers are no longer a luxury in camp with Zodi's new hot water heating systems. Built from rugged stainless steel, these water heaters produce hot water in less than a minute. Using only a 16 oz. propane tank, 100-degree water awaits for 45 five-minute showers. Bulk tanks can provide up to 80 hours of hot water. In addition to the propane water heaters, another product heats water using only your campfire. New items also include a safely vented heating system for your tent or camper without the fear of carbon monoxide poisoning. For more information check out Zodi's web site at: www.zodi.com

Other new products on the market include cozier sleeping bags, smaller and smarter GPS receivers, and high performance fabrics to keep you warmer and drier. New items are appearing daily, which makes it a very exciting time to enjoy Utah's camping experiences. Visit your local outdoor retailer for other unique items arriving this season.

Maps, GPS Units and Compasses

A good old state highway map may be all you need if your destination is along a major road or located in a city or town. But if you're heading for adventure along a back road or in the backcountry, you need a detailed map — and an understanding of how to use it. If you're driving off-road, boating to a particular destination, or backpacking into the wilderness, a GPS unit can also be a big help.

Maps

The Utah Atlas and Gazetteer. This atlas has become a very popular reference for outdoor recreation. Published by DeLorme Mapping, and available at most sporting goods and map stores, it is a booklet containing maps for all areas of the state. The atlas is good enough to meet the needs of most recreationists, showing roads, towns, and major features.

Key advantages: You get the entire state in one booklet, plus enough detail to locate destinations along maintained roads (even backroads).

Key disadvantages: Each booklet page shows only a small area of the state. You often have to look from page to page to trace roads and locate places of interest. The scale is convenient for most uses, but the maps do not show the detail needed for backpacking and serious off-road travel.

USGS Topographical (topo) Maps. The topo maps produced by the United States Geological Survey have long been standards for recreational use. The maps come in various scales:

1:100,000 scale maps are popular because they show key details over a fairly large area.

7.5-minute maps show incredible detail over a much smaller area, and are considered essential for serious backcountry travel and backpacking.

Topo maps are sold in local map stores and also by some government agencies. Computerized versions of these maps are now offered on CD.

Key advantages: Detail! The 7.5-minute maps show details of roads, waterways and other features, along with contour lines that show the location and slope of hills, mountains, and valleys.

Key disadvantages: Most of these maps are based on old surveys. New roads, dams and other man-made features may not be shown.

Other maps. State and federal agencies also offer maps of some areas. Maps produced by the Forest Service are very good — often the best references for recreation in National Forest areas. They are available at Forest District and Ranger offices throughout the state. Recreational maps published by private companies are available for national parks and other key areas. They are also usually very good references.

The bookstore at the Utah Department of Natural Resources Building, 1594 West North Temple, Salt Lake City, sells most of the maps mentioned here, along with guide books and other interesting products. Utah Idaho-Map World operates several retail stores along the Wasatch Front, each offering an extensive line of maps and related products.

GPS

Global Positioning System (GPS) receivers have become extremely valuable when traveling in the backcountry, either by foot, vehicle, or boat. The units use satellite signals to determine your latitude and longitude. GPS receivers are very accurate.

Key advantages: USGS topo maps have latitude and longitude scales along their borders. You can determine your precise location by plotting the coordinates received by the GPS unit onto the map. Alternately, you can use the scales on a map to estimate the coordinates of your destination, then let the GPS unit guide you to that location. Most GPS units allow you to enter coordinates manually. Several screens are provided to help you navigate to your destination. The unit will show the distance to your destination, the direction and speed you are traveling, the direction you need to travel to reach your destination, and other useful information. Push a button and the unit will store your position as a "waypoint." Mark your base camp (or boat ramp, or vehicle) as a waypoint, and then the unit will guide you back as you conclude your outing.

Key disadvantages: A GPS unit may not work in a narrow canyon or where its "view of the sky" is encumbered by other factors. The units require batteries, which can run out when you need them most. The units recommend a direct-line path to your destination, even if the Grand Canyon is between you and your truck.

Compasses

As you can see, topo maps and GPS units have their pros and cons. Many hikers and campers use a compass in conjunction with their maps and GPS unit. While your GPS unit may tell you it's 1.25 miles and 217 degrees to your destination, it's your compass that will show you in what direction the 217 degrees will have you heading.

Furthermore, because you may not be able to see the destination your "Go To" from the GPS unit has given you, some hikers pick landmarks along the way. They use their compass and GPS unit to take them from visible landmark to landmark until they reach their destination.

GPS units and compasses can be purchased through a variety of sources, from catalogs to the Internet, as well as local retail businesses like REI, Gart Brothers, Sportsman's Warehouse, etc.

Camping Safety

Smart camping requires safety precautions. To enjoy your adventures in Utah's outdoors, accept responsibility for your personal safety and the safety of those with you. Watch for potential hazards, heed warning signs, and avoid situations that compromise your well-being.

Planning. Plan your trip so you arrive at the campsite with enough daylight to properly set up camp. Check your site thoroughly for hazards like broken glass or other sharp objects, low hanging branches, etc. Check the slope of the ground for potential trouble if it rains. Watch for areas that might flood or become muddy. Look for level ground with enough area to spread out your camping gear and pitch your tent.

Clean camp. A clean camp is a safe camp. Store your food in a vehicle or food box that can be closed and locked. Leftovers and food scraps left lying around will attract bears and other wildlife. Promptly clean utensils and cookware after eating to limit harmful microbial growth and discourage wandering wildlife with a keen sense of smell. If you have limited means of keeping food cold and preserving it safely, limit prepared quantities to minimize leftovers. Use biodegradable soap for dishwashing and a drop or two of bleach in your rinse water. Avoid leaving sharp objects (knives, hatchets, axes, etc.) around camp where youngsters can play with them, and keep your camp gear in an orderly manner to avoid being an eyesore to others — plus, it makes retrieval easier.

PHOTO: WENDELL CHEEK

Telephoto lenses make possible great shots of wildlife, such as this young moose, without disturbing them — and without incurring the wrath of wild parents.

Campfires. Keep campfires to a minimum. Whenever a fire is lit, make sure an adult is assigned to watch it at all times. Keep water nearby for emergencies. When you put your fire out, use water and dirt. Stir up the ashes to make sure no hot embers are left. Make sure ashes are cool to the touch before you leave.

Carbon monoxide. Carbon monoxide, known as the silent killer, is produced from incomplete combustion of any fuel or gas-operated appliance. Never heat your trailer, tent, or camper with a gas-powered device unless it is properly vented to the outside. Carbon monoxide detectors are worth every penny. If you own a cabin, clean the chimneys regularly and allow for proper ventilation when cooking with liquid propane. Most of your cooking is best conducted outside. Never use a barbecue inside of a closed room, tent, or building.

Wildlife: Observe from a distance. Keeping a distance from wildlife reduces stress for the critters and offers additional safety for you. During certain times of the year, even the most gentle of wildlife can become very aggressive. Spring and early summer months will find very protective parents not far away from baby animals. In the fall, expect to see aggressive males during mating season. If you take your pets camping with you, keep them tethered for their own safety and the safety of the wildlife.

Avoid bear encounters. Campers and outdoor recreationists can generally avoid bear problems by not being careless or reckless. Most bear problems occur because garbage and food are left scattered around camp, or someone attempts to feed one of these large, omnivorous mammals. You create problems for yourself and other campers when you encourage wild animals to rely on humans as food sources. Use the following tips to help avoid problems with these carnivores:

a. Keep a clean camp. Bears, with their extremely good sense of smell, can be attracted to a camp from miles away. Food in the camp and food odors — including fish odors — on clothing will interest these animals. Bears aren't cuddly — they're hungry. Almost every case of black bears damaging property or attacking people has resulted from bears being fed food scraps, pet food, or garbage, or because they could smell food and went looking for it. Since bears will eat anything humans eat, discarded food scraps, food wrappers, vegetable cuttings, and even wash water should be properly taken care of.

b. Separate your cooking area from your sleeping area. Clean camps include separate sleeping areas from cooking and eating areas. Food, coolers, cooking utensils, cleaning rags, and clothing used while cooking should be left in the cooking area, which minimizes the chances of attracting bears to sleeping campers. Fish should be cleaned away from camp. Fish entrails should be buried and the cleaned fish stored in an icebox. Never store food or food-soiled clothing in a tent you will be sleeping in.

c. Suspend food, garbage and game or lock them in your car trunk or camper. In the backcountry, food, garbage, and game should be suspended 12 or more feet above the ground and four feet away from a tree, to keep it out of a bear's reach. Other options include keeping food in a sealed compartment of a vehicle, such as a trunk, or in a camper. Food stored in these locations is usually safe, as long as windows and doors are closed, but bears can break in if they find an opening.

d. Keep yourself clean and odor-free — No cooking odors, perfumes, etc. Leave at home perfumes, makeup, and deodorants, which can attract bears. Blood is an even greater attractant than the former items. Change your clothes after your evening meal, so you don't smell like food when you go to bed.

e. Make noise while hiking. In areas where bears are common, singing or attaching a bell to your backpack will alert bears to your presence and generally help them to move out of your way. Avoid getting between a mother and her cubs.

Bears will not usually attack humans. Most contacts consist of sightings, but occasionally consist of bears damaging property or attacking livestock or pets. A little common sense can prevent most bear problems while in the backcountry.

"I don't like spiders and snakes..."

Reptiles. In general, if you leave snakes and lizards alone, they will leave you alone. Most bites occur when an intruder prods them with a stick or tries to pick one up. Again, it is wise to maintain a safe distance from them. Avoid cornering them and making them feel trapped. If you approach a snake, back up slowly and find another route to your destination. Reptiles are cold-blooded animals and can be found on the south sides of rocks during spring and fall months. When hiking, watch where you put your feet and hands. Step on, not over, obstacles such as logs or large rocks.

The most dangerous reptiles you will encounter in Utah are rattlesnakes and Gila monsters (a poisonous lizard). Gila monsters are native to the southern Utah deserts, but are rarely seen and pose no threat unless you try to pick one up. Rattlesnakes are more common, but are usually encountered away from populated areas. Rattlesnakes make a rapid succession of clicking sounds by shaking their tails to let you know of their presence. If you hear a snake rattle, locate where the sound is coming from before you back away. You can identify a rattlesnake by the shape of its head or the markings on its back. If you encounter a snake, and you aren't sure if it is a rattler, leave it alone anyway. Snakes help keep rodent populations in balance and mean no harm to you. Remember, their fear of you is equal to or greater than your fear of them.

Should you or someone in our group be bitten by a snake:

• Remain calm
• Wash the wound
• Seek professional medical assistance as soon as possible

Don't delay yourselves by attempting to carry the hiker or build a litter, and don't attempt the old advice about cutting open the wound and sucking out the venom. If there is venom in the wound, it will slowly begin damaging the tissue around the bite, but don't worry about movement spreading it into the bloodstream. In some cases, snakes don't inject venom when they bite and all you've got is a puncture wound anyway. But either way, you can do more harm trying to treat it yourself and slowing your progress to trained medical help. Many presumed symptoms of a bite are actually signs of panic. Focus on remaining calm and getting professional help as quickly as possible.

Insects. Utah has the usual insects that can give painful stings and bites, and you are much more likely to get stung by a wasp than get bitten by a snake in the wilds. Insects can make camping less than enjoyable during certain times of the year. When selecting a campsite, avoid marshy areas where mosquitoes thrive. Insect repellents using DEET have been found to be most effective in avoiding these pests. Newer formulations limit your exposure to this harmful substance by time-releasing the chemical slowly, extending the effectiveness of the application without overexposure. Citronella and Avon's Skin-So-Soft also can also work as insect repellents for some people, but you will probably be best off if you have a product with at least 20 percent DEET with you for serious insect encounters. If you are unfortunate enough to receive a number of mosquito bites, try rubbing ammonia on the lumps to minimize the itch associated with them. "After Bite" also makes a very effective product for stopping the itch of mosquito bites.

Next to mosquitoes, you are most apt to be struck by a bee, wasp, hornet, deerfly, or gnat out in the wilds. Trees and logs are favorite nesting areas. Water is breeding ground for many biting insects. Keep an oral antihistamine with you to reduce swelling and itching, protect yourself by closing your collar and cuffs, and wear a bandana or hat to protect your head. If you are allergic to a bite or sting, make sure you have a sting kit suited to your allergy with you at all times.

Ticks pose a greater health risk than mosquitoes, and are a bit frightful for children. Although they can be picked up anywhere, you are more prone to them when hiking through brushy areas or tall grass. Ticks are parasitic insects that burrow into your skin with their heads, leaving the rest of their bodies exposed. Ticks are often found hidden above the hairline. Become familiar with techniques for removing them. Ticks can be carriers of several diseases, including Lyme Disease and Rocky Mountain Spotted Fever. The sooner ticks are removed, the better. Have someone else inspect your body for these pesky bugs and check your scalp carefully. When removing ticks, make sure that you remove the tick's head completely to limit infection. Avoid trying to pinch them or burn them, which will cause them to vomit potential diseases into your bloodstream. Invest in a commercially available tick remover and keep it in your first aid kit.

Scorpions are often found in the warmer, drier areas of southern Utah. Their sting can be painful but is usually not dangerous except to those allergic to their toxins. It is wise to make a habit of checking your footwear before putting them on each morning, and to check your sleeping bag before climbing in each night.

Hantavirus. The Hantavirus should be a concern if you are camping where rodents thrive. Avoid contact with rodent droppings and be careful of breathing dust, which may contain the droppings.

Stinging Nettle, Poison Ivy and Poison Oak. Stinging nettle and poison ivy are the most common backcountry flora to cause you problems. They aren't deadly, but they can cause some moments of pain and anguish for young children. You will often find them near water. The best way to avoid problems is to wear long pants. If you insist on wearing shorts, don't let plants brush up against you.

The Boy Scouts are taught a simple slogan to help them avoid dangerous plants: "Leaves three, let be. Berries white, take flight."

PHOTO: CHEYENNE ROUSE

A couple prepares a meal on Mount Timpanogos. Camping with companions helps protect adventurers from several dangers, including hypothermia.

Wild Berries/Mushrooms. Unless you are extremely good at identifying edible plants such as wild berries and mushrooms, we strongly recommend that you avoid eating them in the backcountry. Some of these can give you a stomachache or worse. Several plant identification guides are available if you are interested in acquiring this knowledge. Guided educational excursions are also available during late summer and early fall to help you acquire these skills. Make sure you obtain your training from qualified individuals to ensure that you do not learn from a very hazardous mistake.

Frostbite and Hypothermia. In Utah's mountains the weather can rapidly change from beautiful warm summer conditions to midwinter blizzards. Frostbite occurs when body tissues are exposed to freezing temperatures. Extremities such as the hands and feet are most often affected. Hypothermia is a condition that occurs when body temperatures drop below normal, often due to exhaustion or exposure to the elements. Trouble usually occurs when the body loses heat faster than it can be produced. Your body loses heat the fastest from your head and feet. Wearing a hat and keeping your feet warm and dry will help prevent heat loss. Hypothermia is a silent killer that can occur any time of the year. To prevent frostbite or hypothermia, try to prevent exposure, eat regularly to maintain energy, get sufficient rest, dress in layers, and do not hike, camp, or swim alone.

Dehydration. Dehydration can occur any time of the year. Recreationists should always keep fluids in their systems, even when they are not thirsty. Under extreme conditions, by the time you feel thirsty, it may be too late. Always pack plenty of water. If you don't need it, you can always dump it out later.

Treating Water in the Backcountry

Camping in Utah's backcountry can be a rewarding, enjoyable experience, but drinking untreated water can leave you with less than fond memories of your vacation. Remember that appearances can be misleading. Even crystal clear water can contain harmful bacteria and parasites, ending your outdoor activities in a hurry. *Giardia lamblia*, responsible for the famous "Rocky Mountain Quickstep" (causing severe diarrhea), is a concern to all backcountry travelers although symptoms won't appear for seven to 10 days after infection. In addition, cryptosporidium, several bacteria and viruses are also concerns for outdoor enthusiasts.

Many harmful microbes and parasites are spread via the fecal-oral route. Water from upstream may be contaminated by run-off, animals, or other humans. Symptoms of giardia include yellow, foul-smelling, frothy diarrhea; bloating; excessive gas; and malaise. For your own safety and well-being, all natural water sources should be considered suspect. Some natural springs have even been contaminated and require treatment.

How should your potable water be treated? Numerous methods are available for limiting parasite and microbe risk, including boiling or filtering the water you drink. Boiling is still the most economical and efficient method today. Research indicates that boiling water for five minutes is possibly one of most effective methods available to backcountry travelers. For elevations above 10,000 feet add one minute for every 1,000 feet in elevation. Keep in mind that boiling the water does nothing for potential chemical pollutants in the water. Watch for water that may be contaminated by mine tailings or questionable sources.

Several chemical purification methods can be effective in destroying water-borne microorganisms and parasites, if you allow the chemicals to work long enough at appropriate temperatures. This can require overnight treatment for water coming from a cold stream. Tincture of iodine or chlorine bleach are the two most common water treatments, with iodine being more effective than chlorine (which is affected by organic matter in the water, and which will not kill cryptosporidium). Several commercially available products are also on the market, including iodine tablets. Follow instructions for individual products carefully and remember that iodine tablets degrade upon contact with moisture, requiring that the bottle be discarded upon returning home.

To purify using liquid iodine: Five drops (1 drop being approximately 0.05 ml) of tincture of iodine (from your first aid kit) can be added to one quart of warm water or 10 drops in cold or cloudy water. Mix thoroughly by stirring or shaking water in the container and allowing it to stand for 30 minutes. Very cold or turbid water may require several hours to overnight treatment. To reduce the Band-aid flavor of iodine treatments add a small amount of vitamin C to the water after the required time frame. Remember to rinse your container thoroughly before trying to treat more water (this prevents the chances of inactivating the next treatment with leftover vitamin C residue). For those who use iodine treatments regularly, some individuals have developed thyroid problems as a side effect. Research also indicates that iodine may not be entirely effective for removing all cryptosporidium.

PHOTO: CHEYENNE ROUSE

A sturdy cast iron kettle can be used to boil water for safety — and then to warm cocoa, tea or soup for chilled campers.

To use liquid bleach (such as used for washing clothes): Add 10 drops (again approximately 0.05 ml) to a quart of clear , warm water or 20 drops to cold or cloudy water. Mix the solution thoroughly and allow it to stand 30 minutes before drinking. If you do not notice a slight chlorine odor at that time, repeat the dosage and let if stand an additional 15 minutes before using. Very cold or cloudy water may also require overnight treatment. Remember that chlorinated water may kill many of the harmful pests, but may not be the magic bullet for all of them. Boiling water has proven itself to be much more effective.

If you want a more high-tech and possibly more reliable solution, consider water filters. Water filtering systems can be expensive and add a lot of weight to your pack, but they are quick and safe, and provide the taste of a clear mountain stream, rather than a drink tainted with Clorox or iodine. Systems with ceramic filters can be reused but are more expensive than their paper filter counterparts. The most important aspect of a filter is to make sure it filters out giardia and other microorganisms.

Filters have certainly grown in popularity in recent years, but buyers need to be informed that all are not created equally. Good filters on the market will remove both cryposporidium and giardia, but research indicates that some are much less effective in filtering out these problem bugs, due to pore size. To limit bacteria from passing through the filter, you need a product with pores less than 0.2 microns. Check this carefully because many filters on the market have a much larger pore size, which allows many of the unwanted nasties through. Buyers should also be aware that an iodine matrix is required to destroy viruses. Addition of a carbon filter will remove some chemical toxins.

Water filters are relatively quick, simple, and offer clean tasting water for recreationists, but remember that the small pore size will require effort and muscle on your part to generate a quart of drinkable water. Smaller pore sizes tend to plug up easily and replacement filters can be costly. With so many filters on the market, check carefully for pore size, cost of replacement filters, durability, weight, and the ability to replace filters in the backcountry without contaminating the filtered water. Many filters tend to be bulky and complicated. Become familiar with yours before using it as your sole source of water purification on your next adventure.

Some individuals worry themselves sick with the possibility of drinking untreated water. Remember that the chances of getting sick are much less important than the possibility of dying from dehydration before you return. If you ever find yourself in the outdoors without the means to properly treat water, try to find the cleanest source available. Look for natural springs or learn how to capture dew. It is not fun to get sick, but if no other options are available, drink enough water to sustain yourself until help arrives or you can return home.

First Aid Kit Master List

- ❑ Dermaplast anesthetic spray — for bug bites and the inevitable scrapes that kids get
- ❑ Antihistamine — Benadryl or something like it to reduce the swelling and itching of bug bites
- ❑ Tweezers
- ❑ Fingernail clippers
- ❑ Alcohol preps
- ❑ Bandage tape
- ❑ Butterfly closures
- ❑ Diaper pins
- ❑ A&D ointment
- ❑ Neosporin Plus
- ❑ Finger splint
- ❑ Small travel size of Vicks VapoRub
- ❑ Regular size bandages
- ❑ Sample size of Myoflex — for those muscle aches hubby might get being "macho"!
- ❑ Ziploc bag with a few Q-tips and cotton squares
- ❑ Emergency blanket
- ❑ Adhesive tape remover pads
- ❑ Hydrocortisone cream for itches
- ❑ Thermometer
- ❑ Disposable razor
- ❑ Bandage scissors
- ❑ Forceps or needle nose pliers for getting fish hooks out
- ❑ Extra-large bandages — great for those skinned knees or elbows after a spill from mountain a bike or in-line skates
- ❑ 1 1/2 x2 inch gauze pads
- ❑ 2x2 inch gauze pads
- ❑ 3x4 inch gauze pads
- ❑ Maxi-pads — for absorbing a lot of blood from a cut
- ❑ Moleskin
- ❑ Antacid
- ❑ Adult pain-relievers
- ❑ Children's pain-reliever/fever reducers — chewables are recommended. Make sure you include a measuring spoon if you use the liquid
- ❑ Laxative
- ❑ Ace Bandage
- ❑ Burn ointment
- ❑ Medicine dropper
- ❑ Any special medicines required by you our your family. Write down the name of the medicine, who it's for, and appropriate dosage on the container

Your first aid kit needs to be stored in a waterproof container. Separate the items into similar groups, then put them in resealable bags. Store these in the waterproof container.

Dressing for Utah Weather

Temperatures in Utah's backcountry can change drastically in a short amount of time. Early morning temperatures may start in the mid-30s and reach the mid-70s by early afternoon. While it is not uncommon to experience snow in May or October, in the high mountains you might experience extreme weather conditions any day of the year.

The key clothing basics to consider are: Be comfortable, and be safe.

You can accomplish both of these basics by dressing in layers. Clothing layers can be mixed and matched to create the proper amount of insulation, ventilation, and weather protection. Most often you will need two to three layers: a base layer, which is next to your skin; an insulation layer, which covers the base layer; and a shell layer, which you will use to cover the insulation layer in wet or windy conditions.

Clothing should be combined and adapted to meet the best and worst of weather conditions. Warm weather clothing should include the following:

- Long-sleeve, loose-fitting shirts
- Loose-fitting pants and shorts
- Comfortable underwear
- Fleece jacket or vest
- Lightweight long underwear
- Lightweight rain shell
- Lightweight rain pants
- Well-ventilated hat with brim
- Bandana
- Wool socks
- Footwear
- Sunscreen and lip balm
- Polarized sunglasses

Because Utah weather can change dramatically in a very short time, it is wise to check weather conditions before heading into the backcountry or hiking in one of the slot canyons of southern Utah's red rock country. On the web, visit www.nws.noaa.gov/, choose "Utah" under the state options, and then click on your specific location (e.g. Bryce Canyon). The National Weather Service hotline in Salt Lake is 524-5133. Nationally, call (900) WEATHER. Carrying a radio can enable you to check up-to-the-minute weather reports while on a trail or choosing a campsite. AM radio signals travel the farthest, especially at night.

Lightning kills many hikers in Utah every year. If you find yourself amid lightning, head to a low elevation and seek shelter in a tent, under a rock outcropping or in a large grove of trees. Avoid high locations and isolated trees.

Flash floods are also a danger, especially during heavy rains after the soil is saturated from late spring run-off, and during the summer monsoon season, especially in August. Always camp above gullies and ravines. Even if it is not raining in your immediate area, rain at a higher elevation could cause a flash flood.

Reservations

Many campgrounds require that you purchase a reservation to camp there, while others don't accept reservations at all. You can save yourself a lot of disappointment if you know the requirements of the campground before you get there. Most of the campgrounds in the state are controlled by federal agencies: The National Forest Service, National Park Service, or the Bureau of Land Management. State-controlled campgrounds are administered by Utah State Parks and Recreation. Permits may be required to camp in unimproved backcountry areas. Winter camping permits are also required in American Fork Canyon. Group size may be limited to reduce impacts on the environment, including in designated wilderness areas.

BLM campgrounds

Most are first-come, first-served. Regulations are available for some developed campgrounds. Call the number listed for the particular campground you want to visit.

National Forest Campgrounds

Campgrounds in Wasatch Front canyons and along Hwy. 150 in the Uintas fill up quickly; advance reservations are needed to obtain a site on summer weekends. Sites may be available midweek on a first-come, first-served basis. Call (800) 280-2267 or (877) 444-6777, or visit www.reserveusa.com.

National Parks & Recreation Areas

Individual campsites are available on a first-come, first-served basis. Sites often fill up by noon, so arrive early. Group sites must be reserved in advance. Call the number listed for the particular park you want to visit, call (800) 365-CAMP, or online see reservations.nps.gov (no "www").

Utah State Parks

Advance reservations for group sites and individual campsites are available at all developed Utah state parks. Parks often fill up on summer weekends. Individual sites may be available on a first-come, first-served basis. Camping at undeveloped parks is first-come, first-served. Call (800) 322-3770, or, in the Salt Lake area, (801) 322-3770.

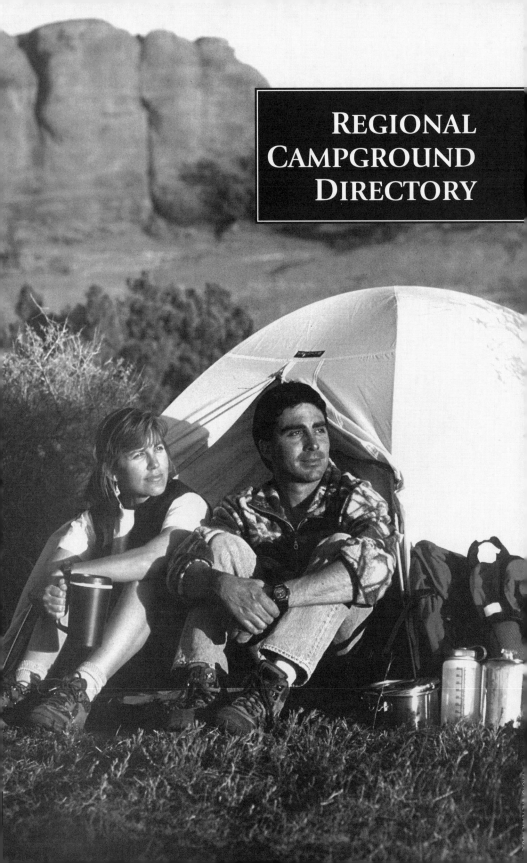

REGIONAL
CAMPGROUND
DIRECTORY

CAMPGROUNDS: NORTHERN REGION

AMERICAN FORK CANYON / ALPINE LOOP

Aspen Grove
🚰 ⛺ 🚐 🚽

Location: Northeast of Pleasant Grove on Hwy. 92, along Alpine Loop
Campsites: 58 RV and tent sites
Max RV Length: 40 feet
Facilities/Accommodations: Drinking water, fishing, handicap facilities, picnic tables, toilets
Reservations: (800) 280-2267
Open: May 25 to October 31
Limit of Stay: 14 days
Fee Charged: Yes
Managing Agency: National Forest Service (Uinta)

Altamont (Reservations Only)
🚰 ⛺ ♿ 🚐 🚽 🚿

Location: 14 miles northeast of Pleasant Grove on Hwy. 92, along Alpine Loop
Campsites: 4 RV sites, 5 tent sites
Max RV Length: 45 feet
Facilities/Accommodations: Drinking water, picnic tables, toilets
Reservations: (800) 280-2267
Open: May 15 to October 1
Limit of Stay: 14 days
Fee Charged: Yes
Managing Agency: National Forest Service (Uinta)

Echo
🚰 🚐 🚽

Location: 10.8 miles northeast of Pleasant Grove off Hwy. 92, in American Fork Canyon
Campsites: 3 RV sites, 5 tent sites
Max RV Length: 40 feet
Facilities/Accommodations: Drinking water, fishing, picnic tables, toilets
Reservations: (800) 280-2267
Open: May 15 to September 30
Limit of Stay: 14 days
Fee Charged: Yes
Managing Agency: National Forest Service (Uinta)

Granite Flat
🚰 ⛺ 🚐 🚽

Location: 14.1 miles northeast of Pleasant Grove off Hwy. 144, in American Fork Canyon
Campsites: 56 RV sites, 32 tent sites
Max RV Length: Unknown
Facilities/Accommodations: Drinking water, fishing, group sites, nondrinkable water, picnic tables, toilets
Reservations: (800) 280-2267
Open: May 24 to September 30
Limit of Stay: 5 days
Fee Charged: Yes
Managing Agency: National Forest Service (Uinta)

SYMBOL LEGEND

🚰 Drinking water	🚐 RV sites
⛺ Group sites	🚽 Toilets
♿ Handicap facilities	🚿 Showers

Idaho

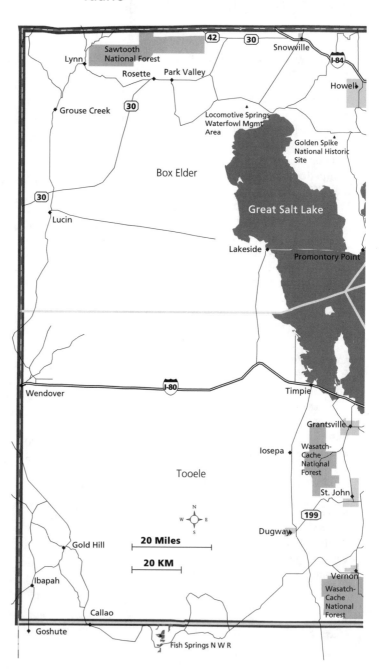

Nevada

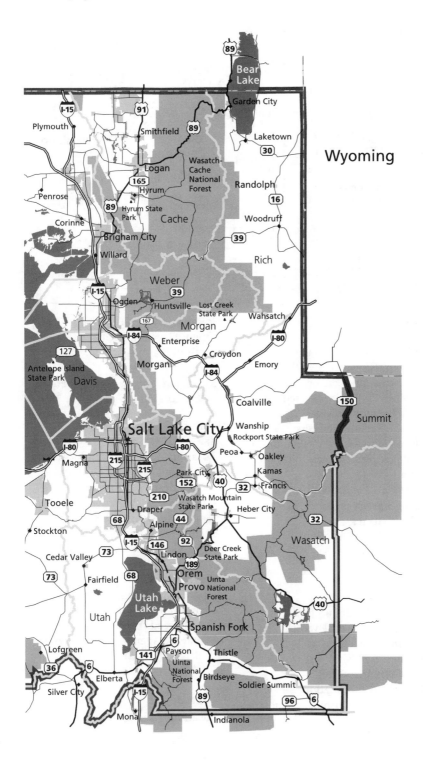

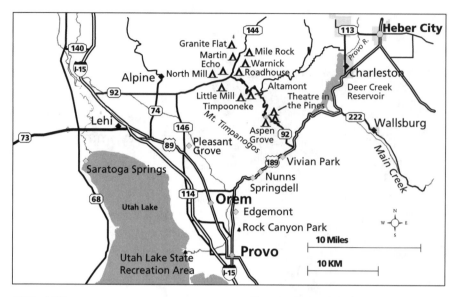

Little Mill
🛶 ♿ 🚐 🚻

Location: 14.1 miles northeast of
Pleasant Grove on Hwy. 92, in
American Fork Canyon
Campsites: 79 RV sites, 46 tent sites
Max RV Length: 45 feet
Facilities/Accommodations:
Drinking water, fishing, handicap
facilities, picnic tables, toilets
Reservations: (800) 280-2267
Open: May 15 to September 30
Limit of Stay: 14 days
Fee Charged: Yes
Managing Agency: National Forest
Service (Uinta)

Martin
🛶 🚻

Location: 11.8 miles northeast of
Pleasant Grove off Hwy. 144, in
American Fork Canyon
Campsites: 5 RV sites, 5 tent sites
Max RV Length: 30 feet
Facilities/Accommodations:
Drinking water, fishing, picnic
tables, toilets

Reservations: (800) 280-2267
Open: May 15 to October 15
Limit of Stay: 14 days
Fee Charged: Yes
Managing Agency: National Forest
Service (Uinta)

Mile Rock
🛶 🚐 🚻

Location: 12.2 miles northeast of
Pleasant Grove off Hwy. 144, in
American Fork Canyon
Campsites: 6 RV sites, 12 tent sites
Max RV Length: 30 feet
Facilities/Accommodations:
Drinking water, fishing, picnic
tables, toilets
Reservations: (800) 280-2267
Open: May 15 to October 15
Limit of Stay: 14 days
Fee Charged: Yes
Managing Agency: National Forest
Service (Uinta)

Mount Timpanogos
🛶 🚐 🚻

Location: 14 miles northeast of

Provo on Hwy. 92, along Alpine
Loop
Campsites: 27 RV sites, 26 tent sites
Max RV Length: 45 feet
Facilities/Accommodations:
Drinking water, picnic tables, toilets
Reservations: (800) 280-2267
Open: June 1 to September 25
Limit of Stay: 14 days
Fee Charged: Yes
Managing Agency: National Forest
Service (Uinta)

North Mill (Reservations Only)

Location: 10.2 miles northeast of
Pleasant Grove on Hwy. 92, in
American Fork Canyon
Campsites: 2 RV sites, 2 tent sites
Max RV Length: 43 feet
Facilities/Accommodations:
Drinking water , fishing, picnic
tables, toilets

Reservations: (800) 280-2267
Open: May 15 to September 30
Limit of Stay: 14 days
Fee Charged: Yes
Managing Agency: National Forest
Service (Uinta)

Roadhouse

Location: 10.9 miles northeast of
Pleasant Grove on Hwy. 92, in
American Fork Canyon
Campsites: 6 RV sites, 10 tent sites
Max RV Length: 40 feet
Facilities/Accommodations:
Drinking water, fishing, toilets
Reservations: (800) 280-2267
Open: May 15 to October 15
Limit of Stay: 14 days
Fee Charged: Yes
Managing Agency: National Forest
Service (Uinta)

A camper finds a great spot on Mount Timpanogos.

PHOTO: CHEYENNE ROUSE

Theatre in the Pines (Reservations Only)

🛶 🚐 🚻

Location: 14 miles north of Provo on Hwy. 92
Campsites: 1 RV site, 150 tent sites
Max RV Length: 45 feet
Facilities/Accommodations: Drinking water, picnic tables, toilets
Reservations: (800) 280-2267
Open: June 1 to September 25
Limit of Stay: 14 days
Fee Charged: Yes
Managing Agency: National Forest Service (Uinta)

Timpooneke

🛶 🚐 🚻

Location: 14.1 miles northeast of Pleasant Grove on Hwy. 92, along Alpine Loop
Campsites: 32 RV and tent sites
Max RV Length: 45 feet
Facilities/Accommodations: Drinking water, picnic tables, toilets
Reservations: (800) 280-2267
Open: May 25 to October 30
Limit of Stay: 14 days
Fee Charged: Yes
Managing Agency: National Forest Service (Uinta)

Warnick

🛶 🚐 🚻

Location: 12.1 miles northeast of Pleasant Grove off Hwy. 144, in American Fork Canyon
Campsites: RV sites, 6 tent sites
Max RV Length: 20 feet
Facilities/Accommodations: Drinking water, fishing, picnic tables, toilets

Reservations: (800) 280-2267
Open: May 15 to October 15
Limit of Stay: 14 days
Fee Charged: Yes
Managing Agency: National Forest Service (Uinta)

ANTELOPE ISLAND STATE PARK

Antelope Island

🛶 ♿ 🚐 🎣 🚻

Location: 15 miles west of Syracuse off I-15 (Exit 335)
Campsites: 64 RV sites, 11 tent sites
Max RV Length: 35 feet
Facilities/Accommodations: Boating, drinking water, fishing, handicap facilities, nondrinkable water, picnic tables, showers, swimming, toilets
Reservations: (800) 322-3770
Open: Year-round
Limit of Stay: 14 days
Fee Charged: Yes
Managing Agency: Utah State Parks

BEAR LAKE

Sunrise

🛶 🚐 🚻

Location: 8.2 miles southwest of Garden City on Hwy. 89, in the mountains above the lake
Campsites: 27 RV and tent sites
Max RV Length: 20 feet
Facilities/Accommodations: Drinking water, picnic tables, toilets
Reservations: (800) 280-2267
Open: June 15 to September 15
Limit of Stay: 7 days
Fee Charged: Yes
Managing Agency: National Forest Service (Wasatch-Cache)

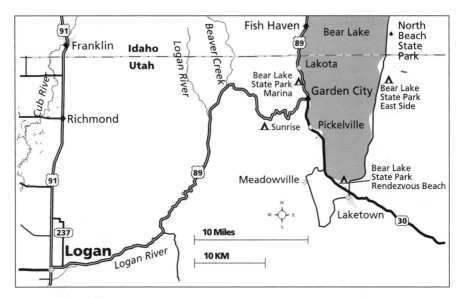

Bear Lake State Park — East Side
🚿 🚐 🚽

Location: East side of the lake, directly across from Garden City
Campsites: 25 RV and tent sites
Max RV Length: None
Facilities/Accommodations: Boating, drinking water, fishing, nondrinkable water, picnic tables, swimming, toilets
Reservations: (800) 322-3770
Open: Year-round
Limit of Stay: 14 days
Fee Charged: Yes
Managing Agency: Utah State Parks

Bear Lake State Park — Marina
🚿 🚐 🍴 🚽

Location: 2 miles north of Garden City on Hwy. 89
Campsites: 13 RV and tent sites
Max RV Length: 32 feet
Facilities/Accommodations: Boating, drinking water, dump sites, fishing, nondrinkable water, picnic tables, showers, swimming, toilets

Reservations: (800) 322-3770
Open: Year-round
Limit of Stay: 14 days
Fee Charged: Yes
Managing Agency: Utah State Parks

Bear Lake State Park — Rendezvous Beach
🚿 ♿ 🚐 🍴 🚽

Location: 2 miles west of Laketown on Hwy. 30
Campsites: 136 RV and tent sites, 136 complete RV hookups, 46 tent sites
Max RV Length: 36 feet
Facilities/Accommodations: Boating, drinking water, dump sites, handicap facilities, picnic tables, showers, swimming, toilets
Reservations: (800) 322-3770
Open: May 1 to October 30
Limit of Stay: 14 days
Fee Charged: Yes
Managing Agency: Utah State Parks

Bear Lake KOA Kampground
🔌 ⛺ 🚐 🌿 🚿

Location: 1 mile north of Garden City on Hwy. 89

Campsites: 150 RV sites, 50 complete RV hookups, 50 tent sites

Max RV Length: 65 feet

Facilities/Accommodations: Boating, drinking water, dump sites, fishing, group sites, laundry, picnic tables, showers, toilets

Reservations: (435) 946-3454

Open: Year-round

Limit of Stay: Unknown

Fee Charged: Yes

Managing Agency: Private

Blue Water Beach Campgrounds
🔌 ♿ 🚐 🌿 🚿

Location: 2126 South Bear Lake Blvd., 2 miles south of Garden City

Campsites: 120 RV sites, 60 complete RV hookups, 60 tent sites

Max RV Length: 35 feet

Facilities/Accommodations: Drinking water, dump sites, fishing, handicap facilities, laundry, nondrinkable water, picnic tables, showers, swimming, toilets

Reservations: (800) 756-6795, (435) 946-3333/2925

Open: May 25 to October 1

Limit of Stay: 7 days

Fee Charged: Yes

Managing Agency: Private

Fay's Trailer Park
🔌 🚐 🚿

Location: 225 N Bear Lake Blvd., Garden City

Campsites: 14 RV sites with complete RV hookups, 10 tent sites

Max RV Length: 34 feet

Facilities/Accommodations: Boating, drinking water, dump sites, fishing, swimming, toilets

Reservations: (435) 773-2415

Open: May 30 to October 1

Limit of Stay: 28 days

Fee Charged: Yes

Managing Agency: Private

Sunrise Village
🔌 🚐 🌿 🚿

Location: 1171 N Bear Lake Blvd., Garden City

Campsites: 24 RV sites with water and electric hookups

Max RV Length: None

Facilities/Accommodations: Boating, drinking water, dump sites, fishing, nondrinkable water, picnic tables, showers, swimming, toilets

Reservations: (435) 946-8620

Open: May 28 to September 5

Limit of Stay: None

Fee Charged: Yes

Managing Agency: Private

Sweetwater RV Park & Marina
🔌 ♿ 🚐 🌿 🚿

Location: Hwy. 30, Garden City

Campsites: 19 RV sites with complete RV hookups

Max RV Length: Unknown

Facilities/Accommodations: Boating, drinking water, dump sites, fishing, handicap facilities, laundry, nondrinkable water, picnic tables, showers, toilets

Reservations: (435) 946-8735 or 735-1701

Open: May 1 to September 30

Limit of Stay: Unknown

Fee Charged: Yes

Managing Agency: Private

BLACKSMITH FORK CANYON

Friendship

Location: 10.5 miles east of Hyrum in left fork of Blacksmith Fork Canyon
Campsites: 6 RV and tent sites
Max RV Length: 20 feet
Facilities/Accommodations: Fishing, group sites, picnic tables, toilets
Reservations: (800) 280-2267
Open: May 15 to September 15
Limit of Stay: 7 days
Fee Charged: Yes
Managing Agency: National Forest Service

Pioneer

Location: 9 miles east of Hyrum on Hwy. 101
Campsites: 18 RV and tent sites
Max RV Length: 20 feet
Facilities/Accommodations: Drinking water, fishing, nondrinkable water, picnic tables, toilets
Reservations: (800) 280-2267
Open: May 25 to November 1
Limit of Stay: 7 days
Fee Charged: Yes
Managing Agency: National Forest Service

Spring

Location: 12.6 miles east of Hyrum in left fork of Blacksmith Fork Canyon
Campsites: 3 RV and tent sites
Max RV Length: 20 feet
Facilities/Accommodations: Drinking water, fishing, nondrinkable water, picnic tables, toilets
Reservations: (800) 280-2267
Open: May 15 to October 31
Limit of Stay: 7 days
Fee Charged: Yes
Managing Agency: National Forest Service

BRIGHAM CITY

Brigham City KOA

Location: I-15 Exit 365 before Brigham City
Campsites: 38 RV sites, 38 RV hookups, 17 tent sites
Max RV Length: Unknown
Facilities/Accommodations: Boating, drinking water, dump sites, fishing, handicap facilities, laundry, nondrinkable water, picnic tables, showers, toilets
Reservations: (435) 723-5503
Open: Year-round
Limit of Stay: Unknown
Fee Charged: Yes
Managing Agency: Private

Doutre's Mobile Home Park

Location: 265 N 300 W, Brigham City
Campsites: 8 RV sites with complete RV hookups
Max RV Length: Unknown
Facilities/Accommodations: Drinking water, dump sites, group sites, handicap facilities, laundry, showers, toilets
Reservations: (435) 257-7500
Open: Year-round
Limit of Stay: Unknown
Fee Charged: Yes
Managing Agency: Private

Golden Spike RV Park

🛥 🚐 🚿 ♨

Location: 905 W 1075 S, Brigham
City
Campsites: 60 RV sites, 55 complete
RV hookups, 31 tent sites
Max RV Length: 70 feet
Facilities/Accommodations:
Drinking water, dump sites, laun-
dry, nondrinkable water, picnic
tables, showers, swimming, toilets
Reservations: (435) 723-8858
Open: Year-round
Limit of Stay: 90 days
Fee Charged: Yes
Managing Agency: Private

CRYSTAL SPRINGS

Crystal Springs Resort

🛥 🏕 ♿ 🚐 🚿 ♨

Location: 8215 North Hwy. 69,
Honeyville (north of Brigham
City)
Campsites: 124 RV sites, 83 com-
plete RV hookups, 41 tent sites
Max RV Length: 90 feet
Facilities/Accommodations:
Drinking water, dump sites, group
sites, handicap facilities, picnic
tables, showers, swimming, toilets
Reservations: (435) 279-8104
Open: Year-round
Limit of Stay: 7 days
Fee Charged: Yes
Managing Agency: Private

CURRANT CREEK RESERVOIR

Currant Creek

🛥 🏕 ♿ 🚐 ♨

Location: 57 miles east of Heber
City off Hwy. 40 and Currant
Creek Road
Campsites: 103 RV and tent sites

Max RV Length: 40 feet
Facilities/Accommodations:
Boating, drinking water, dump
sites, fishing, group sites, handi-
cap facilities, picnic tables, toilets
Reservations: (800) 280-2267
Open: May 25 to October 31
Limit of Stay: 14 days
Fee Charged: Yes
Managing Agency: National Forest
Service (Uinta)

DEER CREEK STATE PARK / MIDWAY

Deer Creek State Park

🛥 🏕 ♿ 🚐 🚿 ♨

Location: On the reservoir, 7 miles
southwest of Heber City along
Hwy. 189
Campsites: 22 RV sites, 10 tent sites
Max RV Length: 35 feet
Facilities/Accommodations:
Boating, drinking water, dump
sites, group sites, handicap facili-
ties, fishing, nondrinkable water,
picnic tables, showers, swimming,
toilets
Reservations: (800) 322-3770; (801)
225-9783
Open: April 1 to November 30
Limit of Stay: 10 days
Fee Charged: Yes
Managing Agency: Utah State Parks

Mountain Spa

🛥 🏕 ♿ 🚐 🚿 ♨

Location: 800 N Mountain Spa
Lane, Midway
Campsites: 20 RV sites, 8 complete
RV hookups, 25 tent sites
Max RV Length: 32 feet
Facilities/Accommodations:
Drinking water, fishing, group
sites, handicap facilities, laundry,
picnic tables, showers, toilets

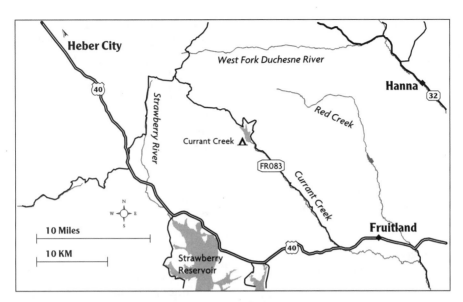

Reservations: (435) 654-0721
Open: April 15 to October 15
Limit of Stay: 30 days
Fee Charged: Yes
Managing Agency: Private

DIAMOND FORK CANYON / HOBBLE CREEK / MAPLETON CANYON

Balsam

Location: 13.1 miles east of Springville in Hobble Creek Canyon
Campsites: 26 RV and tent sites
Max RV Length: 30 feet
Facilities/Accommodations: Drinking water, fishing, group sites, picnic tables, toilets
Reservations: (800) 280-2267
Open: May 25 to October 31
Limit of Stay: 14 days
Fee Charged: Yes
Managing Agency: National Forest Service (Uinta)

Cherry

Location: 8.3 miles east of Springville in Hobble Creek Canyon
Campsites: 18 RV sites, 14 tent sites
Max RV Length: 35 feet
Facilities/Accommodations: Drinking water, fishing, group sites, picnic tables, toilets
Reservations: (800) 280-2267
Open: May 21 to October 31
Limit of Stay: 14 days
Fee Charged: Yes
Managing Agency: National Forest Service (Uinta)

Diamond

Location: 18.5 miles east of Spanish Fork in Diamond Fork Canyon
Campsites: 35 RV and tent sites
Max RV Length: 75 feet
Facilities/Accommodations: Drinking water, fishing, picnic tables, toilets
Reservations: (800) 280-2267

Open: May 15 to October 31
Limit of Stay: 14 days
Fee Charged: Yes
Managing Agency: National Forest
Service

Palmyra (Reservations Only)
🔥 ⫞ 🚐 🛁

Location: 17.5 miles east of Spanish
Fork in Diamond Fork Canyon
Campsites: 15 RV sites, 50 tent sites
Max RV Length: 50 feet
Facilities/Accommodations:
Drinking water, fishing, group
sites, picnic tables, toilets
Reservations: (800) 280-2267
Open: May 15 to October 31
Limit of Stay: 14 days
Fee Charged: Yes
Managing Agency: National Forest
Service

Whiting
🔥 ⫞ 🚐 🛁

Location: 2 miles east of Mapleton
in Mapleton Canyon
Campsites: 27 RV sites, 24 tent sites
Max RV Length: 45 feet
Facilities/Accommodations:
Drinking water, fishing, group
sites, picnic tables, toilets
Reservations: (800) 280-2267
Open: May 1 to October 31
Limit of Stay: 14 days
Fee Charged: Yes
Managing Agency: National Forest
Service (Uinta)

Spanish Fork Canyon RV Resort
🔥 ♿ 🚐 🛁

Location: 13279 East Hwy. 6 in
Spanish Fork Canyon
Campsites: 103 RV sites with com-
plete RV hookups
Max RV Length: 100 feet

Facilities/Accommodations:
Drinking water, handicap facili-
ties, laundry, nondrinkable water,
picnic tables, showers, toilets
Reservationss (801) 489-8128
Open: Year-round
Limit of Stay: 14 days
Fee Charged: Yes
Managing Agency: Private

EAST CANYON STATE PARK

East Canyon
🔥 ⫞ 🚐 🚿 🛁

Location: 10 miles south of Morgan
off Hwy. 66
Campsites: 31 RV sites, 15 tent sites
Max RV Length: 35 feet
Facilities/Accommodations:
Boating, drinking water, dump
sites, fishing, group sites, non-
drinkable water, picnic tables,
showers, swimming, toilets
Reservations: (800) 322-3770
Open: Year-round (limited facilities
in winter)
Limit of Stay: 14 days
Fee Charged: Yes
Managing Agency: Utah State Parks

ECHO RESERVOIR

Holiday Hills Campground
🔥 ⫞ 🚐 🚿 🛁

Location: 500 W 100 S, Coalville
Campsites: 42 RV sites with com-
plete RV hookups, 100 tent sites
Max RV Length: 50 feet
Facilities/Accommodations:
Boating, drinking water, dump
sites, fishing, group sites, laundry,
showers, toilets
Reservations: (435) 336-4421
Open: Year-round
Limit of Stay: Unknown
Fee Charged: Yes
Managing Agency: Private

GRANTSVILLE

Boy Scout

Location: South Willow Creek Canyon, 10.2 miles southwest of Grantsville
Campsites: 9 RV and tent sites
Max RV Length: 20 feet
Facilities/Accommodations: Fishing, picnic tables, toilets
Reservations: (800) 280-2267
Open: May 1 to October 1
Limit of Stay: 7 days
Fee Charged: Yes
Managing Agency: National Forest Service (Wasatch-Cache)

Cottonwood

Location: South Willow Canyon, 9.2 miles southwest of Grantsville
Campsites: 3 RV and tent sites
Max RV Length: 20 feet
Facilities/Accommodations: Fishing, picnic tables, nondrinkable water, toilets
Reservations: (800) 280-2267
Open: May 1 to October 15
Limit of Stay: 7 days
Fee Charged: Yes
Managing Agency: National Forest Service (Wasatch-Cache)

Intake

Location: South Willow Canyon, 13 miles southwest of Grantsville
Campsites: 5 RV and tent sites
Max RV Length: Unknown
Facilities/Accommodations: Fishing, nondrinkable water, picnic tables, toilets
Reservations: (800) 280-2267
Open: May 1 to October 1

Limit of Stay: 7 days
Fee Charged: Yes
Managing Agency: National Forest Service (Wasatch-Cache)

Loop

Location: South Willow Canyon, 13 miles southwest of Grantsville
Campsites: 5 RV and tent sites
Max RV Length: Unknown
Facilities/Accommodations: Nondrinkable water, picnic tables, toilets
Reservations: (800) 280-2267
Open: May 1 to October 1
Limit of Stay: 7 days
Fee Charged: Yes
Managing Agency: National Forest Service (Wasatch-Cache)

Lower Narrows

Location: South Willow Canyon, 10.7 miles southwest of Grantsville
Campsites: 5 tent sites
Max RV Length: NA
Facilities/Accommodations: Nondrinkable water, picnic tables, toilets
Reservations: (800) 280-2267
Open: May 1 to October 1
Limit of Stay: 7 days
Fee Charged: Yes
Managing Agency: National Forest Service (Wasatch-Cache)

Upper Narrows

Location: South Willow Canyon, 11.5 miles southwest of Grantsville
Campsites: 8 RV and tent sites
Max RV Length: Unknown

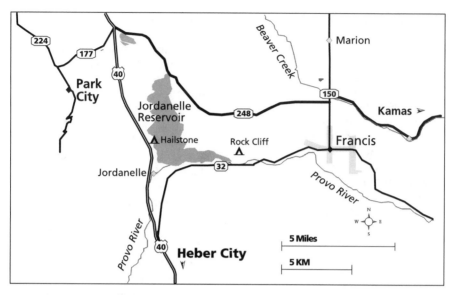

Facilities/Accommodations: Fishing, nondrinkable water, picnic tables, toilets
Reservations: (800) 280-2267
Open: May 1 to October 1
Limit of Stay: 7 days
Fee Charged: Yes
Managing Agency: National Forest Service (Wasatch-Cache)

HEBER CITY

Heber Valley RV Park

Location: 7000 N Old Hwy. 40, Heber
Campsites: 100 RV sites, 34 complete RV hookups, 30 tent sites
Max RV Length: 70 feet
Facilities/Accommodations: Boating, drinking water, fishing, group sites, picnic tables, showers, swimming, toilets
Reservations: (435) 654-4049
Open: Year-round
Limit of Stay: Unknown

Fee Charged: Yes
Managing Agency: Private

HYRUM STATE PARK

Hyrum Lake

Location: Hyrum
Campsites: 40 RV sites, 36 tent sites
Max RV Length: 40 feet
Facilities/Accommodations: Boating, drinking water, fishing, handicap facilities, nondrinkable water, picnic tables, swimming, toilets
Reservations: (800) 322-3770
Open: Year-round
Limit of Stay: 14 days
Fee Charged: Yes
Managing Agency: Utah State Parks

JORDANELLE STATE PARK

Hailstone

Location: On the west shore of the Jordanelle Reservoir off Hwy. 40
Campsites: 103 RV sites, 83 tent sites

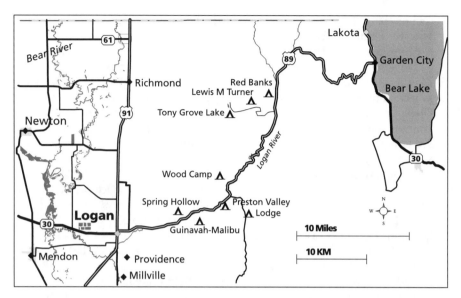

Max RV Length: None
Facilities/Accommodations:
Boating, drinking water, dump sites, fishing, group sites, handicap facilities, laundry, picnic tables, playground, showers, toilets
Reservations: (800) 322-3770
Open: Year-round
Limit of Stay: 14 days
Fee Charged: Yes
Managing Agency: Utah State Parks

Rock Cliff
Location: 2 miles west of Francis off Hwy. 32, on Jordanelle Reservoir
Campsites: 50 tent sites
Max RV Length: NA
Facilities/Accommodations:
Boating, drinking water, fishing, group sites, handicap facilities, picnic tables, showers, toilets; also nature center
Reservations: (800) 322-3770
Open: Year-round

Limit of Stay: 14 days
Fee Charged: Yes
Managing Agency: Utah State Parks

LOGAN / LOGAN CANYON

Guinavah-Malibu
Location: 8 miles east of Logan on Hwy. 89
Campsites: 40 RV and tent sites
Max RV Length: 25 feet
Facilities/Accommodations:
Drinking water, fishing, group sites, nondrinkable water, picnic tables, toilets
Reservations: (800) 280-2267
Open: May 15 to September 30
Limit of Stay: 7 days
Fee Charged: Yes
Managing Agency: National Forest Service (Wasatch-Cache)

Lewis M. Turner
Location: 22.2 miles northeast of Logan off Hwy. 89

Campsites: 10 RV and tent sites
Max RV Length: 20 feet
Facilities/Accommodations:
Drinking water, nondrinkable
water, picnic tables, toilets
Reservations: (800) 280-2267
Open: June 15 to October 31
Limit of Stay: 7 days
Fee Charged: Yes
Managing Agency: National Forest
Service (Wasatch-Cache)

Lodge
Location: 12.7 miles east of Logan
off Hwy. 89, along Right Fork
Campsites: 10 RV and tent sites
Max RV Length: 20 feet
Facilities/Accommodations:
Drinking water, fishing, non-
drinkable water, picnic tables, toi-
lets
Reservations: (800) 280-2267
Open: May 25 to September 15
Limit of Stay: 7 days
Fee Charged: Yes
Managing Agency: National Forest
Service (Wasatch-Cache)

Preston Valley
Location: 10.7 miles east of Logan
on Hwy. 89
Capmsites: 8 RV and tent sites
Max RV Length: 20 feet
Facilities/Accommodations:
Drinking water, fishing, non-
drinkable water, picnic tables, toi-
lets
Reservations: (800) 280-2267
Open: May 15 to September 30
Limit of Stay: 7 days
Fee Charged: Yes
Managing Agency: National Forest
Service (Wasatch-Cache)

Red Banks
Location: 22.7 miles northeast of
Logan on Hwy. 89
Campsites: 12 RV and tent sites
Max RV Length: 20 feet
Facilities/Accommodations:
Drinking water, fishing, non-
drinkable water, picnic tables, toi-
lets
Reservations: (800) 280-2267
Open: June 15 to October 31
Limit of Stay: 7 days
Fee Charged: Yes
Managing Agency: National Forest
Service (Wasatch-Cache)

Smithfield Canyon
Location: 5 miles northeast of
Smithfield in Smithfield Canyon
Campsites: 16 RV and tent sites
Max RV Length: 25 feet
Facilities/Accommodations:
Drinking water, fishing, non-
drinkable water, picnic tables, toi-
lets
Reservations: (800) 280-2267
Open: May 15 to September 15
Limit of Stay: 7 days
Fee Charged: Yes
Managing Agency: National Forest
Service (Wasatch-Cache)

Spring Hollow
Location: 6.5 miles east of Logan on
Hwy. 89
Campsites: 12 RV and tent sites
Max RV Length: 20 feet
Facilities/Accommodations:
Drinking water, fishing, group
sites, nondrinkable water, picnic
tables, toilets
Reservations: (800) 280-2267

Open: May 15 to November 1
Limit of Stay: 7 days
Fee Charged: Yes
Managing Agency: National Forest Service (Wasatch-Cache)

Tony Grove Lake

Location: About 15 miles west of Bear Lake off Hwy. 89
Campsites: 36 RV and tent sites
Max RV Length:
Facilities/Accommodations: Drinking water, fishing, swimming, toilets
Reservations: (800) 280-2267; (877) 444-6777
Open: July to September
Limit of Stay: 14 days
Fee Charged: Yes
Managing Agency: National Forest Service (Wasatch-Cache)

Wood Camp

Location: 12.4 miles northeast of Logan on Hwy. 89
Campsites: 6 RV and tent sites
Max RV Length: 20 feet
Facilities/Accommodations: Fishing, group sites, nondrinkable water, picnic tables, toilets
Reservations: (800) 280-2267
Open: May 15 to October 31
Limit of Stay: 7 days
Fee Charged: Yes
Managing Agency: National Forest Service (Wasatch-Cache)

Bandits Cove

Location: 590 S Main, Logan
Campsites: 12 RV sites with complete RV hookups, 4 tent sites
Max RV Length: 55 feet

Facilities/Accommodations: Drinking water, dump sites, fishing, group sites, handicap facilities, laundry, picnic tables, showers, toilets
Reservations: (435) 753-0508
Open: Year-round
Limit of Stay: Unknown
Fee Charged: Yes
Managing Agency: Private

Beaver Mountain RV Park

Location: Top of Logan Canyon off Hwy. 89
Campsites: RV and tent sites, some complete RV hookups
Max RV Length: Unknown
Facilities/Accommodations: Drinking water, dump sites, fishing, toilets
Reservations: (435) 753-0921
Open: Year-round
Limit of Stay: Unknown
Fee Charged: Yes
Managing Agency: Private

Riverside RV Park and Campgrounds

Location: 445 W 1700 S (1 mile south of Logan on Hwy. 89)
Campsites: 14 RV sites with complete RV hookups, 10 tent sites
Max RV Length: 40 feet
Facilities/Accommodations: Drinking water, dump sites, fishing, group sites, handicap facilities, nondrinkable water, picnic tables, showers, toilets
Reservations: (435) 245-4469
Open: Year-round
Limit of Stay: Unknown
Fee Charged: Yes
Managing Agency: Private

Western Park Camp

Location: 350 W 800 S, Logan
Campsites: 15 RV sites with complete RV hookups, 5 tent sites
Max RV Length: 40 feet
Facilities/Accommodations: Drinking water, fishing, picnic tables, showers, toilets
Reservations: (435) 752-6424
Open: Year-round
Limit of Stay: Unknown
Fee Charged: Yes
Managing Agency: Private

LOST CREEK

Lost Creek

Location: 10 miles northeast of Croydon off I-84, in Weber Canyon
Campsites: Primitive camping
Max RV Length: NA
Facilities/Accommodations: Boating, drinking water, fishing, nondrinkable water, picnic tables, toilets
Reservations: NA
Open: Year-round (check on status of reservoir for current recreation possibilities)
Limit of Stay: 14 days
Fee Charged: Yes
Managing Agency: Bureau of Reclamation(downgraded from state park status as of 2000)

MANTUA

Box Elder

Location: On the west edge of Mantua off Hwy. 89
Campsites: 26 RV and tent sites
Max RV Length: 25 feet
Facilities/Accommodations: Boating, drinking water, fishing, group sites, handicap facilities, nondrinkable water, picnic tables, toilets
Reservations: (800) 280-2267
Open: May 15 to September 30
Limit of Stay: 7 days
Fee Charged: Yes
Managing Agency: National Forest Service (Wasatch-Cache)

Willard Basin

Location: 8 miles south of Mantua on F.R. 84
Campsites: 4 RV and tent sites
Max RV Length: Unknown
Facilities/Accommodations: Picnic tables, toilets
Reservations: (800) 280-2267
Open: June 1 to September 30
Limit of Stay: 7 days
Fee Charged: Yes
Managing Agency: National Forest Service (Wasatch-Cache)

Mountain Haven Campground and RV Park

Location: 130 N Main, Mantua
Campsites: 54 RV sites with complete RV hookups, 10 tent sites
Max RV Length: 36 feet
Facilities/Accommodations: Boating, drinking water, dump sites, fishing, group sites, picnic tables, showers, toilets
Reservations: (435) 723-1292
Open: May 1 to September 30
Limit of Stay: None
Fee Charged: Yes
Managing Agency: Private

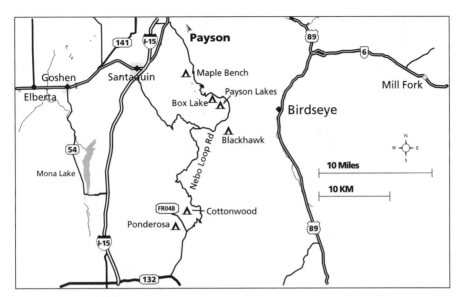

NEBO LOOP / PAYSON / PAYSON LAKES

Blackhawk

Location: 16 miles southeast of Payson off Nebo Loop Road
Campsites: 30 RV and tent sites
Max RV Length: 35 feet
Facilities/Accommodations: Drinking water, dump sites, group sites, handicap facilities, picnic tables, toilets
Reservations: (800) 280-2267
Open: June 1 to September 30
Limit of Stay: 14 days
Fee Charged: Yes
Managing Agency: National Forest Service (Uinta)

Box Lake

Location: 12 miles south of Payson on Nebo Loop Road
Campsites: 2 RV and tent sites
Max RV Length: Unknown
Facilities/Accommodations: Group sites, picnic tables, toilets
Reservations: (800) 280-2267
Open: July 1 to September 30
Limit of Stay: Unknown
Fee Charged: Yes
Managing Agency: National Forest Service

Maple Bench

Location: 5 miles south of Payson on Nebo Loop Road
Campsites: 10 RV and tent sites
Max RV Length: 35 feet
Facilities/Accommodations: Drinking water, fishing, picnic tables, toilets
Reservations: (800) 280-2267
Open: May 25 to October 1
Limit of Stay: 14 days
Fee Charged: Yes
Managing Agency: National Forest Service (Uinta)

Payson Lakes

🚰 ⛺ ♿ 🚐 🚻

Location: 12 miles southeast of Payson on Nebo Loop Road
Campsites: 99 RV and tent sites
Max RV Length: 45 feet
Facilities/Accommodations: Boating, drinking water, fishing, group sites, handicap facilities, picnic tables, swimming, toilets
Reservations: (800) 280-2267
Open: June 1 to September 30
Limit of Stay: 14 days
Fee Charged: Yes
Managing Agency: National Forest Service (Uinta)

Tinney Flat

🚰 ⛺ 🚐 🚻

Location: 8 miles southeast of Santaquin in Santaquin Canyon
Campsites: 16 RV and tent sites
Max RV Length: 45 feet
Facilities/Accommodations: Drinking water, fishing, group sites, nondrinkable water, picnic tables, toilets
Reservations: (800) 280-2267
Open: June 5 to October 30
Limit of Stay: 14 days
Fee Charged: Yes
Managing Agency: National Forest Service (Uinta)

Uintah

🚰 🚻

Location: Outside Nephi on Nebo Loop Road
Campsites: 99 tent sites
Max RV Length: NA
Facilities/Accommodations: Drinking water, fishing, picnic tables, swimming, toilets
Reservations: (800) 280-2267
Open: June 15 to September 10

Limit of Stay: 14 days
Fee Charged: Yes
Managing Agency: National Forest Service

Dale Draper RV Park

🚰 🚐

Location: 160 W 800 S, Payson
Campsites: 9 RV sites with complete RV hookups
Max RV Length: 40 feet
Facilities/Accommodations: Drinking water
Reservations: (801) 465-4775
Open: April 1 to November 1
Limit of Stay: Unknown
Fee Charged: Yes
Managing Agency: Private

OGDEN

Fort Buenaventura (Group Site)

🚰 ⛺ ♿ 🚐 🚻

Location: 2450 A Avenue, Ogden
Campsites: 25 RV and tent sites
Max RV Length: Unknown
Facilities/Accommodations: Boating, drinking water, fishing, group sites, handicap facilities, picnic tables, swimming, toilets
Reservations: (800) 322-3770
Open: March 1 to November 30
Limit of Stay: 14 days
Fee Charged: Yes
Managing Agency: Utah State Parks

Century RV Park

🚰 🚐 🎣 🚻

Location: 1300 W 2100 S, Ogden
Campsites: 140 RV sites, 110 complete RV hookups, 30 tent sites
Max RV Length: Unknown
Facilities/Accommodations: Drinking water, dump sites, laundry, nondrinkable water, picnic tables, showers, swimming, toilets

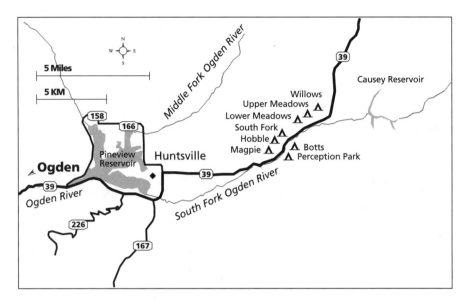

Reservations: (801) 731-3800
Open: Year-round
Limit of Stay: Unknown
Fee Charged: Yes
Managing Agency: Private

OGDEN RIVER — SOUTH FORK

Botts

Location: 6.5 miles east of
   Huntsville on Hwy. 39
Campsites: 8 RV and tent sites
Max RV Length: 20 feet
Facilities/Accommodations:
   Drinking water, fishing, non-
   drinkable water, picnic tables,
   swimming, toilets
Reservations: (800) 280-2267
Open: May 15 to October 31
Limit of Stay: 7 days
Fee Charged: Yes
Managing Agency: National Forest
   Service (Wasatch-Cache)

Hobble

Location: 6 miles east of Huntsville
   on Hwy. 39
Campsites: 8 RV and tent sites
Max RV Length: 20 feet
Facilities/Accommodations: Fishing,
   nondrinkable water, picnic tables,
   swimming, toilets
Reservations: (800) 280-2267
Open: May 15 to October 31
Limit of Stay: 7 days
Fee Charged: Yes
Managing Agency: National Forest
   Service (Wasatch-Cache)

Lower Meadows

Location: 8 miles east of Huntsville
   on Hwy. 39
Campsites: 15 RV sites, 17 tent sites
Max RV Length: 20 feet
Facilities/Accommodations:
   Drinking water, fishing, non-
   drinkable water, picnic tables,
   swimming, toilets

Reservations: (800) 280-2267
Open: May 15 to October 31
Limit of Stay: 7 days
Fee Charged: Yes
Managing Agency: National Forest
Service (Wasatch-Cache)

Magpie

Location: 6 miles east of Huntsville
on Hwy. 39
Campsites: 27 RV and tent sites
Max RV Length: 20 feet
Facilities/Accommodations:
Drinking water, fishing, non-
drinkable water, picnic tables,
swimming, toilets
Reservations: (800) 280-2267
Open: May 15 to October 31
Limit of Stay: 7 days
Fee Charged: Yes
Managing Agency: National Forest
Service (Wasatch-Cache)

Perception Park

Location: 7.5 miles east of
Huntsville on Hwy. 39
Campsites: 24 RV and tent sites
Max RV Length: 35 feet
Facilities/Accommodations:
Drinking water, group sites, hand-
icap facilities, nondrinkable water,
picnic tables, swimming, toilets
Reservations: (800) 280-2267
Open: May 15 to October 31
Limit of Stay: 7 days
Fee Charged: Yes
Managing Agency: National Forest
Service (Wasatch-Cache)

South Fork

Location: 7 miles east of Huntsville
on Hwy. 39

Campsites: 32 RV sites, 37 tent sites
Max RV Length: 25 feet
Facilities/Accommodations:
Drinking water, fishing, non-
drinkable water, picnic tables,
swimming, toilets
Reservations: (800) 280-2267
Open: May 15 to October 31
Limit of Stay: 7 days
Fee Charged: Yes
Managing Agency: National Forest
Service (Wasatch-Cache)

Upper Meadows

Location: 8 miles east of Huntsville
on Hwy. 39
Campsites: 9 RV and tent sites
Max RV Length: 20 feet
Facilities/Accommodations:
Drinking water, fishing, non-
drinkable water, picnic tables,
swimming, toilets
Reservations: (800) 280-2267
Open: May 15 to October 31
Limit of Stay: 7 days
Fee Charged: Yes
Managing Agency: National Forest
Service (Wasatch-Cache)

Willows

Location: 8 miles east of Huntsville
on Hwy. 39
Campsites: 10 RV sites, 13 tent sites
Max RV Length: 20 feet
Facilities/Accommodations:
Drinking water, fishing, non-
drinkable water, picnic tables,
swimming, toilets
Reservations: (800) 280-2267
Open: May 15 to October 31
Limit of Stay: 7 days
Fee Charged: Yes

Managing Agency: National Forest Service (Wasatch-Cache)

PARK CITY

Hidden Haven Campground

Location: 2200 Rasmussen Road, Park City

Campsites: 50 RV sites, 15 complete RV hookups, 18 tent sites

Max RV Length: 45 feet

Facilities/Accommodations: Boating, drinking water, dump sites, fishing, group sites, laundry, nondrinkable water, picnic tables, showers, toilets

Reservations: (435) 649-8935

Open: Year-round

Limit of Stay: Unknown

Fee Charged: Yes

Managing Agency: Private

PINEVIEW RESERVOIR

Anderson Cove

Location: 2.5 miles southwest of Huntsville on Hwy. 39

Campsites: 29 RV sites, 74 tent sites

Max RV Length: 40 feet

A couple relaxes in a campsite near Park City.

PHOTO: CHEYENNE ROUSE

Facilities/Accommodations:
Boating, drinking water, dump sites, group sites, nondrinkable water, picnic tables, swimming, toilets
Reservations: (800) 280-2267
Open: May 1 to September 30
Limit of Stay: 7 days
Fee Charged: Yes
Managing Agency: National Forest Service (Wasatch-Cache)

Jefferson Hunt

Location: 2 miles south of Huntsville on Hwy. 39
Campsites: 29 RV and tent sites
Max RV Length: 40 feet
Facilities/Accommodations:
Boating, drinking water, fishing, handicap facilities, nondrinkable water, picnic tables, toilets
Reservations: (800) 280-2267
Open: June 1 to September 30
Limit of Stay: 7 days
Fee Charged: Yes
Managing Agency: National Forest Service (Wasatch-Cache)

PLYMOUTH

Belmont Hot Springs

Location: 1 mile south of Plymouth on Hwy. 80
Campsites: 71 RV sites with complete RV hookups, 100 tent sites
Max RV Length: Unknown
Facilities/Accommodations:
Drinking water, dump sites, fishing, group sites, picnic tables, showers, swimming, toilets
Reservations: (435) 458-3200
Open: April 1 to October 15
Limit of Stay: Unknown

Fee Charged: Yes
Managing Agency: Private

PROVO / OREM

Hope

Location: 10 miles northeast of Provo off Hwy. 189
Campsites: 24 RV and tent sites
Max RV Length: 45 feet
Facilities/Accommodations:
Drinking water, picnic tables
Reservations: (800) 280-2267
Open: May 25 to October 15
Limit of Stay: 14 days
Fee Charged: Yes
Managing Agency: National Forest Service (Uinta)

Rock Canyon

Location: 12 miles northeast of Provo off Hwy. 189
Campsites: 40 RV and tent sites
Max RV Length: 50 feet
Facilities/Accommodations:
Drinking water, picnic tables, toilets
Reservations: (800) 280-2267
Open: June 1 to September 30
Limit of Stay: 14 days
Fee Charged: Yes
Managing Agency: National Forest Service (Uinta)

Utah Lake State Park

Location: 5 miles west of Provo off I-15
Campsites: 73 RV and tent sites
Max RV Length: 40 feet
Facilities/Accommodations:
Boating, drinking water, dump

sites, fishing, group sites, handicap facilities, nondrinkable water, showers, swimming
Reservations: (800) 322-3770
Open: Year-round
Limit of Stay: 14 days
Fee Charged: Yes
Managing Agency: Utah State Parks

Deer Creek Park

Location: In Provo Canyon off Hwy. 189
Campsites: 90 RV sites, 60 complete RV hookups, 20 tent sites
Max RV Length: Unknown
Facilities/Accommodations:
Boating, drinking water, dump sites, fishing, handicap facilities, nondrinkable water, picnic tables, showers, toilets
Reservations: (801) 225-9783
Open: April 1 to September 30
Limit of Stay: 30 days
Fee Charged: Yes
Managing Agency: Private

Frazier Trailer Park

Location: 3 miles east of Orem in Provo Canyon
Campsites: 26 RV sites, 8 complete RV hookups
Max RV Length: Unknown
Facilities/Accommodations:
Drinking water, dump sites, fishing, group sites, nondrinkable water, picnic tables, showers, toilets
Reservations: (801) 225-5346
Open: March 20 to November 1
Limit of Stay: Unknown
Fee Charged: Yes
Managing Agency: Private

KOA Kampground

Location: 320 N 2050 W, Provo
Campsites: 75 RV sites, 41 complete RV hookups, 25 tent sites
Max RV Length: 60 feet
Facilities/Accommodations:
Drinking water, dump sites, fishing, group sites, laundry, nondrinkable water, picnic tables, showers, swimming, toilets
Reservations: (801) 375-2994
Open: Year-round
Limit of Stay: Unknown
Fee Charged: Yes
Managing Agency: Private

Lakeside Campground

Location: 4000 W Center, Provo
Campsites: 148 RV sites, 100 complete RV hookups, 34 tent sites
Max RV Length: 65 feet
Facilities/Accommodations:
Boating, drinking water, fishing, group sites, laundry, picnic tables, showers, swimming, toilets
Reservations: (801) 373-5267
Open: Year-round
Limit of Stay: Unknown
Fee Charged: Yes
Managing Agency: Private

Riverbend Trailer Park

Location: 7 miles east of Orem in Provo Canyon
Campsites: 64 RV sites, 50 complete RV hookups
Max RV Length: Unknown
Facilities/Accommodations:
Drinking water, dump sites, fishing, group sites, laundry, nondrinkable water, showers, toilets

Reservations: (801) 225-1836
Open: April 15 to October 15
Limit of Stay: Unknown
Fee Charged: Yes
Managing Agency: Private

Silver Fox Campground
🛶 🚐 🚿 🚽
Location: 101 W 1500 S, Provo
Campsites: 102 RV sites with complete RV hookups, 16 tent sites
Max RV Length: 45 feet
Facilities/Accommodations: Drinking water, dump sites, laundry, picnic tables, showers, swimming, toilets
Reservations: (800) 833-1379
Open: Year-round
Limit of Stay: 30 days
Fee Charged: Yes
Managing Agency: Private

Wagon Wheel Trailer Park
🛶 🚐 🚿
Location: 500 S Main, Springville
Campsites: 4 RV sites with complete RV hookups
Max RV Length: 30 feet
Facilities/Accommodations: Drinking water, showers
Reservations: (801) 489-4783
Open: Year-round
Limit of Stay: 14 days
Fee Charged: Yes
Managing Agency: Private

RANDOLPH/WOODRUFF

Birch Creek
🚐 🚽
Location: 9 miles west of Woodruff off Hwy. 39
Campsites: 5 RV sites, 4 tent sites
Max RV Length: 20 feet

Facilities/Accommodations: Fishing, nondrinking water, picnic tables, toilets
Reservations: (801) 977-4300
Open: June 1 to October 1
Limit of Stay: 14 days
Fee Charged: Yes
Managing Agency: BLM

Monte Cristo
🛶 🚐 🚽
Location: 22 miles southwest of Woodruff off Hwy. 39
Campsites: 47 RV and tent sites
Max RV Length: 25 feet
Facilities/Accommodations: Drinking water, picnic tables, toilets
Reservations: (800) 280-2267
Open: July 1 to September 30
Limit of Stay: 7 days
Fee Charged: Yes
Managing Agency: National Forest Service (Wasatch-Cache)

Barker Trailer Court
🛶 🏕 ♿
Location: 80 W Pond, Randolph
Campsites: 24 RV sites with complete RV hookups, tent sites
Max RV Length: Unknown
Facilities/Accommodations: Boating, drinking water, dump sites, fishing, group sites, handicap facilities, laundry
Reservations: (435) 793-5535
Open: Year-round
Limit of Stay: Unknown
Fee Charged: Yes
Managing Agency: Private

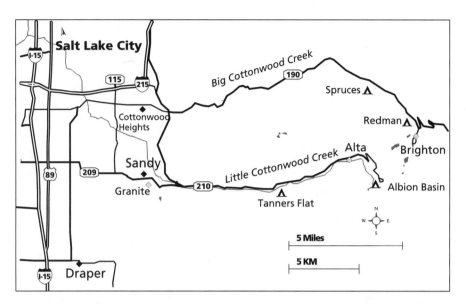

ROCKPORT STATE PARK

Rockport Reservoir

🔧 ⋕ 🚐 🚻

Location: 4 miles south of Wanship on S.R. 32 off Hwy. 189

Campsites: 36 RV sites, 200 tent sites, some complete RV hookups

Max RV Length: 40 feet

Facilities/Accommodations: Boating, drinking water, fishing, group sites, picnic tables, swimming, toilets

Reservations: (800) 322-3770; accepted May 10-September 15

Open: Year-round

Limit of Stay: 14 days

Fee Charged: Yes

Managing Agency: Utah State Parks

SALT LAKE / WASATCH FRONT

Albion Basin

🔧 ⋕ 🚐 🚻

Location: Little Cottonwood Canyon, 18.4 miles southeast of Salt Lake City

Campsites: 24 RV sites, tent sites

Max RV Length: 20 feet

Facilities/Accommodations: Drinking water, fishing, group sites, picnic tables, toilets

Reservations: (800) 280-2267

Open: June 15 to October 15

Limit of Stay: 7 days

Fee Charged: Yes

Managing Agency: National Forest Service (Wasatch-Cache)

Bountiful Peak

🔧 ⋕ 🚻

Location: 9.3 miles northeast of Farmington on F.R. 007

Campsites: 42 tent sites

Max RV Length: NA

Facilities/Accommodations: Drinking water, fishing, group sites, picnic tables, toilets

Reservations: (800) 280-2267

Open: June 15 to September 7

Limit of Stay: 7 days

Fee Charged: Yes

Managing Agency: National Forest Service (Wasatch-Cache)

Redman

🔌 ♨ 🚐 🚽

Location: Big Cottonwood Canyon, 16.4 miles southeast of Salt Lake City
Campsites: 37 RV sites, tent sites
Max RV Length: 20 feet
Facilities/Accommodations: Drinking water, fishing, group sites, picnic tables, toilets
Reservations: (800) 280-2267
Open: July 1 to October 1
Limit of Stay: 7 days
Fee Charged: Yes
Managing Agency: National Forest Service (Wasatch-Cache)

Spruces

🔌 ♨ ♿ 🚐 🚽

Location: Big Cottonwood Canyon, 13.7 miles southeast of Salt Lake City
Campsites: 86 RV sites, tent sites
Max RV Length: 30 feet
Facilities/Accommodations: Drinking water, fishing, group sites, handicap facilities, picnic tables, toilets
Reservations: (800) 280-2267
Open: June 5 to October 15
Limit of Stay: 7 days
Fee Charged: Yes
Managing Agency: National Forest Service (Wasatch-Cache)

Sunset

🔌 ♨

Location: 4 miles northeast of Farmington on F.R. 007
Campsites: 10 tent sites
Max RV Length: NA
Facilities/Accommodations: Drinking water, fishing, group sites, picnic tables

Reservations: (800) 280-2267
Open: May 1 to October 15
Limit of Stay: 14 days
Fee Charged: Yes
Managing Agency: National Forest Service (Wasatch-Cache)

Tanners Flat

🔌 ♨ 🚐 🚽

Location: Little Cottonwood Canyon, 11.7 miles southeast of Salt Lake City
Campsites: 36 RV sites, tent sites
Max RV Length: 20 feet
Facilities/Accommodations: Drinking water, fishing, group sites, picnic tables, toilets
Reservations: (800) 280-2267
Open: June 15 to October 15
Limit of Stay: 7 days
Fee Charged: Yes
Managing Agency: National Forest Service (Wasatch-Cache)

American Campground

🔌 🚐 🍴 🚽

Location: I-15 Exit 279, American Fork
Campsites: 52 RV sites with complete hookups
Max RV Length: 35 feet
Facilities/Accommodations: Drinking water, dump sites, laundry, picnic tables, showers, toilets
Reservations: (801) 756-5502
Open: Year-round
Limit of Stay: 7 days
Fee Charged: Yes
Managing Agency: Private

Camp VIP

🔌 ♨ 🚐 🍴 🚽

Location: 1400 W North Temple, Salt Lake City

Campsites: 396 RV sites, 142 complete RV hookups, 52 tent sites
Max RV Length: 65 feet
Facilities/Accommodations: Drinking water, dump sites, group sites, laundry, nondrinkable water, picnic tables, showers, swimming, toilets
Reservations: (801) 328-0224
Open: Year-round
Limit of Stay: Unknown
Fee Charged: Yes
Managing Agency: Private

Cherry Hill Campground
Location: 1325 S Main, Kaysville
Campsites: 162 RV sites, 119 complete RV hookups, 83 tent sites
Max RV Length: 40 feet
Facilities/Accommodations: Drinking water, dump sites, group sites, handicap facilities, nondrinking water, picnic tables, showers, swimming, toilets
Reservations: (801) 451-5379
Open: April 1 to November 1

A woman hikes beside Lake Blanche, up Big Cottonwood Canyon near Salt Lake City.

PHOTO: DAVID WHITTEN

Limit of Stay: Unknown
Fee Charged: Yes
Managing Agency: Private

Circle L Mobile Home Park

Location: 229 North Main, Layton
Campsites: 15 RV sites with complete RV hookups, 15 tent sites
Max RV Length: 70 feet
Facilities/Accommodations: Drinking water, dump sites, laundry, picnic tables, showers, toilets
Reservations: (801) 544-8945
Open: Year-round
Limit of Stay: Unknown
Fee Charged: Yes
Managing Agency: Private

Lagoon's RV Park & Campground

Location: 175 N Lagoon Lane, Farmington
Campsites: 205 RV sites, 98 complete RV hookups, 10 tent sites
Max RV Length: 40 feet
Facilities/Accommodations: Drinking water, dump sites, handicap facilities, laundry, picnic tables, toilets
Reservations: (801) 451-8000/8100
Open: May 1 To September 30
Limit of Stay: Six days
Fee Charged: Yes
Managing Agency: Private

Mountain Shadows RV Park

Location: 13275 S Minuteman Drive, Draper
Campsites: 106 RV sites, 88 complete RV hookups, 12 tent sites
Max RV Length: 40 feet

Facilities/Accommodations: Drinking water, dump sites, laundry, picnic tables, showers, swimming, toilets
Reservations: (801) 571-4024
Open: Year-round
Limit of Stay: Unknown
Fee Charged: Yes
Managing Agency: Private

Saratoga Resort

Location: 5 miles southwest of Lehi on Utah Lake
Campsites: 40 RV sites with complete RV hookups, tent sites
Max RV Length: Unknown
Facilities/Accommodations: Boating, drinking water, dump sites, group sites, nondrinkable water, picnic tables, showers, swimming, toilets
Reservations: (801) 768-8206
Open: May 1 to September 2
Limit of Stay: 7 days
Fee Charged: Yes
Managing Agency: Private

Shady Haven RV Park

Location: 8875 S 225 W, Sandy
Campsites: 58 RV sites, 40 complete RV hookups, 15 tent sites
Max RV Length: 40 feet
Facilities/Accommodations: Drinking water, handicap facilities, laundry, nondrinkable water, picnic tables, showers, toilets
Reservations: (801) 561-1744
Open: May 1 to October 1
Limit of Stay: Unknown
Fee Charged: Yes
Managing Agency: Private

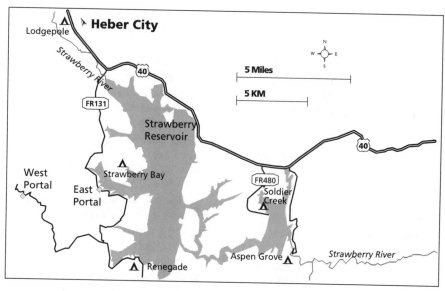

SNOWVILLE

Clear Creek

Location: 30 miles west of Snowville
Campsites: 10 tent sites
Max RV Length: NA
Facilities/Accommodations:
   Drinking water, fishing, picnic
   tables, toilets
Reservations: (800) 280-2267
Open: June 1 to September 30
Limit of Stay: 7 days
Fee Charged: Yes
Managing Agency: National Forest
   Service (Sawtooth)

Lottie Dell Campground

Location: Snowville
Campsites: 85 RV and tent sites
Max RV Length: None
Facilities/Accommodations:
   Laundry, picnic tables, showers,
   toilets; also cabins and tepees
Reservations: (435) 872-8273
Open: March to November

Limit of Stay: None
Fee Charged: Yes
Managing Agency: Private

STRAWBERRY RESERVOIR

Aspen Grove

Location: On the southeast shore of
   Strawberry
Campsites: 54 RV and tent sites
Max RV Length: Unknown
Facilities/Accommodations:
   Boating, drinking water, fishing,
   toilets
Reservations: NA
Open: May 25 to October 31
Limit of Stay: 14 days
Fee Charged: Yes
Managing Agency: National Forest
   Service (Uinta)

Lodgepole

Location: 16 miles southeast of
   Heber City off Hwy. 40
Campsites: 35 RV sites, 50 tent sites

Max RV Length: 30 feet
Facilities/Accommodations:
Drinking water, dump sites, fishing, handicap facilities, nondrinkable water, picnic tables, toilets
Reservations: (800) 280-2267
Open: May 25 to October 31
Limit of Stay: 14 days
Fee Charged: Yes
Managing Agency: National Forest Service (Uinta)

Renegade

Location: On the south shore of Strawberry, about 37 miles southeast of Heber City off Hwy. 40
Campsites: 80 RV and tent sites
Max RV Length: 40 feet
Facilities/Accommodations:
Boating, drinking water, fishing, handicap facilities, picnic tables, toilets
Reservations: (800) 280-2267
Open: May 25 to October 31
Limit of Stay: 14 days
Fee Charged: Yes
Managing Agency: National Forest Service (Uinta)

Soldier Creek

Location: Off Hwy. 40 on the Soldier Creek Marina road, about 34 miles southeast of Heber
Campsites: 165 RV and tent sites
Max RV Length: Unknown
Facilities/Accommodations:
Boating, drinking water, dump sites, fishing, picnic tables, toilets
Reservations: (800) 280-2267; (877) 444-6777
Open: May to October
Limit of Stay: 14 days
Fee Charged: Yes

Managing Agency: National Forest Service (Uinta)

Strawberry Bay

Location: On the west short of Strawberry, about 23 miles southeast of Heber City off Hwy. 40
Campsites: 551 RV and tent sites, 27 complete RV hookups
Max RV Length: 40 feet
Facilities/Accommodations:
Boating, drinking water, dump sites, fishing, group sites, handicap facilities, picnic tables, toilets
Reservations: (800) 280-2267
Open: May 25 to October 31
Limit of Stay: 14 days
Fee Charged: Yes
Managing Agency: National Forest Service (Uinta)

TOOELE

Clover Spring

Location: 15 miles south of Tooele off Hwy. 36
Campsites: 12 RV and tent sites
Max RV Length: Unknown
Facilities/Accommodations: Fishing, group sites, toilets
Reservations: (801) 977-4300
Open: April 1 to October 31
Limit of Stay: 14 days
Fee Charged: Yes
Managing Agency: BLM

UINTAS — MIRROR LAKE HIGHWAY (HWY. 150)

Bear River

Location: About 35 miles northwest of Kamas on Hwy. 150
Campsites: 4 RV and tent sites

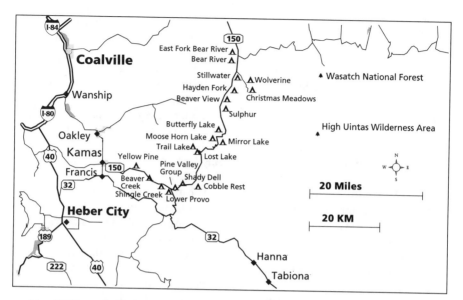

Max RV Length: Unknown
Facilities/Accommodations:
Drinking water, fishing, handicap facilities, toilets
Reservations: NA
Open: June to October
Limit of Stay: 14 days
Fee Charged: Yes
Managing Agency: National Forest Service (Wasatch-Cache)

Beaver Creek
🛶 🚐 🍴

Location: 8.4 miles east of Kamas on Hwy. 150
Campsites: 14 RV and tent sites
Max RV Length: 60 feet
Facilities/Accommodations:
Drinking water, fishing, non-drinkable water, picnic tables, toilets
Reservations: (800) 280-2267
Open: June 1 to September 20
Limit of Stay: 7 days
Fee Charged: Yes
Managing Agency: National Forest Service (Wasatch-Cache)

Beaver View
🛶 🚐 🍴

Location: About 33 miles northeast of Kamas on Hwy. 150
Campsites: 8 RV and tent sites
Max RV Length: Unknown
Facilities/Accommodations:
Drinking water, fishing, picnic tables, toilets
Reservations: NA
Open: June to October
Limit of Stay: 14 days
Fee Charged: Yes
Managing Agency: National Forest Service (Wasatch-Cache)

Butterfly Lake
🛶 🚐 🍴

Location: About 30 miles northeast of Kamas on Hwy. 150
Campsites: 20 RV and tent sites
Max RV Length: Unknown
Facilities/Accommodations:
Drinking water, fishing, picnic tables, toilets
Reservations: NA

Open: July to September
Limit of Stay: 14 days
Fee Charged: Yes
Managing Agency: National Forest
  Service (Wasatch-Cache)

Christmas Meadows
🔥 🚐 🛁

Location: About 35 miles northwest
  of Kamas off Hwy. 150
Campsites: 11 RV and tent sites
Max RV Length: Unknown
Facilities/Accommodations:
  Drinking water, fishing, toilets
Reservations: NA
Open: June to October
Limit of Stay: 14 days
Fee Charged: Yes
Managing Agency: National Forest
  Service (Wasatch-Cache)

Cobble Rest
🔥 🚐 🛁

Location: 19.1 miles east of Kamas
  on Hwy. 150
Campsites: 18 RV and tent sites
Max RV Length: 30 feet
Facilities/Accommodations:
  Drinking water, fishing, non-
  drinkable water, picnic tables, toi-
  lets
Reservations: (800) 280-2267
Open: June 15 to September 15
Limit of Stay: 7 days
Fee Charged: Yes
Managing Agency: National Forest
  Service (Wasatch-Cache)

East Fork Bear River
🔥 🚐 🛁

Location: About 35 miles northeast
  of Kamas on Hwy. 150
Campsites: 8 RV and tent sites
Max RV Length: Unknown

Facilities/Accommodations:
  Drinking water, fishing, toilets
Reservations: NA
Open: June to October
Limit of Stay: 14 days
Fee Charged: Yes
Managing Agency: National Forest
  Service (Wasatch-Cache)

Haydenfork
🔥 🚐 🛁

Location: About 33 miles northeast
  of Kamas on Hwy. 150
Campsites: 9 RV and tent sites
Max RV Length: Unknown
Facilities/Accommodations:
  Drinking water, fishing, toilets
Reservations: NA
Open: June to October
Limit of Stay: 14 days
Fee Charged: Yes
Managing Agency: National Forest
  Service (Wasatch-Cache)

Lost Lake
🔥 🚐 🛁

Location: About 20 miles northeast
  of Kamas on Hwy. 150
Campsites: 34 RV and tent sites
Max RV Length: Unknown
Facilities/Accommodations:
  Drinking water, fishing, toilets
Reservations: NA
Open: July to September
Limit of Stay: 14 days
Fee Charged: Yes
Managing Agency: National Forest
  Service (Wasatch-Cache)

Lower Provo
🔥 🚐 🛁

Location: 12 miles southeast of
  Kamas off Hwy. 150
Campsites: 10 RV and tent sites

Max RV Length: 40 feet
Facilities/Accommodations:
  Drinking water, fishing, non-drinkable water, picnic tables, toilets
Reservations: (800) 280-2267
Open: June 8 to September 15
Limit of Stay: 7 days
Fee Charged: Yes
Managing Agency: National Forest Service (Uinta)

Mill Hollow

Location: About 25 miles west of Heber City off Hwy. 35
Campsites: 26 RV and tent sites
Max RV Length: Unknown
Facilities/Accommodations:
  Drinking water, fishing, toilets
Reservations: NA
Open: June to September
Limit of Stay: 14 days
Fee Charged: Yes
Managing Agency: National Forest Service (Uinta)

Mirror Lake

Location: About 25 miles northeast of Kamas on Hwy. 150
Campsites: 85 RV and tent sites
Max RV Length: Unknown
Facilities/Accommodations:
  Boating, drinking water, fishing, handicap facilities, picnic tables, toilets
Reservations: NA
Open: July to September
Limit of Stay: 14 days
Fee Charged: Yes
Managing Agency: National Forest Service (Wasatch-Cache)

Moose Horn Lake

Location: About 25 miles northeast of Kamas on Hwy. 150
Campsites: 33 RV and tent sites
Max RV Length: Unknown
Facilities/Accommodations:
  Drinking water, fishing, toilets
Reservations: NA
Open: July to September
Limit of Stay: 14 days
Fee Charged: Yes
Managing Agency: National Forest Service (Wasatch-Cache)

Pine Valley (Group Site)

Location: 11 miles east of Kamas on Hwy. 150
Campsites: 16 RV and tent sites
Max RV Length: 30 feet
Facilities/Accommodations:
  Drinking water, handicap facilities, picnic tables, toilets
Reservations: (800) 280-2267
Open: June 15 to September 10
Limit of Stay: 7 days
Fee Charged: Yes
Managing Agency: National Forest Service (Wasatch-Cache)

Shady Dell

Location: 17.3 miles east of Kamas on Hwy. 150
Campsites: 20 RV and tent sites
Max RV Length: 25 feet
Facilities/Accommodations:
  Drinking water, fishing, non-drinkable water, picnic tables, toilets
Reservations: (800) 280-2267
Open: June 8 to September 15
Limit of Stay: 7 days
Fee Charged: Yes

Managing Agency: National Forest Service (Wasatch-Cache)

Shingle Creek

🛶 🚐 🚻

Location: 9.5 miles east of Kamas on Hwy. 150
Campsites: 21 RV and tent sites
Max RV Length: 60 feet
Facilities/Accommodations: Drinking water, nondrinkable water, picnic tables, toilets
Reservations: (800) 280-2267
Open: June 1 to September 15
Limit of Stay: 7 days
Fee Charged: Yes
Managing Agency: National Forest Service (Wasatch-Cache)

Soapstone

🛶 🚻 🚐 🚻

Location: 15.8 miles east of Kamas on Hwy. 150
Campsites: 33 RV and tent sites
Max RV Length: 40 feet
Facilities/Accommodations: Drinking water, fishing, group sites, nondrinkable water, picnic tables, toilets
Reservations: (800) 280-2267
Open: June 8 to September 15
Limit of Stay: 7 days
Fee Charged: Yes
Managing Agency: National Forest Service (Wasatch-Cache)

Stillwater

🛶 🚻 🚐 🚻

Location: About 34 miles northeast of Kamas on Hwy. 150
Campsites: 21 RV and tent sites
Max RV Length: Unknown
Facilities/Accommodations: Drinking water, fishing, group sites, picnic tables, toilets

Reservations: (800) 280-2267
Open: June to October
Limit of Stay: 15 days
Fee Charged: Yes
Managing Agency: National Forest Service (Wasatch-Cache)

Sulphur

🛶 🚐 🚻

Location: About 32 miles northeast of Kamas on Hwy. 150
Campsites: 21 RV and tent sites
Max RV Length: Unknown
Facilities/Accommodations: Drinking water, fishing, picnic tables, toilets
Reservations: NA
Open: June to October
Limit of Stay: 14 days
Fee Charged: Yes
Managing Agency: National Forest Service (Wasatch-Cache)

Trial Lake

🛶 ♿ 🚐 🚻

Location: About 20 miles east of Kamas on Hwy. 150
Campsites: 60 RV and tent sites
Max RV Length: Unknown
Facilities/Accommodations: Drinking water, fishing, handicap facilities, toilets facilities
Reservations: NA
Open: July to September
Limit of Stay: 14 days
Fee Charged: Yes
Managing Agency: National Forest Service (Wasatch-Cache)

Wolf Creek

🛶 🚐 🚻

Location: 18 miles southeast of Francis on F.R. 91 off S.R. 35
Campsites: 6 RV and tent sites
Max RV Length: Unknown

Facilities/Accommodations:
Drinking water, toilets
Reservations: (800) 280-2267
Open: June-September
Limit of Stay: Unknown
Fee Charged: Yes
Managing Agency: National Forest
Service (Uinta)

Wolverine
₪ ⌂

Location: About 35 miles northeast
of Kamas off Hwy. 150
Campsites: 6 RV and tent sites
Max RV Length: Unknown
Facilities/Accommodations: Fishing,
toilets
Reservations: NA
Open: June to October
Limit of Stay: 14 days
Fee Charged: Yes
Managing Agency: National Forest
Service (Wasatch-Cache)

Yellow Pine
⚓ ⅃ ₪ ⌂

Location: 6.8 miles east of Kamas on
Hwy. 150
Campsites: 12 RV sites, 29 tent sites
Max RV Length: 22 feet
Facilities/Accommodations: Fishing,
handicap facilities, nondrinkable
water, picnic tables, toilets
Reservations: (800) 280-2267
Open: May 29 to September 20
Limit of Stay: 16 days
Fee Charged: Yes
Managing Agency: National Forest
Service (Ashley)

VERNON / PONY EXPRESS TRAIL

Little Valley
₪ ⌂

Location: 10.5 miles southeast of
Vernon off Hwy. 36

Campsites: 5 RV and tent sites
Max RV Length: Unknown
Facilities/Accommodations: Fishing,
picnic tables, toilets
Reservations: (800) 280-2267
Open: May 1 to October 31
Limit of Stay: 10 days
Fee Charged: Yes
Managing Agency: National Forest
Service (Wasatch-Cache)

Simpson Springs
⅃ ₪ ⌂

Location: 31 miles west of Vernon
on the Pony Express Trail
Campsites: 20 RV and tent sites
Max RV Length: 30 feet
Facilities/Accommodations:
Handicap facilities, picnic tables,
toilets
Reservations: (801) 977-4300
Open: Year-round
Limit of Stay: 14 days
Fee Charged: No
Managing Agency: BLM

WASATCH MOUNTAIN STATE PARK

Little Deer Creek
⚓ ⋮⋮⋮ ⌂

Location: 15 miles southwest of
Midway
Campsites: 17 primitive tent sites
Max RV Length: NA
Facilities/Accommodations:
Drinking water, group sites, non-
drinkable water, toilets
Reservations: (800) 322-3770
Open: May to September
Limit of Stay: 14 days
Fee Charged: Yes
Managing Agency: Utah State Parks

Mahogany

Location: 3 miles northwest of Midway
Campsites: 35 RV and tent sites
Max RV Length: 35 feet
Facilities/Accommodations: Drinking water, dump sites, nondrinkable water, showers, toilets
Reservations: (800) 322-3770
Open: April to October
Limit of Stay: 14 days
Fee Charged: Yes
Managing Agency: Utah State Parks

Oak Hollow

Location: 3 miles northwest of Midway
Campsites: 40 RV and tent sites, some complete RV hookups
Max RV Length: 35 feet
Facilities/Accommodations: Drinking water, nondrinkable water, showers, toilets
Reservations: (800) 322-3770
Open: April to October
Limit of Stay: 14 days
Fee Charged: Yes
Managing Agency: Utah State Parks

Cottonwood

Location: 2 miles northwest of Midway off Hwy. 220/224
Campsites: 46 RV sites, 15 complete RV hookups
Max RV Length: 30 feet
Facilities/Accommodations: Boating, drinking water, handicap facilities, nondrinkable water, showers, toilets
Reservations: (800) 322-3770
Open: Year-round
Limit of Stay: 14 days
Fee Charged: Yes
Managing Agency: Utah State Parks

WEBER CANYON / SMITH AND MOREHOUSE RESERVOIR

Ledgefork

Location: 12 miles east of Oakley, above the reservoir
Campsites: 73 RV and tent sites
Max RV Length: 50 feet
Facilities/Accommodations: Boating, drinking water, fishing, nondrinkable water, picnic tables, toilets
Reservations: (800) 280-2267
Open: June 20 to September 15
Limit of Stay: 7 days
Fee Charged: Yes
Managing Agency: National Forest Service (Wasatch-Cache)

Smith and Morehouse

Location: 11 miles east of Oakley, at the reservoir
Campsites: 34 RV and tent sites
Max RV Length: 45 feet
Facilities/Accommodations: Boating, drinking water, fishing, nondrinkable water, picnic tables, toilets
Reservations: (800) 280-2267
Open: June 20 to September 15
Limit of Stay: 7 days
Fee Charged: Yes
Managing Agency: National Forest Service (Wasatch-Cache)

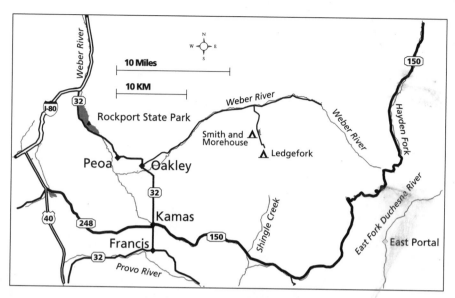

WILLARD BAY STATE PARK

Willard Bay — North Marina

Location: 15 miles north of Ogden off I -15
Campsites: 62 RV sites, 40 tent sites
Max RV Length: Unknown
Facilities/Accommodations:
Boating, drinking water, fishing, group sites, handicap facilities, nondrinkable water, toilets
Reservations: (800) 322-2770
Open: Year-round
Limit of Stay: 14 days
Fee Charged: Yes
Managing Agency: Utah State Parks

Willard Bay — South Marina

Location: 8 miles north of Ogden off I -15
Campsites: 30 RV sites, 12 tent sites
Max RV Length: Unknown
Facilities/Accommodations:
Boating, drinking water, fishing, group sites, handicap facilities, nondrinkable water, toilets
Reservations: NA
Open: April 1 to October 31
Limit of Stay: 14 days
Fee Charged: Yes
Managing Agency: Utah State Parks

CAMPGROUNDS: EASTERN REGION

CASTLE DALE

Esquire Estates Park
🍗 ⚌ ♿ 🚐 🚽

Location: 270 W 380 N, Castle Dale
Campsites: 40 RV sites with complete RV hookups
Max RV Length: 70 feet
Facilities/Accommodations: Boating, drinking water, dump sites, fishing, group sites, handicap facilities, laundry, nondrinkable water, swimming, toilets
Reservations: (435) 381-2778
Open: Year-round
Limit of Stay: Unknown
Fee Charged: Yes
Managing Agency: Private

DINOSAUR NATIONAL MONUMENT

Green River Campground
🍗 🚐 🚽

Location: 5 miles east of Dinosaur Quarry (east from Vernal on Hwy. 149)
Campsites: 88 RV and tent sites
Max RV Length: 35 feet
Facilities/Accommodations: Drinking water, firewood, fishing, picnic tables, toilets
Reservations: (970) 374-3000 or (435) 789-2115
Open: April 15 to October 15
Limit of Stay: 14 days
Fee Charged: Yes
Managing Agency: National Park Service

Rainbow Park Campground
🚐 🚽

Location: 20 miles northeast of Vernal
Campsites: 4 RV and tent sites
Max RV Length: Unknown
Facilities/Accommodations: Fishing, nondrinkable water, picnic tables, toilets
Reservations: (970) 374-3000 or (435) 789-2115
Open: Year-round
Limit of Stay: 14 days
Fee Charged: Yes
Managing Agency: National Park Service

Split Mountain Campground
⚌ 🚐 🚽

Location: 4 miles northeast of Dinosaur Quarry (east from Vernal on Hwy. 149)
Campsites: 15 RV and tent sites
Max RV Length: 35 feet
Facilities/Accommodations: Boating, fishing, group sites, toilets
Reservations: (970) 374-3000 or (435) 789-2115
Open: October 16 to April 14
Limit of Stay: Unknown
Fee Charged: Yes

SYMBOL LEGEND

🍗 Drinking water   🚐 RV sites
⚌ Group sites   🚽 Toilets
♿ Handicap facilities   🎇 Showers

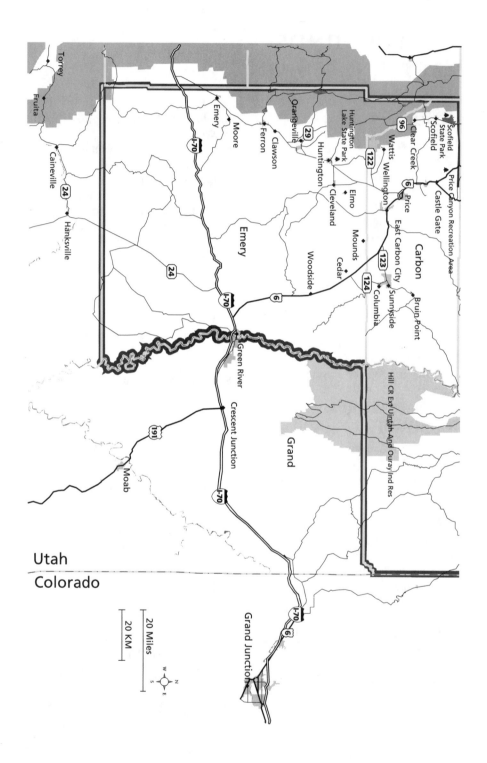

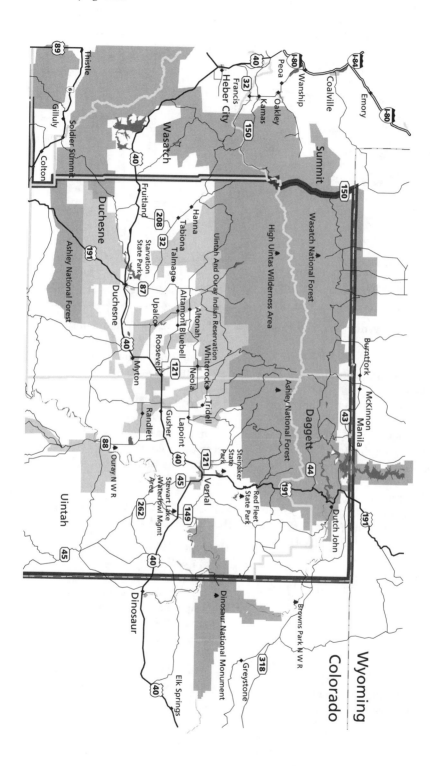

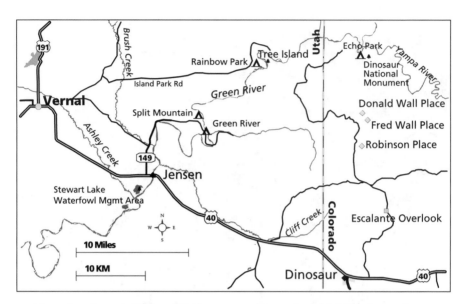

Managing Agency: National Park
Service

Echo Park Campground
🛅 🚐 🚾

Location: 38 miles north of monument headquarters
Campsites: 13 tent sites
Max RV Length: NA
Facilities/Accommodations:
Drinking water, picnic tables, toilets; no fires allowed
Reservations: (970) 374-3000
Open: Year-round (high waters can block off from late May-late June)
Limit of Stay: 14 days
Fee Charged: Yes
Managing Agency: National Park
Service

DUCHESNE

Avintaquin
🛅 🚐 🚾

Location: 20 miles south of
Duchesne off Hwy. 191

Campsites: 24 RV and tent sites
Max RV Length: Unknown
Facilities/Accommodations:
Drinking water, picnic tables, toilets
Reservations: NA
Open: June to September
Limit of Stay: 16 days
Fee Charged: Yes
Managing Agency: National Forest
Service (Ashley)

FLAMING GORGE NATIONAL RECREATION AREA

Antelope Flat
🛅 ⛺ ♿ 🚾

Location: 10.9 miles northwest of
Dutch John off Hwy. 191
Campsites: 12 tent sites
Max RV Length: NA
Facilities/Accommodations:
Boating, drinking water, dump sites, fishing, group sites, handicap facilities, nondrinkable water, picnic tables, swimming, toilets

Reservations: (800) 280-2267
Open: May 20 To September 22
Limit of Stay: 16 days
Fee Charged: Yes
Managing Agency: National Forest
Service (Ashley)

Arch Dam

Location: Just south of Dutch John
off Hwy. 19
Campsites: 40 tent sites
Max RV Length: NA
Facilities/Accommodations:
Boating, drinking water, picnic
tables, toilets
Reservations: (800) 280-2267
Open: May 31 to September 5
Limit of Stay: 16 days
Fee Charged: Yes
Managing Agency: National Forest
Service (Ashley)

Buckboard Crossing

Location: 15 miles south of Green
River, Wyo., off Hwy. 530
Campsites: 68 RV and tent sites
Max RV Length: Unknown
Facilities/Accommodations:
Boating, drinking water, fishing,
picnic tables, toilets
Reservations: NA
Open: May to October
Limit of Stay: 16 days
Fee Charged: Yes
Managing Agency: National Forest
Service (Ashley)

Cedar Springs

Location: 5 miles west of Dutch
John off Hwy. 191
Campsites: 23 RV and tent sites

Max RV Length: 40 feet
Facilities/Accommodations:
Drinking water, dump sites, fish-
ing, group sites, handicap facili-
ties, picnic tables, toilets
Reservations: (800) 280-2267
Open: May 1 to October 15
Limit of Stay: 16 days
Fee Charged: Yes
Managing Agency: National Forest
Service (Ashley)

Deer Run

Location: 4.5 miles west of Dutch
John off Hwy. 191
Campsites: 19 RV and tent sites
Max RV Length: 45 feet
Facilities/Accommodations:
Drinking water, dump sites, fish-
ing, group sites, handicap facili-
ties, picnic tables, toilets
Reservations: (800) 280-2267
Open: May 20 to September 12
Limit of Stay: 16 days
Fee Charged: Yes
Managing Agency: National Forest
Service (Ashley)

Firefighters Memorial

Location: 6 miles west of Dutch
John off Hwy. 191
Campsites: 94 RV and tent sites
Max RV Length: 45 feet
Facilities/Accommodations:
Drinking water, dump sites, hand-
icap facilities, picnic tables, toilets
Reservations: (800) 280-2267
Open: May 17 to September 12
Limit of Stay: 16 days
Fee Charged: Yes
Managing Agency: National Forest
Service (Ashley)

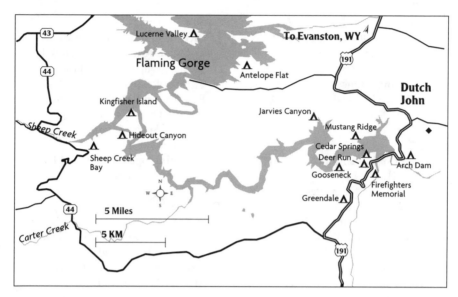

Firehole

🛶 ♨ 🚐 📷

Location: East of Green River, Wyo., about five miles down F. R. 106 off Hwy. 191

Campsites: 40 RV and tent sites

Max RV Length: Unknown

Facilities/Accommodations: Boating, drinking water, group sites, picnic tables, swimming, toilets

Reservations: NA

Open: May to October

Limit of Stay: 16 days

Fee Charged: Yes

Managing Agency: National Forest Service (Ashley)

Gooseneck

🛶 ♨ 📷

Location: Boat access only — 14.9 miles uplake from Dutch John

Campsites: 6 tent sites

Max RV Length: NA

Facilities/Accommodations: Boating, drinking water, fishing, group sites, nondrinkable water, picnic tables, toilets

Reservations: (800) 280-2267

Open: Year-round

Limit of Stay: 16 days

Fee Charged: Yes

Managing Agency: National Forest Service (Ashley)

Greendale

🛶 🚐 📷

Location: West of Dutch John off Hwy. 191, near Flaming Gorge Lodge

Campsites: 8 RV and tent sites

Max RV Length: 40 feet

Facilities/Accommodations: Boating, drinking water, picnic tables, toilets

Reservations: 9800) 280-2267

Open: May 20 To December 31

Limit of Stay: 16 days

Fee Charged: Yes

Managing Agency: National Forest Service (Ashley)

Greendale (Group Site)

Location: West of Dutch John off Hwy. 191, near Flaming Gorge Lodge
Campsites: 24 RV and tent sites
Max RV Length: 45 feet
Facilities/Accommodations: Boating, drinking water, fishing, picnic tables, toilets
Reservations: (800) 280-2267
Open: May 17 to October 1
Limit of Stay: 16 days
Fee Charged: Yes
Managing Agency: National Forest Service (Ashley)

Hideout Canyon

Location: Boat access only — On the southern shore about 1 mile south of Sheep Creek Bay
Campsites: 19 tent sites
Max RV Length: NA
Facilities/Accommodations: Boating, drinking water, fishing, swimming, toilets
Reservations: NA
Open: June to September
Limit of Stay: 16 days
Fee Charged: Yes
Managing Agency: National Forest Service (Ashley)

Jarvies Canyon

Location: Boat access only — About 4 miles uplake from the dam
Campsites: 8 tent sites
Max RV Length: NA
Facilities/Accommodations: Boating, fishing, nondrinkable water, picnic tables, toilets
Reservations: (877) 444-6777; TDD (877) 833-6777
Open: June 7 to December 31
Limit of Stay: 16 days
Fee Charged: Yes
Managing Agency: National Forest Service (Ashley)

PHOTO: WENDELL CHEEK

A broad view of land, sky and water across Flaming Gorge.

Kingfisher Island
🛟

Location: Boat access only — near Sheep Creek Bay
Campsites: 8 tent sites
Max RV Length: NA
Facilities/Accommodations: Boating, fishing, nondrinkable water, picnic tables, toilets
Reservations: (800) 280-2267
Open: April 1 to December 31
Limit of Stay: 16 days
Fee Charged: Yes
Managing Agency: National Forest Service (Ashley)

Lucerne Point
🛟 ♨ 🚐 🛟

Location: 8.7 miles east of Manila off Hwy. 43
Campsites: 4 RV sites, 20 tent sites
Max RV Length: 40 feet
Facilities/Accommodations: Boating, drinking water, dump sites, group sites, nondrinkable water, picnic tables, swimming, toilets
Reservations: (800) 280-2267
Open: May 20 to September 12
Limit of Stay: 16 days
Fee Charged: Yes
Managing Agency: National Forest Service (Ashley)

Lucerne Valley
🛟 ♿ 🚐 🛟

Location: 8.5 miles east of Manila off Hwy. 43
Campsites: 157 RV and tent sites
Max RV Length: 40 feet
Facilities/Accommodations: Boating, drinking water, dump sites, fishing, handicap facilities, nondrinkable water, picnic tables, swimming, toilets

Reservations: (800) 280-2267
Open: May 17 to September 12
Limit of Stay: 16 days
Fee Charged: Yes
Managing Agency: National Forest Service (Ashley)

Mustang Ridge
🛟 🚐 🛟

Location: On the reservoir, 4 miles northwest of Dutch John
Campsites: 73 RV and tent sites
Max RV Length: 45 feet
Facilities/Accommodations: Boating, drinking water, fishing, picnic tables, swimming, toilets
Reservations: (800) 280-2267
Open: May 17 to September 12
Limit of Stay: 16 days
Fee Charged: Yes
Managing Agency: National Forest Service (Ashley)

Sheep Creek Bay
♿ 🛟

Location: About five miles south of Manila off Hwy. 44
Campsites: 8 RV and tent sites
Max RV Length: Unknown
Facilities/Accommodations: Handicap facilities, nondrinkable water, toilets
Reservations: NA
Open: May to October
Limit of Stay: 16 days
Fee Charged: Yes
Managing Agency: National Forest Service (Ashley)

Flaming Gorge KOA
🛟 ♨ 🚐 🎣 🛟

Location: 3 W at Hwy. 43, Manila
Campsites: 40 RV sites, 37 complete RV hookups, 12 tent sites
Max RV Length: 65 feet

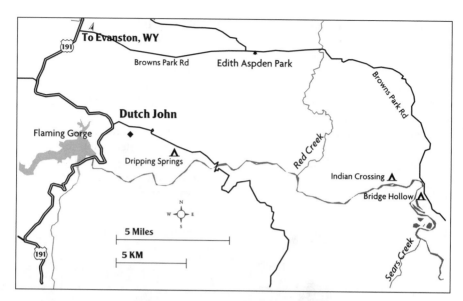

Facilities/Accommodations:
Drinking water, dump sites, fishing, group sites, laundry, picnic tables, showers, swimming, toilets
Reservations: (435) 784-3184
Open: April 15 to October 15
Limit of Stay: Unknown
Fee Charged: Yes
Managing Agency: Private

Tex's Travel Camp, Inc.

Location: Hwy. 374, Green River, Wyo.
Campsites: 49 RV sites with complete RV hookups, 23 tent sites
Max RV Length: Unknown
Facilities/Accommodations:
Drinking water, dump sites, laundry, showers, toilets
Reservations: (307) 875-2630
Open: May 1 to October 1
Limit of Stay: Unknown
Fee Charged: Yes
Managing Agency: Private

GREEN RIVER (BELOW FLAMING GORGE DAM)

Bridge Hollow

Location: East of Flaming Gorge, on the river off Browns Park Road
Campsites: 12 RV and tent sites
Max RV Length: Unknown
Facilities/Accommodations:
Boating, drinking water, fishing, group sites, handicap facilities, nondrinkable water, picnic tables, toilets
Reservations: (435) 789-1362 or 259-6111
Open: Year-round
Limit of Stay: 14 days
Fee Charged: Yes
Managing Agency: BLM

Indian Crossing

Location: On the river, off Browns Park Road
Campsites: 20 RV and tent sites
Max RV Length: 25 feet

Facilities/Accommodations:
Boating, drinking water, fishing,
group sites, handicap facilities,
nondrinkable water, picnic tables,
toilets
Reservations: (800) 280-2267
Open: Year-round
Limit of Stay: 14 days
Fee Charged: Yes
Managing Agency: BLM

Dripping Springs

Location: 3 miles southeast of Dutch
John on F.S. Road 75, above the
Green River
Campsites: 21 RV and tent sites
Max RV Length: 45 feet
Facilities/Accommodations:
Drinking water, group sites, hand-
icap facilities, picnic tables, toilets
Reservations: (800) 280-2267
Open: Year-round
Limit of Stay: 16 days

**Canoeists traverse the Green River, taking in the sights
while finding the perfect campsite.**

Fee Charged: Yes
Managing Agency: National Forest
Service (Ashley)

HUNTINGTON

Forks of Huntington Canyon
🛶 ⛺ 🚐 🚻

Location: 18 miles northwest of
Huntington on Hwy. 31
Campsites: RV sites, 6 tent sites
Max RV Length: 20 feet
Facilities/Accommodations:
Drinking water, fishing, group
sites, picnic tables, toilets
Reservations: (800) 280-2267
Open: June 1 to September 15
Limit of Stay: 16 days
Fee Charged: Yes
Managing Agency: National Forest
Service (Manti-La Sal)

Old Folks Flat
🛶 ⛺ 🚐 🚻

Location: 21 miles northwest of
Huntington on Hwy. 31
Campsites: 8 RV and tent sites
Max RV Length: 30 feet
Facilities/Accommodations:
Drinking water, fishing, group
sites, nondrinkable water, picnic
tables, toilets
Reservations: (800) 280-2267
Open: June 1 to September 15
Limit of Stay: 16 days
Fee Charged: Yes
Managing Agency: National Forest
Service (Manti-La Sal)

Huntington State Park
🛶 ⛺ ♿ 🚐 🚿 🚻

Location: 2 miles north of
Huntington off Hwy. 10
Campsites: 22 RV and tent sites
Max RV Length: 30 feet

Facilities/Accommodations:
Boating, drinking water, dump
sites, fishing, group sites, handi-
cap facilities, nondrinkable water,
picnic tables, showers, swimming,
toilets
Reservations: (800) 322-3770
Open: Year-round
Limit of Stay: 14 days
Fee Charged: Yes
Managing Agency: Utah State Parks

JOE'S VALLEY

Indian Creek
🛶 🚐 🚻

Location: North of Joe's Valley on
F.R. 017
Campsites: 28 RV and tent sites
Max RV Length: Unknown
Facilities/Accommodations:
Boating, drinking water, fishing,
nondrinkable water, picnic tables,
toilets
Reservations: (800) 280-2267
Open: June 30 to September 20
Limit of Stay: 16 days
Fee Charged: Yes
Managing Agency: National Forest
Service (Manti-La Sal)

Joe's Valley Reservoir
🛶 ♿ 🚐 🚻

Location: 17 miles from Orangeville
off Hwy. 29
Campsites: 45 RV sites, 46 tent sites
Max RV Length: Unknown
Facilities/Accommodations:
Boating, drinking water, fishing,
handicap facilities, nondrinkable
water, picnic tables, toilets
Reservations: (800) 280-2267
Open: May 25 to October 25
Limit of Stay: 16 days

Fee Charged: Yes
Managing Agency: National Forest Service (Manti-La Sal)

Joe's Valley Boat ramp

Location: 17 miles from Orangeville off Hwy. 29
Campsites: 18 RV sites
Max RV Length: 38 feet
Facilities/Accommodations: Boating, drinking water, fishing, handicap facilities, nondrinkable water, picnic tables, toilets
Reservations: (800) 280-2267
Open: May 25 to October 25
Limit of Stay: 16 days
Fee Charged: Yes
Managing Agency: National Forest Service (Manti-La Sal)

PRICE

El Rancho Motel & RV

Location: 145 N Carbonville Rd., Price
Campsites: 34 RV sites with complete RV hookups
Max RV Length: 40 feet
Facilities/Accommodations: Drinking water, dump sites, laundry, showers, swimming, toilets
Reservations: (435) 637-2424
Open: Year-round
Limit of Stay: Unknown
Fee Charged: Yes
Managing Agency: Private

ROOSEVELT

Pelican Lake

Location: 25 miles southeast of Hwy. 40 on Hwy. 88
Campsites: 12 RV and tent sites

Max RV Length: Unknown
Facilities/Accommodations: Boating, fishing, nondrinkable water, picnic tables, toilets
Reservations: (435) 789-1362 or 259-6111
Open: Year-round
Limit of Stay: 14 days
Fee Charged: Yes
Managing Agency: BLM

Country Village Trailer Park

Location: 8 miles east of Roosevelt on Hwy. 40
Campsites: 19 RV sites, 15 complete RV hookups, 10 tent sites
Max RV Length: Unknown
Facilities/Accommodations: Boating, drinking water, dump sites, fishing, picnic tables, toilets
Reservations: (435) 722-2890
Open: March 1 to November 1
Limit of Stay: Unknown
Fee Charged: Yes
Managing Agency: Private

SCOFIELD

Scofield State Park— Madsen Bay

Location: On the northwest shore of the reservoir off Hwy. 96
Campsites: 37 tent sites
Max RV Length: NA
Facilities/Accommodations: Boating, drinking water, dump sites, fishing, group sites, handicap facilities, nondrinkable water, picnic tables, toilets
Reservations: (800) 322-3770
Open: May to November
Limit of Stay: 14 days
Fee Charged: Yes
Managing Agency: Utah State Parks

Scofield State Park — Mountain View

⚓ ⊞ ♿ 🚐 🚿 🚽

Location: On the east shore off Hwy. 96
Campsites: 34 RV sites
Max RV Length: 30 feet
Facilities/Accommodations: Boating, drinking water, dump sites, fishing, group sites, handicap facilities, nondrinkable water, picnic tables, showers, toilets
Reservations: (800) 322-3770
Open: May to November
Limit of Stay: 14 days
Fee Charged: Yes
Managing Agency: Utah State Parks

Lazy Anchor Campground

⚓ ♿ 🚐 🚿 🚽

Location: In Scofield on Hwy. 96
Campsites: 9 RV sites with complete RV hookups, 6 tent sites
Max RV Length: 70 feet
Facilities/Accommodations: Boating, drinking water, dump sites, handicap facilities, laundry, picnic tables, showers, toilets
Reservations: (435) 448-9697
Open: May 1 to November 15
Limit of Stay: Unknown
Fee Charged: Yes
Managing Agency: Private

STARVATION STATE PARK

Starvation Reservoir

⚓ ⊞ 🚐 🚿 🚽

Location: Northwest of Duchesne off Hwy. 40
Campsites: 55 RV sites, 3 tent sites
Max RV Length: 30 feet

Facilities/Accommodations: Boating, drinking water, dump sites, fishing, group sites, non-drinkable water, showers, swimming, toilets
Reservations: (800) 322-3770
Open: Year-round
Limit of Stay: 14 days
Fee Charged: Yes
Managing Agency: Utah State Parks

UINTAS — HWY. 191/44

Browne Lake

🚐 🚽

Location: 20.5 miles southwest of Manila off the Sheep Creek Loop
Campsites: 8 RV and tent sites
Max RV Length: 30 feet
Facilities/Accommodations: Boating, fishing, picnic tables, toilets
Reservations: (800) 280-2267
Open: June 1 to October 1
Limit of Stay: 16 days
Fee Charged: No
Managing Agency: National Forest Service (Ashley)

Canyon Rim

⚓ 🚐 🚽

Location: Above the lake near Red Canyon Visitor Center, off Hwy. 44
Campsites: 19 RV and tent sites
Max RV Length: Unknown
Facilities/Accommodations: Drinking water, picnic tables, toilets
Reservations: NA
Open: June to September
Limit of Stay: 16 days
Fee Charged: Yes
Managing Agency: National Forest Service (Ashley)

Carmel/Navajo Cliffs

Location: 2 miles south of Manila off Hwy. 44
Campsites: 13 RV and tent sites
Max RV Length: Unknown
Facilities/Accommodations: Drinking water, fishing, non-drinkable water, picnic tables, toilets
Reservations: NA
Open: June to September
Limit of Stay: 16 days
Fee Charged: No
Managing Agency: National Forest Service (Ashley)

Deep Creek

Location: 21.5 miles southwest of Manila on F.R. 539 off Hwy. 44
Campsites: 17 RV and tent sites
Max RV Length: 30 feet
Facilities/Accommodations: Drinking water, fishing, non-drinkable water, picnic tables, toilets
Reservations: (800) 280-2267
Open: June 1 to October 1
Limit of Stay: 16 days
Fee Charged: No
Managing Agency: National Forest Service (Ashley)

Dowd Spring

Location: South of Manila on Hwy. 44
Campsites: 6 RV and tent sites
Max RV Length: Unknown
Facilities/Accommodations: Drinking water, picnic tables, toilets
Reservations: NA
Open: May 15 to September

Limit of Stay: 16 days
Fee Charged: Yes
Managing Agency: National Forest Service

East Park

Location: 12 miles north of Vernal on Hwy.191, left on F.R. 20, then right to the reservoir
Campsites: 21 RV and tent sites
Max RV Length: Unknown
Facilities/Accommodations: Boating, drinking water, fishing, picnic tables, toilets
Reservations: NA
Open: June to September
Limit of Stay: 16 days
Fee Charged: Yes
Managing Agency: National Forest Service (Ashley)

Green's Lake

Location: About 9 miles south of Manila off Hwy. 44
Campsites: 20 RV and tent sites
Max RV Length: 40 feet
Facilities/Accommodations: Drinking water, group sites, laundry, picnic tables, showers, toilets
Reservations: (800) 280-2267
Open: May 20 to September 12
Limit of Stay: 16 days
Fee Charged: Yes
Managing Agency: National Forest Service (Ashley)

Kaler Hollow

Location: From 2500 West in Vernal, go north onto F.R. 044 then about 12 miles
Campsites: 4 RV and tent sites

Max RV Length: Unknown
Facilities/Accommodations: Picnic
  tables, toilets
Reservations: NA
Open: June to September
Limit of Stay: 16 days
Fee Charged: No
Managing Agency: National Forest
  Service (Ashley)

Lodgepole Springs

Location: 15 miles north of Vernal
  along Hwy. 191
Campsites: 35 RV and tent sites
Max RV Length: Unknown
Facilities/Accommodations:
  Drinking water, group sites, picnic
  tables, toilets

PHOTO: CHEYENNE ROUSE

A hiker pauses to take in some High Uintas peaks.

Reservations: NA
Open: June to September
Limit of Stay: 16 days
Fee Charged: Yes
Managing Agency: National Forest
Service (Ashley)

Oaks Park
🛏 🚽

Location: From 2500 West in Vernal,
go north onto F.R. 044 then 15
miles to the reservoir
Campsites: 11 RV and tent sites
Max RV Length: Unknown
Facilities/Accommodations:
Boating, fishing, picnic tables, toi-
lets
Reservations: NA
Open: June to September
Limit of Stay: 16 days
Fee Charged: Yes
Managing Agency: National Forest
Service (Ashley)

Palisades Memorial Park
🛏 🚽 🚻

Location: About 6 miles south of
Manila on F.R. 221
Campsites: 3 RV and tent sites
Max RV Length: Unknown
Facilities/Accommodations:
Drinking water, picnic tables, toi-
lets
Reservations: NA
Open: June to September
Limit of Stay: 16 days
Fee Charged: No
Managing Agency: National Forest
Service (Ashley)

Skull Creek
🛏 🚽 🚻

Location: 12 miles northwest of
Dutch John off Hwy. 44
Campsites: 17 RV and tent sites

Max RV Length: 40 feet
Facilities/Accommodations:
Drinking water, picnic tables, toi-
lets
Reservations: (800) 280-2267
Open: May 20 to September 12
Limit of Stay: 16 days
Fee Charged: Yes
Managing Agency: National Forest
Service (Ashley)

UINTAS — NORTH SLOPE

Bridger Lake
🚻 🛏 🚽

Location: Just south of Stateline
Reservoir, out of Mountain View,
Wyo.
Campsites: 10 RV and tent sites
Max RV Length: 20 feet
Facilities/Accommodations:
Drinking water, fishing, non-
drinkable water, picnic tables
Reservations: (800) 280-2267
Open: June 30 to September 15
Limit of Stay: 7 days
Fee Charged: Yes
Managing Agency: National Forest
Service (Wasatch-Cache)

China Meadows
🛏 🚽

Location: About 3 miles south of
Stateline Reservoir (From
Mountain View, Wyo., take Hwy.
410 south for 7 miles, then F.R.
072 to the lake and campground)
Campsites: 12 RV and tent sites
Max RV Length: Unknown
Facilities/Accommodations:
Boating, fishing, toilets
Reservations: NA
Open: June to October
Limit of Stay: 14 days
Fee Charged: Yes

Managing Agency: National Forest Service (Wasatch-Cache)

East Fork Blacks Fork
🏕 🚽

Location: From Mountain View, Wyo., go south on Hwy. 410 about 5 miles to F.R. 073, then south on it about 30 miles
Campsites: 8 RV and tent sites
Max RV Length: Unknown
Facilities/Accommodations: Fishing, toilets
Reservations: NA
Open: June to October
Limit of Stay: 14 days
Fee Charged: No
Managing Agency: National Forest Service (Wasatch-Cache)

Henry's Fork
🚽

Location: From Lonetree, Wyo., south on the Henry's Fork Road
Campsites: 7 tent sites
Max RV Length: NA
Facilities/Accommodations: Fishing, toilets
Reservations: NA
Open: June to October
Limit of Stay: 14 days
Fee Charged: No
Managing Agency: National Forest Service (Wasatch-Cache)

Hoop Lake
🚤 🏕 🚽

Location: From Lonetree, Wyo., south on the Hole in the Rock Road
Campsites: 44 RV and tent sites
Max RV Length: Unknown
Facilities/Accommodations: Boating, drinking water, fishing, toilets

Reservations: NA
Open: June to October
Limit of Stay: 14 days
Fee Charged: Yes
Managing Agency: National Forest Service (Wasatch-Cache)

Marsh Lake
🚤 🏕 🚽

Location: About 2 miles south of Stateline Reservoir (1 mile above China Meadows; see China Meadows for directions)
Campsites: 38 RV and tent sites
Max RV Length: Unknown
Facilities/Accommodations: Boating, drinking water, fishing, nondrinkable water, toilets
Reservations: NA
Open: June to October
Limit of Stay: 14 days
Fee Charged: Yes
Managing Agency: National Forest Service (Wasatch-Cache)

Meeks Cabin
🚤 🏕 🚽

Location: From Mountain View, Wyo., go south to Robertson, then west to Meeks Cabin Road (F.R. 271)
Campsites: 24 RV and tent sites
Max RV Length: Unknown
Facilities/Accommodations: Boating, drinking water, fishing, toilets
Reservations: NA
Open: June to October
Limit of Stay: 14 days
Fee Charged: Yes
Managing Agency: National Forest Service (Wasatch-Cache)

Spirit Lake

🚶 🚐 🚽

Location: South of Green River, Wyo., on F.R. 221 off Hwy. 530
Campsites: 24 RV and tent sites
Max RV Length: Unknown
Facilities/Accommodations: Drinking water, picnic tables, toilets
Reservations: NA
Open: July to September
Limit of Stay: 16 days
Fee Charged: Yes
Managing Agency: National Forest Service (Ashley)

Stateline

♿ 🚐 🚽

Location: About 20 miles south of Mountain View, Wyo. (take Hwy. 410 south, then continue south on F.R. 072)
Campsites: 41 RV and tent sites
Max RV Length: Unknown
Facilities/Accommodations: Boating, fishing, handicap facilities, toilets
Reservations: NA
Open: June to October
Limit of Stay: 14 days
Fee Charged: Yes
Managing Agency: National Forest Service (Wasatch-Cache)

UINTAS — SOUTH SLOPE

Aspen Grove

🚶 🚐 🚽

Location: 4 miles north of Hanna on F.R. 144, on the Duchesne River
Campsites: 33 RV and tent sites
Max RV Length: Unknown

Facilities/Accommodations: Drinking water, fishing, picnic tables, toilets
Reservations: NA
Open: June to September
Limit of Stay: 16 days
Fee Charged: Yes
Managing Agency: National Forest Service (Ashley)

Bridge

🚶 🚐 🚽

Location: 17.6 miles north of Altamont on F.R. 268, on the Yellowstone River
Campsites: 5 RV and tent sites
Max RV Length: 15 feet
Facilities/Accommodations: Drinking water, fishing, nondrinkable water, picnic tables, toilets
Reservations: NA
Open: May 25 to September 10
Limit of Stay: 14 days
Fee Charged: Yes
Managing Agency: National Forest Service (Ashley)

Hades

🚶 🚐 🚽

Location: 5 miles north of Hanna on F.R. 144, on the Duchesne River
Campsites: 17 RV and tent sites
Max RV Length: Unknown
Facilities/Accommodations: Drinking water, fishing, picnic tables, toilets
Reservations: NA
Open: June to September
Limit of Stay: 16 days
Fee Charged: Yes
Managing Agency: National Forest Service (Ashley)

A secluded campsite beneath the Uintas' Kings Peak (the view just north of sites in Bridge, Swift Creek and other nearby south slope camping areas).

Iron Mine

⚓ 🚐 🚻

Location: 6 miles north of Hanna on F.R. 144, on the Duchesne River

Campsites: 27 RV and tent sites

Max RV Length: Unknown

Facilities/Accommodations: Drinking water, fishing, picnic tables, toilets

Reservations: NA

Open: June to September

Limit of Stay: 16 days

Fee Charged: Yes

Managing Agency: National Forest Service (Ashley)

Iron Springs

⚓ ⛺ 🚐 🚻

Location: 25 miles northwest of Vernal off Hwy. 191 along Red Cloud Loop

Campsites: 18 RV and tent sites

Max RV Length: Unknown

Facilities/Accommodations: Drinking water, fishing, group sites, picnic tables, toilets

Reservations: (800) 280-2267

Open: May 25 to October 31

Limit of Stay: 16 days

Fee Charged: Yes

Managing Agency: National Forest Service (Ashley)

Miners Gulch

🚐 🚻

Location: 18 miles northwest of Mountain Home off Hwy. 87 on F.R. 134 (left at Rock Creek Store)

Campsites: 5 RV and tent sites

Max RV Length: 22 feet

Facilities/Accommodations: Fishing, toilets

Reservations: NA

Open: May 25 to September 10

Limit of Stay: 16 days
Fee Charged: Yes
Managing Agency: National Forest
Service (Ashley)

Moon Lake

Location: 35.5 miles northwest of
Altamont off Hwy. 87 on F.R. 131
Campsites: 18 RV and tent sites
Max RV Length: 22 feet
Facilities/Accommodations:
Boating, drinking water, fishing,
group sites, nondrinkable water,
picnic tables, swimming, toilets
Reservations: Group sites only.
(800) 280-2267
Open: June 1 to September 10
Limit of Stay: 16 days
Fee Charged: Yes
Managing Agency: National Forest
Service (Ashley)

Pole Creek Lake

Location: North of Neola on F.R.
117
Campsites: 18 RV and tent sites
Max RV Length: Unknown
Facilities/Accommodations: Picnic
tables, toilets
Reservations: NA
Open: June to September
Limit of Stay: 16 days
Fee Charged: No
Managing Agency: National Forest
Service (Ashley)

Reservoir

Location: 16 miles north of
Altamont on F.R. 124, on the
Yellowstone River
Campsites: 4 RV sites, 5 tent sites

Max RV Length: 22 feet
Facilities/Accommodations: Fishing,
nondrinkable water, picnic tables,
toilets
Reservations: NA
Open: May 25 to September 10
Limit of Stay: 14 days
Fee Charged: Yes
Managing Agency: National Forest
Service (Ashley)

Riverview

Location: 18.5 miles north of
Altamont on F.R. 124, on the
Yellowstone River
Campsites: 19 RV and tent sites
Max RV Length: 22 feet
Facilities/Accommodations:
Drinking water, fishing, non-
drinkable water, picnic tables
Reservations: (800) 280-2267
Open: May 25 to September 10
Limit of Stay: 16 days
Fee Charged: Yes
Managing Agency: National Forest
Service (Ashley)

Swift Creek

Location: 22.5 miles north of
Altamont on F.R. 124 off Hwy.
121, on the Yellowstone River
Campsites: 11 RV and tent sites
Max RV Length: 22 feet
Facilities/Accommodations:
Drinking water, fishing, non-
drinkable water, picnic tables, toi-
lets
Reservations: NA
Open: May 20 to September 10
Limit of Stay: 16 days
Fee Charged: Yes
Managing Agency: National Forest
Service (Ashley)

Uinta Canyon

Location: 24 miles northwest of Roosevelt on F.R. 118 off Hwy. 121

Campsites: 24 RV and tent sites

Max RV Length: 40 feet

Facilities/Accommodations: Drinking water, fishing, nondrinkable water, picnic tables, toilets

Reservations: NA

Open: May 25 to September 10

Limit of Stay: 16 days

Fee Charged: Yes

Managing Agency: National Forest Service (Ashley)

Uinta River

Location: 24 miles northwest of Roosevelt on F.R. 118 off Hwy. 121

Campsites: 5 RV and tent sites

Max RV Length: 20 feet

Facilities/Accommodations: Drinking water, fishing, group sites, nondrinkable water, picnic tables, toilets

Reservations: (800) 280-2267

Open: May 25 to September 10

Limit of Stay: 16 days

Fee Charged: Yes

Managing Agency: National Forest Service (Ashley)

Wandin

Location: 25.5 miles northwest of Roosevelt on F.R. 18 off Hwy. 121, on the Uinta River

Campsites: 4 RV and tent sites

Max RV Length: 15 feet

Facilities/Accommodations: Fishing, nondrinkable water, picnic tables, toilets

Reservations: (800) 280-2267

Open: May 25 to September 10

Limit of Stay: 16 days

Fee Charged: Yes

Managing Agency: National Forest Service

Whiterocks

Location: North of Neola on F.R. 492, on the Whiterocks River

Campsites: 21 RV and tent sites

Max RV Length: Unknown

Facilities/Accommodations: Drinking water, fishing, picnics tables, toilets

Reservations: NA

Open: June to September

Limit of Stay: 16 days

Fee Charged: Yes

Managing Agency: National Forest Service (Ashley)

Yellowpine

Location: 20 miles northwest of Mountain Home off Hwy. 87 on F.R. 134 (left at Rock Creek Store)

Campsites: 29 RV and tent sites

Max RV Length: 22 feet

Facilities/Accommodations: Drinking water, fishing, handicap facilities, nondrinkable water, toilets

Reservations: NA

Open: May 25 to September 10

Limit of Stay: 16 days

Fee Charged: Yes

Managing Agency: National Forest Service (Ashley)

Yellowstone

Location: 14.5 miles north of Altamont on F.R. 119, on the Yellowstone River
Campsites: 11 RV and tent sites
Max RV Length: 22 feet
Facilities/Accommodations: Drinking water, fishing, non-drinkable water, picnic tables, toilets
Reservations: NA
Open: May 25 to September 10
Limit of Stay: 16 days
Fee Charged: Yes
Managing Agency: National Forest Service (Ashley)

Rock Creek Ranch

Location: 22miles northwest of Mountain Home on F.R. 134(left at Rock Creek Store)
Campsites: RV and tent sites
Max RV Length: 40 feet
Facilities/Accommodations: Drinking water, fishing, group sites, nondrinkable water, picnic tables, toilets; also cabins
Reservations: (435) 454-3332
Open: Year-round
Limit of Stay: None
Fee Charged: Yes
Managing Agency: Private

VERNAL / RED FLEET STATE PARK / STEINAKER STATE PARK

Dry Fork

Location: 15 miles northwest of Vernal in Dry Fork Canyon, along Red Cloud Loop
Campsites: 5 tent sites
Max RV Length: NA

Facilities/Accommodations: Group sites, picnic tables, toilets
Reservations: (800) 280-2267
Open: April 1 to November 1
Limit of Stay: 14 days
Fee Charged: Yes
Managing Agency: National Forest Service (Ashley)

Red Fleet State Park

Location: 13 miles north of Vernal off Hwy. 191
Campsites: 29 RV and tent sites
Max RV Length: 35 feet
Facilities/Accommodations: Boating, drinking water, dump sites, fishing, handicap facilities, nondrinkable water, picnic tables, swimming, toilets
Reservations: (800) 322-3770
Open: Year-round
Limit of Stay: 14 days
Fee Charged: Yes
Managing Agency: Utah State Parks

Steinaker State Park

Location: 7 miles north of Vernal off Hwy. 191
Campsites: 31 RV and tent sites
Max RV Length: 35 feet
Facilities/Accommodations: Boating, drinking water, fishing, group sites, nondrinkable water, swimming, toilets
Reservations: (800) 322-3770
Open: Year-round
Limit of Stay: 14 days
Fee Charged: Yes
Managing Agency: Utah State Parks

Campground Dina

Location: 930 N Vernal Ave., Vernal

Campsites: 100 RV sites, 66 complete RV hookups, 100 tent sites
Max RV Length: 70 feet
Facilities/Accommodations:
Boating, drinking water, dump sites, fishing, group sites, laundry, picnic tables, showers, swimming, toilets
Reservations: (800) 245-2148; (435) 789-2148
Open: March 1 to November 30
Limit of Stay: Unknown
Fee Charged: Yes
Managing Agency: Private

Dinosaur Village

Location: 7000 E Hwy. 40, Vernal
Campsites: 32 RV sites, 16 complete RV hookups, 10 tent sites
Max RV Length: 30 feet
Facilities/Accommodations:
Drinking water, dump sites, fishing, group sites, handicap facilities, picnic tables, showers, toilets
Reservations: (435) 789-5552
Open: Year-round
Limit of Stay: Unknown
Fee Charged: Yes
Managing Agency: Private

Fossil Valley RV

Location: 999 W Hwy. 40, Vernal
Campsites: 45 RV sites with complete RV hookups, 4 tent sites
Max RV Length: 55 feet
Facilities/Accommodations:
Boating, drinking water, dump sites, fishing, group sites, handicap facilities, laundry, picnic tables, showers, toilets
Reservations: (435) 789-6450
Open: April 1 to November 1
Limit of Stay: Unknown

Fee Charged: Yes
Managing Agency: Private

Outlaw Country RV Park

Location: Vernal
Campsites: 25 RV and tent sites
Max RV Length: None
Facilities/Accommodations:
Drinking water, picnic tables, toilets
Reservations: (435) 789-8935
Open: March through August
Limit of Stay: No
Fee Charged: Yes
Managing Agency: Private

Western Heritage RV Park

Location: 271 S 500 E, Vernal
Campsites: 32 RV sites
Max RV Length: 60 feet
Facilities/Accommodations:
Boating, drinking water, dump sites, fishing, handicap facilities, laundry, picnic tables, showers, toilets
Reservations: (435) 781-1347
Open: April 1 to October 30
Limit of Stay: Unknown
Fee Charged: Yes
Managing Agency: Private

CAMPGROUNDS: CENTRAL REGION

DELTA

Antelope Valley RV Park
🔖 ⛺ ♿ 🚐 🚽

Location: 776 W Main, Delta, west of the overpass
Campsites: 96 RV sites with complete RV hookups, 96 tent sites
Max RV Length: Unknown
Facilities/Accommodations: Boating, drinking water, dump sites, fishing, group sites, handicap facilities, laundry, showers, toilets
Reservations: (435) 864-1813
Open: Year-round
Limit of Stay: Unknown
Fee Charged: Yes
Managing Agency: Private

FILLMORE

Fillmore KOA
🔖 ⛺ 🚐 🚽

Location: 800 S 270 W, Fillmore
Campsites: 49 RV sites, 42 complete RV hookups, 7 tent sites
Max RV Length: 65 feet
Facilities/Accommodations: Drinking water, dump sites, group sites, laundry, picnic tables, showers, swimming, toilets
Reservations: (800) 562-1516
Open: March 1 to December 15
Limit of Stay: Unknown
Fee Charged: Yes
Managing Agency: Private

Wagons West RV Camp
🔖 🚐 🍴 🚽

Location: 545 N Main Street, Fillmore
Campsites: 50 RV sites, 40 complete RV hookups, 8 tent sites
Max RV Length: Unknown
Facilities/Accommodations: Boating, drinking water, dump sites, fishing, laundry, picnic tables, showers, swimming, toilets
Reservations: (435) 743-6188
Open: Year-round
Limit of Stay: Unknown
Fee Charged: Yes
Managing Agency: Private

FISH LAKE

Bowery Creek
🔖 ⛺ 🚐 🚽

Location: At Fish Lake on Hwy. 25
Campsites: 43 RV sites with complete hookups, tent sites
Max RV Length: 22 feet
Facilities/Accommodations: Boating, drinking water, fishing, group sites, picnic tables, toilets
Reservations: (800) 280-2267; (877) 444-6777
Open: May 17 to September 20

S Y M B O L   L E G E N D

🔖 Drinking water   🚐 RV sites
⛺ Group sites   🚽 Toilets
♿ Handicap facilities   🍴 Showers

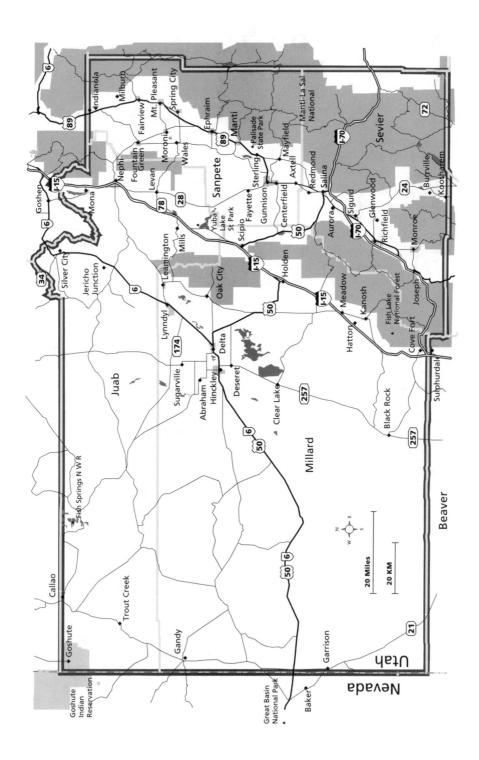

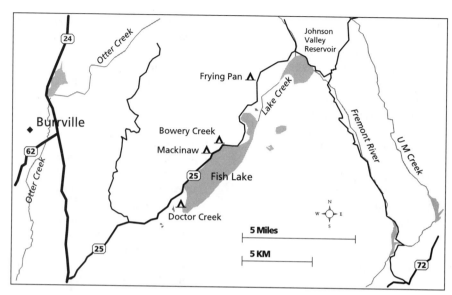

Limit of Stay: 14 days
Fee Charged: Yes
Managing Agency: National Forest
Service (Fishlake)

Doctor Creek
🚰 ⛲ 🚐 ⛺
Location: At Fish Lake on Hwy. 25
Campsites: 13 RV sites, 29 tent sites
Max RV Length: 22 feet
Facilities/Accommodations:
Boating, drinking water, dump
sites, fishing, group sites, picnic
tables, toilets
Reservations: (800) 280-2267
Open: June 4 to September 9
Limit of Stay: 10 days
Fee Charged: Yes
Managing Agency: National Forest
Service (Fishlake)

Frying Pan
🚰 ⛲ 🚐 ⛺
Location: Between Fish Lake and
Johnson Reservoir on Hwy. 25
Campsites: 12 RV and tent sites
Max RV Length: 22 feet

Facilities/Accommodations:
Boating, drinking water, fishing,
group sites, picnic tables, toilets
Reservations: (800) 280-2267
Open: May 27 to September 30
Limit of Stay: 16 days
Fee Charged: Yes
Managing Agency: National Forest
Service (Fishlake)

Mackinaw
🚰 ⛲ 🚐 ⛺
Location: At Fish Lake on Hwy. 25
Campsites: 68 RV and tent sites
Max RV Length: 22 feet
Facilities/Accommodations:
Boating, drinking water, fishing,
group sites, nondrinkable water,
picnic tables, toilets
Reservations: (800) 280-2267
Open: May 27 to September 16
Limit of Stay: 10 days
Fee Charged: Yes
Managing Agency: National Forest
Service (Fishlake)

Bowery Haven Resort

Location: At Fish Lake on Hwy. 25
Campsites: 69 RV sites with complete hookups
Max RV Length: Unknown
Facilities/Accommodations:
Boating, drinking water, fishing, laundry, picnic tables, showers, toilets
Reservations: (435) 638-1040
Open: May 15 to November 1
Limit of Stay: Unknown
Fee Charged: Yes
Managing Agency: Private

Lakeside Resort

Location: At Fish Lake on Hwy. 25
Campsites: 24 RV sites with complete hookups
Max RV Length: 121 feet
Facilities/Accommodations:
Boating, drinking water, dump sites, fishing, laundry, picnic tables, showers, toilets
Reservations: (435) 638-1000
Open: May 15 to October 25
Limit of Stay: 14 days
Fee Charged: Yes
Managing Agency: Private

FREMONT INDIAN STATE PARK

Castle Rock

Location: South of I-70 (Exit 17), near Fremont Indian State Park, southwest of Richfield
Campsites: 30 RV and tent sites
Max RV Length: 24 feet
Facilities/Accommodations:
Laundry, picnic tables, showers, toilets

Reservations: (800) 280-2267
Open: April 1 to October 31
Limit of Stay: 14 days
Fee Charged: Yes
Managing Agency: National Forest Service (Fishlake)

Fremont

Location: 21 miles southwest of Richfield off I-70
Campsites: 31 RV sites, tent sites
Max RV Length: 30 feet
Facilities/Accommodations:
Drinking water, handicap facilities, nondrinkable water, picnic tables, toilets
Reservations: (800) 322-3770
Open: Year-round
Limit of Stay: 14 days
Fee Charged: Yes
Managing Agency: Utah State Parks

GUNNISON

Gunnison

Location: 240 S Main, Gunnison
Campsites: 15 RV sites, 12 complete RV hookups, 8 tent sites
Max RV Length: 40 feet
Facilities/Accommodations:
Drinking water, fishing, group sites, picnic tables, toilets
Reservations: (435) 528-3366
Open: March 1 to November 30
Limit of Stay: Unknown
Fee Charged: Yes
Managing Agency: Private

Lunds Drive-In & Campground

Location: 230 S Main, Gunnison
Campsites: 15 RV and tent sites

Max RV Length: Unknown
Facilities/Accommodations:
Drinking water, picnic tables,
showers, toilets
Reservations: (435) 528-3366
Open: Year-round
Limit of Stay: None
Fee Charged: Yes
Managing Agency: Private

JOSEPH

Flying U Campground

Location: 45 S State, Joseph
Campsites: 10 RV sites, 7 RV
hookups
Max RV Length: Unknown
Facilities/Accommodations:
Drinking water, dump sites, laundry, showers, toilets
Reservations: (435) 527-4758
Open: May 15 to October 30
Limit of Stay: 10 days
Fee Charged: Yes
Managing Agency: Private

KANOSH

Adelaide

Location: 6 miles east of Kanosh on
F.R.106
Campsites: 20 RV sites, 15 tent sites
Max RV Length: Unknown
Facilities/Accommodations:
Drinking water, fishing, group
sites, picnic tables, toilets
Reservations: (800) 280-2267.
Open: May 21 to October 30
Limit of Stay: 14 days
Fee Charged: Yes
Managing Agency: National Forest
Service (Fishlake)

LEVAN

Chicken Creek

Location: 6 miles southeast of Levan
on Chicken Creek Canyon Road
Campsites: 9 RV and tent sites
Max RV Length: Unknown
Facilities/Accommodations:
Drinking water, fishing, group
sites, nondrinkable water, picnic
tables, toilets
Reservations: (800) 280-2267
Open: June 1 to September 10
Limit of Stay: 16 days
Fee Charged: Yes
Managing Agency: National Forest
Service (Manti-La Sal)

MANTI / EPHRAIM

Manti Community

Location: 7 miles east of Manti on
Manti Canyon Road
Campsites: 9 RV and tent sites
Max RV Length: Unknown
Facilities/Accommodations:
Drinking water, fishing, group
sites, nondrinkable water, picnic
tables, toilets
Reservations: (800) 280-2267
Open: June 15 to September 10
Limit of Stay: 16 days
Fee Charged: Yes
Managing Agency: National Forest
Service (Manti-La Sal)

Lake Hill

Location: About 6 miles east of
Ephraim on Hwy. 29
Campsites: 12 RV and tent sites
Max RV Length: Unknown

Facilities/Accommodations:
Drinking water, fishing, group
sites, toilets
Reservations: NA
Open: June to October
Limit of Stay: 14 days
Fee Charged: Yes
Managing Agency: National Forest
Service (Manti-LaSal)

Spring City

Location: East of Spring City on F.R.
036 off Hwy. 89
Campsites: 6 RV and tent sites
Max RV Length: Unknown
Facilities/Accommodations:
Drinking water, fishing, group
sites, picnic tables, toilets
Reservations: NA
Open: June to October
Limit of Stay: 14 days
Fee Charged: Yes
Managing Agency: National Forest
Service (Manti-LaSal)

Palisade State Park

Location: Southeast of Manti (2
miles east of Sterling) off Hwy. 89
Campsites: 53 RV sites, 43 tent sites
Max RV Length: 45 feet
Facilities/Accommodations:
Boating, drinking water, dump
sites, fishing, group sites, non-
drinking water, picnic tables,
showers, swimming, toilets
Reservations: (800) 322-3770
Open: Year-round
Limit of Stay: 14 days
Fee Charged: Yes
Managing Agency: Utah State Parks

Yogi Bear's Jellystone Park

Location: North end of Manti off
Hwy. 89
Campsites: 54 RV sites with com-
plete RV hookups, 17 tent sites
Max RV Length: 40 feet
Facilities/Accommodations:
Drinking water, dump sites, laun-
dry, nondrinkable water, picnic
tables, showers, swimming, toilets
Reservations: (435) 835-2267
Open: Year-round
Limit of Stay: Unknown
Fee Charged: Yes
Managing Agency: Private

MONROE

Mystic Hot Springs

Location: 575 E 100 N, Monroe
Campsites: 32 RV sites with com-
plete RV hookups, 30 tent sites
Max RV Length: Unknown
Facilities/Accommodations:
Drinking water, dump sites, group
sites, laundry, nondrinkable
water, picnic tables, showers,
swimming, toilets
Reservations: (435) 527-3286
Open: Year-round
Limit of Stay: Unknown
Fee Charged: Yes
Managing Agency: Private

MORONI

Maple Canyon

Location: 2 miles northwest of
Freedom (7 miles west of
Moroni)
Campsites: 7 RV sites, 12 tent sites
Max RV Length: Unknown

Facilities/Accommodations:
Drinking water, group sites, picnic tables, toilets
Reservations: (800) 280-2267
Open: June 1 to September 10
Limit of Stay: 16 days
Fee Charged: Yes
Managing Agency: National Forest Service (Manti-La Sal)

MOUNT PLEASANT

Discover Utah, Inc.

Location: 1468 Pine Creek Drive, Mount Pleasant
Campsites: 20 RV sites, 30 tent sites
Max RV Length: Unknown
Facilities/Accommodations:
Drinking water, picnic tables, showers, swimming, toilets
Reservations: (435) 462-2781
Open: June 1 to October 30

Limit of Stay: Unknown
Fee Charged: Yes
Managing Agency: Private

Horseshoe Mountain

Location: 310 S Main, Spring City
Campsites: 2 RV sites, 20 tent sites
Max RV Length: 30 feet
Facilities/Accommodations:
Boating, drinking water, group sites, laundry, nondrinkable water, picnic tables, showers, toilets
Reservations: (435) 462-2671
Open: April 1 to November 30
Limit of Stay: Unknown
Fee Charged: Yes
Managing Agency: Private

Pine Creek Ranch

Location: 1468 Pine Creek Drive, Mount Pleasant

Sagebrush, aspens and evergreens dot the shore of Fish Lake.

PHOTO: MARCIA DIBBLE

Campsites: 20 RV sites, 10 tent sites
Max RV Length: Unknown
Facilities/Accommodations:
  Boating, drinking water, fishing,
  picnic tables, showers, swimming,
  toilets
Reservations: (435) 462-2781
Open: May 31 to September 15
Limit of Stay: Unknown
Fee Charged: Yes
Managing Agency: Private

NEPHI

Bear Canyon
Location: 13 miles northeast of
  Nephi off F.R. 048 off Nebo Loop
Campsites: 9 RV sites, 20 tent sites
Max RV Length: 35 feet
Facilities/Accommodations:
  Drinking water, fishing, group
  sites, picnic tables, toilets
Reservations: (800) 280-2267
Open: May 1 to October 31
Limit of Stay: 14 days
Fee Charged: Yes
Managing Agency: National Forest
  Service (Uinta)

Ponderosa
Location: 5 miles northeast of Nephi
  on F.R. 048, off Nebo Loop Road
  east of Hwy. 11
Campsites: 22 RV sites, 10 tent sites
Max RV Length: Unknown
Facilities/Accommodations:
  Drinking water, fishing, toilets
Reservations: (800) 280-2267
Open: May 15 to October 31
Limit of Stay: 14 days
Fee Charged: Yes
Managing Agency: National Forest
  Service (Uinta)

High Country RV Camp
Location: 899 S Main, Nephi
Campsites: 45 RV sites, 40 complete
  RV hookups, 8 tent sites
Max RV Length: 50 feet
Facilities/Accommodations:
  Drinking water, dump sites, fish-
  ing, group sites, handicap facili-
  ties, laundry, nondrinkable water,
  picnic tables, showers, toilets
Reservations: (435) 623-2624
Open: Year-round
Limit of Stay: Unknown
Fee Charged: Yes
Managing Agency: Private

Nephi KOA Campground
Location: 5 miles east of Nephi on
  Hwy. 132
Campsites: 67 RV sites, 28 complete
  RV hookups, 20 tent sites
Max RV Length: 40 feet
Facilities/Accommodations:
  Drinking water, dump sites, fish-
  ing, laundry, nondrinkable water,
  picnic tables, showers, swimming,
  toilets
Reservations: (435) 623-0811
Open: May 15 to September 30
Limit of Stay: 5 days
Fee Charged: Yes
Managing Agency: Private

OAK CITY

Oak Creek
Location: 4.5 miles southeast of Oak
  City on F.R. 089 off Hwy. 135
Campsites: 23 RV sites, 9 tent sites
Max RV Length: Unknown

Facilities/Accommodations:
Drinking water, fishing, group sites, nondrinkable water, picnic tables, toilets
Reservations: (800) 280-2267
Open: May 21 to September 30
Limit of Stay: 14 days
Fee Charged: Yes
Managing Agency: National Forest Service (Fishlake)

RICHFIELD

J.R. Munchies Campground

Location: 745 S Main (Hwy. 89), Richfield
Campsites: 22 RV sites
Max RV Length: 40 feet
Facilities/Accommodations:
Drinking water, dump sites, laundry, showers
Reservations: (435) 896-9340
Open: Year-round
Limit of Stay: Unknown
Fee Charged: Yes
Managing Agency: Private

KOA Campground

Location: 600 W 600 S, Richfield
Campsites: 83 RV sites with complete RV hookups, 60 tent sites
Max RV Length: 45 feet
Facilities/Accommodations:
Drinking water, dump sites, group sites, laundry, nondrinkable water, picnic tables, showers, swimming, toilets
Reservations: (435) 896-6674
Open: March 1 to October 31
Limit of Stay: Unknown
Fee Charged: Yes
Managing Agency: Private

Big Rock Candy Mountains

Location: 20 miles south of Richfield on Hwy. 89
Campsites: 40 RV sites
Max RV Length: Unknown
Facilities/Accommodations:
Drinking water, fishing, group sites, handicap facilities, picnic tables
Reservations: (435) 326-4263
Open: March 1 to October 31
Limit of Stay: Unknown
Fee Charged: Yes
Managing Agency: Private

SALINA

Gooseberry

Location: 18 miles southeast of Salina on F.R. 640 off Hwy. 70
Campsites: 7 RV and tent sites
Max RV Length: Unknown
Facilities/Accommodations:
Drinking water, nondrinkable water, picnic tables, toilets
Reservations: (800) 280-2267
Open: June 15 to September 10
Limit of Stay: 16 days
Fee Charged: Yes
Managing Agency: National Forest Service (Fishlake)

Piute

Location: About 20 miles southeast of Salina on F.R. 640 off Hwy. 70
Campsites: 48 RV and tent sites
Max RV Length: Unknown
Facilities/Accommodations:
Boating, fishing, toilets
Reservations: NA
Open: May to October
Limit of Stay: 14 days

Fee Charged: Yes
Managing Agency: National Forest
Service (Fisklake)

Butch Cassidy Campground
🔌 ⛺ 🚿 🎣 🚽
Location: 1100 S State, Salina
Campsites: 70 RV sites, 45 complete
RV sites, 50 tent sites
Max RV Length: Unknown
Facilities/Accommodations:
Boating, drinking water, dump
sites, fishing, group sites, laundry,
picnic tables, showers, swimming,
toilets
Reservations: (800) 551-6842
Open: April 1 to November 1
Limit of Stay: Unknown
Fee Charged: Yes
Managing Agency: Private

Salina Creek RV & Camp
🔌 ⛺ 🚿 🎣 🚽
Location: 1385 S State, Salina
Campsites: 26 RV sites with com-
plete RV hookups
Max RV Length: 45 feet
Facilities/Accommodations:
Drinking water, dump sites, fish-
ing, laundry, showers, toilets
Reservations: (435) 529-3711
Open: Year-round
Limit of Stay: Unknown
Fee Charged: Yes
Managing Agency: Private

Don's Texaco Campground
🔌 ♿ ⛺ 🚿 🚽
Location: 215 W Main, Salina
Campsites: 12 RV sites, 8 tent sites
Max RV Length: Unknown
Facilities/Accommodations:
Drinking water, dump sites, hand-
icap facilities, showers, toilets

Reservations: (435) 529-3531
Open: Year-round
Limit of Stay: Unknown
Fee Charged: Yes
Managing Agency: Private

SCIPIO

Maple Grove
🔌 ⛺ ♿ 🏕 🚽
Location: Southeast of Scipio off
Hwy. 50
Campsites: 11 RV and tent sites
Max RV Length: Unknown
Facilities/Accommodations:
Drinking water, fishing, group
sites, handicap facilities, non-
drinkable water, picnic tables, toi-
lets
Reservations: (800) 280-2267
Open: May 21 to October 30
Limit of Stay: 14 days
Fee Charged: Yes
Managing Agency: National Forest
Service (Fishlake)

SKYLINE DRIVE

Flat Canyon
🔌 ⛺ ♿ 🏕 🚽
Location: 12 miles east of Fairview
on Hwy. 264, off Hwy. 31 above
Electric Lake
Campsites: 13 RV and tent sites
Max RV Length: 30 feet
Facilities/Accommodations:
Drinking water, fishing, group
sites, handicap facilities, picnic
tables, toilets
Reservations: (800) 280-2267
Open: June 15 to September 15
Limit of Stay: 16 days
Fee Charged: Yes
Managing Agency: National Forest
Service (Manti-La Sal)

Gooseberry

🎣 ⛺ 🚐 🚽

Location: 9.9 miles northeast of Fairview off Hwy. 31 by lower Gooseberry Reservoir
Campsites: 2 RV sites, 8 tent sites
Max RV Length: 25 feet
Facilities/Accommodations: Drinking water, fishing, group sites, picnic tables, toilets
Reservations: (800) 280-2267
Open: June 15 to September 15
Limit of Stay: 16 days
Fee Charged: Yes
Managing Agency: National Forest Service (Manti-La Sal)

Twelve Mile Flat

🎣 ⛺ 🚐 🚽

Location: 19 miles east of Mayfield, on Mayfield-Ferron Road
Campsites: 16 RV and tent sites
Max RV Length: Unknown
Facilities/Accommodations: Drinking water, fishing, group sites, picnic tables, toilets
Reservations: (800) 280-2267
Open: July 1 to September 10
Limit of Stay: 16 days
Fee Charged: Yes
Managing Agency: National Forest Service (Manti-La Sal)

YUBA STATE PARK

Oasis

🎣 ⛺ ♿ 🚐 🚿 🚽

Location: 30 miles south of Nephi off I-15, west end of Yuba Reservoir
Campsites: 26 RV and tent sites
Max RV Length: 45 feet
Facilities/Accommodations: Boating, drinking water, dump sites, fishing, group sites, handicap facilities, picnic tables, showers, swimming, toilets
Reservations: (800) 322-3770
Open: Year-round
Limit of Stay: 14 days
Fee Charged: Yes
Managing Agency: Utah State Parks

Painted Rocks

♿ 🚐 🚽

Location: 30 miles south of Nephi off I-15, east end of Yuba Reservoir
Campsites: 20 RV and tent sites
Max RV Length: 45 feet
Facilities/Accommodations: Boating, fishing, handicap facilities, picnic tables, swimming, toilets
Reservations: (800) 322-3770
Open: Year-round
Limit of Stay: 14 days
Fee Charged: Yes
Managing Agency: Utah State Parks

CAMPGROUNDS: SOUTHEASTERN REGION

ARCHES NATIONAL PARK / MOAB

Devils Garden
🚰 ⠿ ♿ 🚐 🚽

Location: In Arches NP, 20 miles north of the Visitor's Center
Campsites: 54 RV sites, tent sites
Max RV Length: 35 feet
Facilities/Accommodations: Drinking water, group sites, handicap facilities, picnic tables, toilets
Reservations: Only group sites may be reserved; registration begins at 7:30 a.m. daily. (453) 259-8161; recorded information (435) 719-2313
Open: Year-round after renovations scheduled for Nov. 1, 2000 to Feb. 15, 2001
Limit of Stay: 7 days
Fee Charged: Yes
Managing Agency: National Park Service

Big Bend
⠿ ♿ 🚐 🚽

Location: On the Colorado, eight miles northeast of Moab on Hwy. 128
Campsites: 29 RV sites, 11 tent sites
Max RV Length: 24 feet
Facilities/Accommodations: Fishing, group sites, handicap facilities, nondrinkable water, picnic tables, toilets
Reservations: (435) 259-6111
Open: Year-round
Limit of Stay: 14 days

Fee Charged: Yes
Managing Agency: BLM

Oowah Lake
🚐 🚽

Location: Off the La Sal Mountain Loop Road southeast of Moab
Campsites: 6 RV and tent sites
Max RV Length: Unknown
Facilities/Accommodations: Fishing, picnic tables, toilets
Reservations: (800) 280-2267
Open: May 29 to October 1
Limit of Stay: 16 days
Fee Charged: Yes
Managing Agency: National Forest Service (Manti-La Sal)

Warner
🚰 ⠿ 🚐 🚽

Location: Off the La Sal Mountain Loop Road southeast of Moab
Campsites: 27 RV and tent sites
Max RV Length: Unknown
Facilities/Accommodations: Drinking water, fishing, group sites, picnic tables, toilets
Reservations: NA
Open: July-October
Limit of Stay: 14 days
Fee Charged: Yes
Managing Agency: National Forest Service (Manti-La Sal)

SYMBOL LEGEND

🚰 Drinking water   🚐 RV sites
⠿ Group sites   🚽 Toilets
♿ Handicap facilities   🚿 Showers

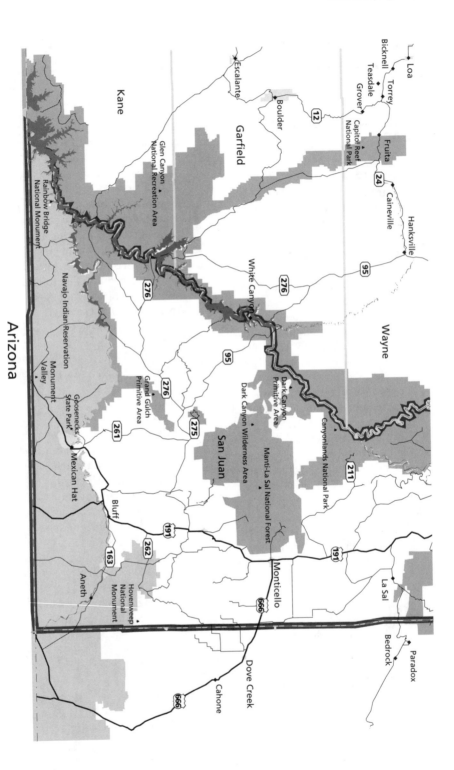

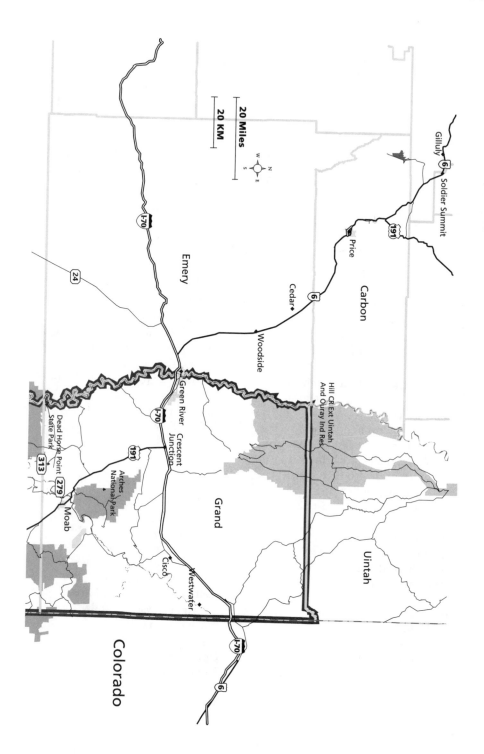

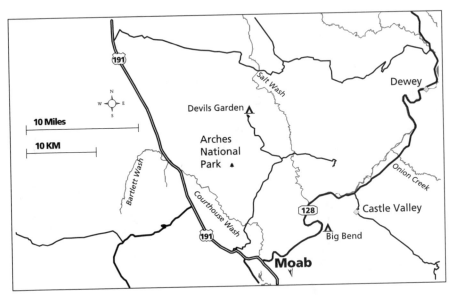

Arch View Campark

⚡ ⊞ 🚐 ⚲ 🚿

Location: 7 miles north of Moab on Hwy. 191
Campsites: 52 RV sites with complete RV hookups, 31 tent sites
Max RV Length: 40 feet
Facilities/Accommodations: Drinking water, dump sites, group sites, laundry, nondrinkable water, picnic tables, showers, swimming, toilets
Reservations: (800) 813-6622; (435) 259-7854
Open: Year-round
Limit of Stay: Unknown
Fee Charged: Yes
Managing Agency: Private

Canyonlands Campground

⚡ ⊞ 🚐 ⚲ 🚿

Location: 555 S Main, Moab
Campsites: 70 RV sites with complete RV hookups, 35 tent sites
Max RV Length: 65 feet
Facilities/Accommodations: Boating, drinking water, fishing, group sites, laundry, picnic tables, showers, swimming, toilets
Reservations: (800) 522-6848; (435) 259-6848
Open: Year-round
Limit of Stay: Unknown
Fee Charged: Yes
Managing Agency: Private

Creekside Court

⚡ 🚐 ⚲ 🚿

Location: 1251 S Millcreek Drive, Moab
Campsites: 8 RV sites with complete RV hookups, 10 tent sites
Max RV Length: 70 feet
Facilities/Accommodations: Drinking water, laundry, picnic tables, showers, toilets
Reservations: (435) 259-7813
Open: Year-round
Limit of Stay: Unknown
Fee Charged: Yes
Managing Agency: Private

Holiday Haven RV Park

🚿 ⛺ ♿ 🚐 🎣 🚽

Location: 400 N 5 W, Moab
Campsites: 82 RV sites with complete RV hookups
Max RV Length: 65 feet
Facilities/Accommodations: Drinking water, group sites, handicap facilities, laundry, picnic tables, showers, swimming, toilets
Reservations: (435) 259-8526
Open: Year-round
Limit of Stay: Unknown

Fee Charged: Yes
Managing Agency: Private

Moab KOA

🚿 ⛺ ♿ 🚐 🎣 🚽

Location: 3225 S Hwy. 191, Moab
Campsites: 60 RV sites, 39 complete RV hookups, 60 tent sites
Max RV Length: 60 feet
Facilities/Accommodations: Drinking water, dump sites, group sites, handicap facilities, laundry, picnic tables, showers, swimming, toilets

PHOTO: DAVID WHITTEN

Visitors hike around Turret Arch in Arches National Park.

Reservations: (800) 562-0372; (435)
259-6682
Open: March 15 to October 15
Limit of Stay: Unknown
Fee Charged: Yes
Managing Agency: Private

Moab Valley RV and Campark
↻ ⋮⋮⋮ ♿ 🚐 🚿 ⛽

Location: 1773 N Hwy. 191,
MoabCampsites: 68 RV sites with
complete RV hookups, 62 tent
sites
Max RV Length: 60 feet
Facilities/Accommodations:
Drinking water, dump sites, group
sites, handicap facilities, laundry,
picnic tables, showers, toilets; also
cabins
Reservations: (435) 459-4469
Open: March 1 to October 31
Limit of Stay: Unknown
Fee Charged: Yes
Managing Agency: Private

Pack Creek Moblehome Estates and Campground
↻ ⋮⋮⋮ ♿ 🚐 🚿 ⛽

Location: 1520 Murphy Lane, Moab
Campsites: 40 RV sites, 26 complete
RV hookups, 9 tent sites
Max RV Length: 55 feet
Facilities/Accommodations:
Drinking water, dump sites, group
sites, handicap facilities, laundry,
picnic tables, showers, toilets
Reservations: (435) 259-2982
Open: Year-round
Limit of Stay: 30 days
Fee Charged: Yes
Managing Agency: Private

Portal RV Park and Fishery
⋮⋮⋮ 🚐 🚿 ⛽

Location: Moab

Campsites: 36 RV sites, 10 tents
Max RV Length: None
Facilities/Accommodations: Fishing,
group sites, laundry, picnic tables,
showers, toilets
Reservations: (435) 259-6108
Open: Year-round
Limit of Stay: NA
Fee Charged: Yes
Managing Agency: Private

Slickrock Campground
↻ ⋮⋮⋮ ♿ 🚐 🚿 ⛽

Location: 1 mile north of Moab on
Hwy. 191
Campsites: 116 RV sites, 85 com-
plete RV hookups, 65 tent sites
Max RV Length: 65 feet
Facilities/Accommodations:
Drinking water, dump sites, group
sites, handicap facilities, laundry,
picnic tables, showers, swimming,
toilets
Reservations: (800) 448-8873; (435)
459-7660
Open: Year-round
Limit of Stay: Unknown
Fee Charged: Yes
Managing Agency: Private

Spanish Trail RV Park and Campground
↻ 🚐 🚿 ⛽

Location: 3 miles south of Moab
Campsites: 65 RV sites, 13 tent sites
Max RV Length: 70 feet
Facilities/Accommodations:
Drinking water, dump sites, picnic
tables, showers, toilets
Reservations: (800) RVPARK1
Open: February to December
Limit of Stay: 30 days
Fee Charged: Yes
Managing Agency: Private

Up the Creek

Location: 210 E 300 S, Moab
Campsites: 20 tent sites
Max RV Length: NA
Facilities/Accommodations:
Boating, drinking water, picnic
tables, showers, toilets
Reservations: NA. General informa-
tion: (435) 259-6995
Open: March 15 to October 31
Limit of Stay: 7 days
Fee Charged: Yes
Managing Agency: Private

BLANDING

Kampark

Location: 861 S Main St., Blanding
Campsites: 53 RV sites with com-
plete RV hookups, 16 tent sites
Max RV Length: 65 feet
Facilities/Accommodations:
Drinking water, dump sites, group
sites, laundry, picnic tables, show-
ers, toilets
Reservations: (435) 678-2770
Open: Year-round
Limit of Stay: Unknown
Managing Agency: Private

PHOTO: CHEYENNE ROUSE

A backpacker pauses a moment to take in a view at Canyonlands National Park.

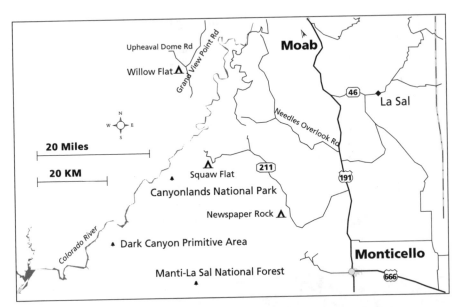

BLUFF

Sand Island

Location: 2 miles west of Bluff on San Juan River
Campsites: 6 tent sites
Max RV Length: NA
Facilities/Accommodations: Boating, fishing, nondrinkable water, picnic tables, toilets
Reservations: (435) 259-6111
Open: Year-round
Limit of Stay: 14 days
Fee Charged: Yes
Managing Agency: BLM

Cadillac Ranch

Location: Hwy. 191, Bluff
Campsites: 15 RV sites with hookups, 10 tent sites
Max RV Length: 35 feet
Facilities/Accommodations: Drinking water, picnic tables, toilets
Reservations: (800) 538-6185; (435) 672-2262
Open: March 1 to November 30
Limit of Stay: Unknown
Fee Charged: Yes
Managing Agency: Private

Turquoise RV Park

Location: In Bluff at Hwy. 191 at 5 West
Campsites: 8 RV sites with complete RV hookups
Max RV Length: 28 feet
Facilities/Accommodations: Drinking water, picnic tables
Reservations: (435) 672-2219
Open: Year-round
Limit of Stay: Unknown
Fee Charged: Yes
Managing Agency: Private

CANYONLANDS NATIONAL PARK

Canyonlands National Park — Squaw Flat (Needles District)

🛶 🚻 🏕

Location: 82 miles southwest of Moab off Hwy. 211

Campsites: 26 RV and tent sites, plus 3 sites for groups of 11-50 people (up to 10 vehicles)

Max RV Length: 20 feet

Facilities/Accommodations: Drinking water, group sites, picnic tables

Reservations: (435) 259-4351 or 259-7164

Open: Year-round

Limit of Stay: 7 days

Fee Charged: Yes

Managing Agency: National Park Service

Canyonlands National Park — Willow Flat (Island District)

🏕

Location: 42 miles southwest of Moab off Upheaval Dome Road

Campsites: 12 RV and tent sites

Max RV Length: 23 feet

Facilities/Accommodations: Picnic tables

Reservations: (435) 259-4351 or 259-7164

Open: Year-round

PHOTO: CHEYENNE ROUSE

A couple enjoys a big-sky sunset in Canyonlands.

Limit of Stay: 7 days
Fee Charged: Yes
Managing Agency: National Park
Service

Newspaper Rock

Location: 20 miles northwest of
Monticello along S.R. 211
Campsites: 8 tent sites
Max RV Length: NA
Facilities/Accommodations:
Handicap facilities, picnic tables,
toilets
Reservations: (435) 259-6111
Open: Year-round
Limit of Stay: 14 days
Fee Charged: No
Managing Agency: BLM

DEAD HORSE POINT STATE PARK

Dead Horse Point

Location: 32 miles west of Moab on
Hwy. 313 off Hwy. 191
Campsites: 21 RV and tent sites
Max RV Length: 45 feet
Facilities/Accommodations:
Drinking water, picnic tables, toilets
Reservations: (800) 322-3770
Open: Year-round
Limit of Stay: 14 days
Fee Charged: Yes
Managing Agency: Utah State Parks

GLEN CANYON NATIONAL RECREATION AREA

Bullfrog RV Park

Location: Bullfrog Marina, 70 miles
south of Hanksville on Lake
Powell

Campsites: 86 RV and tent sites, 24
complete RV hookups
Max RV Length: 35 feet
Facilities/Accommodations:
Boating, drinking water, fishing,
group sites, handicap facilities,
laundry, picnic tables, showers,
swimming, toilets
Reservations: (800) 528-6154; (520)
608-6404
Open: Year-round
Limit of Stay: 14 days
Fee Charged: Yes
Managing Agency: National Park
Service concessionaire

Farley Canyon

Location: Eastern end of Lake
Powell, southwest of Hite Marina
Campsites: Not designated; an open
beach
Max RV Length: NA
Facilities/Accommodations:
Boating, fishing, swimming, toilets
Reservations: NA
Open: Year-round
Limit of Stay: None
Fee Charged: No
Managing Agency: National Park
Service

Halls Crossing RV

Location: Halls Crossing, 95 miles
southwest of Blanding on Hwy.
276, across the lake from Bullfrog
Campsites: 65 RV sites, 32 complete
RV hookups, tent sites
Max RV Length: Unknown

An incredible overlook at Dead Horse Point State Park.

Facilities/Accommodations:
Boating, drinking water, dump sites, fishing, handicap facilities, laundry, nondrinkable water, picnic tables, showers, swimming, toilets
Reservations: (435) 684-2261
Open: Year-round
Limit of Stay: 14 days
Fee Charged: Yes
Managing Agency: National Park Service concessionaire

Hite

Location: 66 miles south of Hanksville off Hwy. 95
Campsites: Not designated; an open beach
Max RV Length: None
Facilities/Accommodations:
Boating, drinking water, swimming, toilets
Reservations: (520) 608-6404

Open: Year-round
Limit of Stay: 14 days
Fee Charged: Yes
Managing Agency: National Park Service concessionaire

Lees Ferry

Location: Lees Ferry, Ariz., 15.3 miles down the river from Glen Canyon Dam
Campsites: 51 RV and tent sites
Max RV Length: None
Facilities/Accommodations:
Boating, drinking water, fishing, nondrinkable water, picnic tables, showers, toilets
Reservations: NA
Open: Year-round
Limit of Stay: 14 days
Fee Charged: Yes
Managing Agency: National Park Service

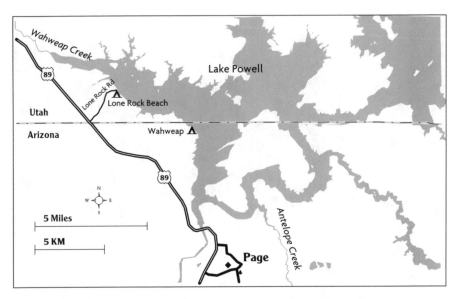

Lone Rock Beach

Location: Western tip of Lake Powell, north of Glen Canyon Dam and Wahweap Marina

Campsites: Not designated; an open beach

Max RV Length: None

Facilities/Accommodations: Boating, fishing, swimming, toilets

Reservations: NA

Open: Year-round

Limit of Stay: None

Fee Charged: No

Managing Agency: National Park Service

Wahweap Marina

Location: On Lake Powell near Page, Ariz.

Campsites: 116 RV sites with complete RV hookups, tent sites

Max RV Length: 45 feet

Facilities/Accommodations: Boating, drinking water, fishing, laundry, nondrinkable water, picnic tables, showers, toilets

Reservations: (800) 528-6154, (520) 645-2433

Open: Year-round

Limit of Stay: 14 days

Fee Charged: Yes

Managing Agency: National Park Service concessionaire

GOBLIN VALLEY STATE PARK

Goblin Valley

Location: 35 miles northwest of Hanksville off Hwy. 24

Campsites: 21 RV and tent sites

Max RV Length: 30 feet

Facilities/Accommodations: Drinking water, dump sites, group sites, picnic tables, showers, toilets

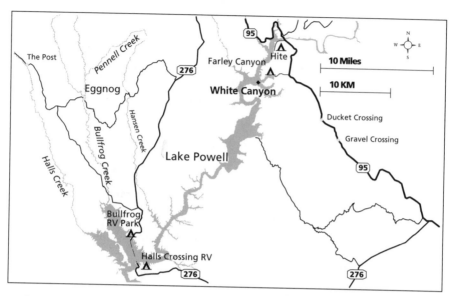

Reservations: (800) 322-3770
Open: Year-round
Limit of Stay: 14 days
Fee Charged: Yes
Managing Agency: Utah State Parks

GOOSENECKS STATE PARK / MEXICAN HAT

Goosenecks of San Juan
&

Location: 4 miles north of Mexican Hat off Hwy. 261
Campsites: 4 primitive RV and tent sites
Max RV Length: 30 feet
Facilities/Accommodations: Handicap facilities, picnic table
Reservations: (800) 322-3770
Open: Year-round
Limit of Stay: 14 days
Fee Charged: No
Managing Agency: Utah State Parks

Burches Trading Post

Location: Mexican Hat

Campsites: 10 RV sites with complete RV hookups
Max RV Length: 50 feet
Facilities/Accommodations: Drinking water, fishing, laundry, picnic tables, showers, toilets
Reservations: (435) 683-2221
Open: Year-round
Limit of Stay: Unknown
Fee Charged: Yes
Managing Agency: Private

Valle's Trailer Park

Location: Hwy. 163, Mexican Hat
Campsites: 20 RV sites with complete RV hookups, 8 tent sites
Max RV Length: 40 feet
Facilities/Accommodations: Boating, drinking water, fishing, group sites, laundry, picnic tables, showers, toilets
Reservations: (435) 683-2226
Open: Year-round
Limit of Stay: Unknown
Fee Charged: Yes
Managing Agency: Private

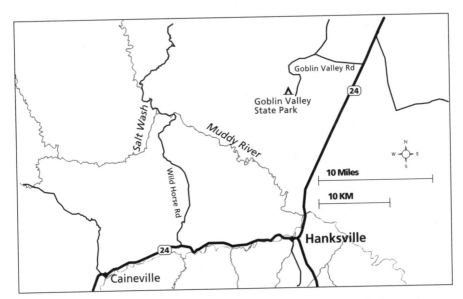

GREEN RIVER

Green River State Park

🪝 ⛺ ♿ 🚐 🍽 🚿

Location: Green River
Campsites: 42 RV sites, tent sites
Max RV Length: 45 feet
Facilities/Accommodations:
    Boating, drinking water, dump
    sites, fishing, group sites, handi-
    cap facilities, nondrinkable water,
    picnic tables, showers, toilets
Reservations: (800) 322-3770
Open: Year-round
Limit of Stay: 14 days
Fee Charged: Yes
Managing Agency: Utah State Parks

Green River KOA

🪝 ⛺ ♿ 🚐 🍽 🚿

Location: 550 S Green River Blvd,
    Green River
Campsites: 77 RV sites, 25 complete
    RV hookups, 25 tent sites
Max RV Length: 105 feet

Facilities/Accommodations:
    Boating, drinking water, dump
    sites, fishing, group sites, handi-
    cap facilities, laundry, picnic
    tables, showers, swimming, toilets
Reservations: (435) 564-3651
Open: April 1 to October 15
Limit of Stay: Unknown
Fee Charged: Yes
Managing Agency: Private

Shady Acres RV Park

🪝 ⛺ ♿ 🚐 🍽 🚿

Location: 360 E Main, Green River
Campsites: 105 RV sites, 65 com-
    plete RV hookups, 27 tent sites
Max RV Length: 100 feet
Facilities/Accommodations:
    Drinking water, group sites, hand-
    icap facilities, laundry, picnic
    tables, showers, swimming, toilets
Reservations: (800) 537-8674
Open: Year-round
Limit of Stay: Unknown
Fee Charged: Yes
Managing Agency: Private

United Campground of Green River

Location: 910 E Main, Green River
Campsites: 65 RV sites with complete RV hookups, 15 tent sites
Max RV Length: 45 feet
Facilities/Accommodations:
Boating, drinking water, dump sites, group sites, laundry, picnic tables, showers, swimming, toilets
Reservations: (435) 564-8195
Open: Year-round
Limit of Stay: Unknown
Fee Charged: Yes
Managing Agency: Private

HANKSVILLE / HENRY MOUNTAINS

Lonesome Beaver

Location: 23 miles south of Hanksville on Lonesome Beaver Road
Campsites: 5 RV and tent sites
Max RV Length: Unknown
Facilities/Accommodations:
Drinking water, group sites, picnic tables, toilets
Reservations: (435) 586-2401
Open: May 1 to October 30
Limit of Stay: 14 days
Fee Charged: Yes
Managing Agency: BLM

McMillan Springs

Location: 33 miles south of Hanksville south of Lonesome Beaver
Campsites: 10 tent sites
Max RV Length: Unknown
Facilities/Accommodations:
Drinking water, picnic tables, toilets
Reservations: (435) 586-2401
Open: Unknown
Limit of Stay: 14 days

A kayaker wends his way through Glen Canyon.

Fee Charged: Yes
Managing Agency: BLM

Ekker Campground

Location: 110 Center St., Hanksville
Campsites: 15 RV sites, 6 complete
RV hookups, 1 tent site
Max RV Length: 70 feet
Facilities/Accommodations:
Drinking water, picnic tables, toilets
Reservations: (801) 524-3283
Open: Year-round
Limit of Stay: Unknown
Fee Charged: Yes
Managing Agency: Private

Jurassic RV Park

Location: 110 S Center, Hanksville
Campsites: 17 RV sites with complete RV hookups, 20 tent sites
Max RV Length: 70 feet
Facilities/Accommodations:
Boating, drinking water, dump sites, fishing, group sites, nondrinkable water, picnic tables
Reservations: (800) 524-3433
Open: Year-round
Limit of Stay: Unknown
Fee Charged: Yes
Managing Agency: Private

Red Rock Campground

Location: Junction of S.R. 95 and S.R. 24, Hanksville
Campsites: 45 RV sites, 45 complete RV hookups, 18 tent sites
Max RV Length: 60 feet
Facilities/Accommodations:
Boating, drinking water, dump sites, fishing, laundry, picnic tables, showers, toilets

Reservations: (435) 542-3235
Open: March 15 to October 31
Limit of Stay: Unknown
Fee Charged: Yes
Managing Agency: Private

HOVENWEEP NATIONAL MONUMENT

Square Tower Ruin

Location: 20 miles north of Aneth off Hwy. 262, on Hovenweep Road
Campsites: 31 RV and tent sites
Max RV Length: 24 feet
Facilities/Accommodations:
Drinking water, handicap facilities, picnic tables, toilets
Reservations: (970) 749-0510
Open: Year-round
Limit of Stay: 14 days
Fee Charged: Yes
Managing Agency: National Park Service

MILLSITE STATE PARK / FERRON

Millsite

Location: 4 miles west of Ferron on F.R. 022 off Hwy. 10
Campsites: 20 RV sites, 10 tent sites
Max RV Length: 30 feet
Facilities/Accommodations:
Boating, drinking water, dump sites, fishing, group sites, handicap facilities, nondrinkable water, picnic tables, showers, toilets
Reservations: (800) 322-3770
Open: Year-round
Limit of Stay: 14 days
Fee Charged: Yes
Managing Agency: Utah State Parks

Ferron Canyon
⠿ 🚐 🛁
Location: About 9 miles west of Ferron on F.R. 022
Campsites: 4 RV and tent sites
Max RV Length: Unknown
Facilities/Accommodations: Fishing, group sites, picnic tables, toilets
Reservations: NA
Open: May to October
Limit of Stay: 14 days
Fee Charged: No
Managing Agency: National Forest Service (Manti-LaSal)

Ferron Revervior
⠿ 🚐 🛁
Location: About 18 miles west of Ferron on F.R. 022
Campsites: 30 RV and tent sites
Max RV Length: Unknown
Facilities/Accommodations: Boating, drinking water, fishing, group sites, picnic tables, toilets
Reservations: NA
Open: June to October
Limit of Stay: 14 days
Fee Charged: Yes
Managing Agency: National Forest Service (Manti-LaSal)

MONTICELLO

Buck Board
⠿ 🚐 🛁
Location: 6.5 miles west of Monticello on North Creek Road (F.R. 105) off Hwy. 191
Campsites: 8 RV and tent sites
Max RV Length: 25 feet
Facilities/Accommodations: Drinking water, group sites, picnic tables, toilets
Reservations: (800) 280-2267
Open: May 20 to October 15
Limit of Stay: 16 days

Fee Charged: Yes
Managing Agency: National Forest Service (Manti-La Sal)

Dalton Springs
⠿ 🚐 🛁
Location: 5 miles west of Monticello on North Creek Road (F.R. 105) off Hwy. 191
Campsites: 18 RV sites, 13 tent sites
Max RV Length: 30 feet
Facilities/Accommodations: Drinking water, picnic tables, toilets
Reservations: (800) 280-2267
Open: May 20 to October 15
Limit of Stay: 16 days
Fee Charged: Yes
Managing Agency: National Forest Service (Manti-La Sal)

Devils Canyon
⠿ 🚐 🛁
Location: South of Monticello off Hwy. 191
Campsites: 33 RV and tent sites
Max RV Length: 30 feet
Facilities/Accommodations: Drinking water, group sites, picnic tables, toilets
Reservations: NA
Open: May 15 to October 30
Limit of Stay: 14 days
Fee Charged: Yes
Managing Agency: National Forest Service (Manti-LaSal)

Nizhoni
⠿ 🚐 🛁
Location: 7 miles southwest of Monticello on F.R. 079 off Hwy. 191
Campsites: 21 RV and tent sites
Max RV Length: 40 feet

Facilities/Accommodations:
Drinking water, group sites, handicap facilities, picnic tables, toilets
Reservations: (800) 280-2267; (435) 587-2041
Open: May 15 to October 30
Limit of Stay: 16 days
Fee Charged: Yes
Managing Agency: National Forest Service (Manti-La Sal)

Monticello Canyonlands KOA

Location: 5.5 miles east of Monticello on Hwy. 666
Campsites: 30 RV sites, 7 complete RV hookups, 20 tent sites
Max RV Length: 60 feet
Facilities/Accommodations:
Drinking water, dump sites, fishing, laundry, picnic tables, showers, swimming, toilets
Reservations: (435) 587-2884
Open: May 1 to October 1
Limit of Stay: Unknown
Fee Charged: Yes
Managing Agency: Private

Mountain View RV Park

Location: 648 N Main, Monticello
Campsites: 29 RV sites, 20 complete RV hookups, 10 tent sites
Max RV Length: 50 feet
Facilities/Accommodations:
Boating, drinking water, dump sites, group sites, laundry, nondrinkable water, picnic tables, showers, toilets
Reservations: (435) 587-2974
Open: Year-round
Limit of Stay: Unknown
Fee Charged: Yes
Managing Agency: Private

Roughlock Campground

Location: 8 miles north of Monticello on Hwy. 191
Campsites: 16 RV sites, 10 complete RV hookups, 16 tent sites
Max RV Length: 75 feet
Facilities/Accommodations:
Drinking water, group sites, handicap facilities, picnic tables, showers, toilets; also cabins
Reservations: (435) 587-2351
Open: Year-round
Limit of Stay: Unknown
Fee Charged: Yes
Managing Agency: Private

Rowley's Trailer Park

Location: 480 N Main, Monticello
Campsites: 17 RV sites with complete RV hookups, 3 tent sites
Max RV Length: 45 feet
Facilities/Accommodations:
Boating, drinking water, fishing, laundry, showers, toilets
Reservations: (435) 587-2762
Open: Year-round
Limit of Stay: Unknown
Fee Charged: Yes
Managing Agency: Private

Westerner Trailer Park

Location: 516 S Main, Monticello
Campsites: 28 RV sites with complete RV hookups, 28 tent sites
Max RV Length: 70 feet
Facilities/Accommodations:
Drinking water, fishing, laundry, nondrinkable water, picnic tables, showers, toilets
Reservations: (435) 587-2762
Open: Year-round
Limit of Stay: Unknown

PHOTO: CHEYENNE ROUSE

An excellent spot overlooking Monument Valley.

Fee Charged: Yes
Managing Agency: Private

MONUMENT VALLEY

Goulding's
🛶 ⠿ 🚐 🌿 🚽
Location: Monument Valley, off Hwy. 163
Campsites: 66 RV sites with complete RV hookups, 40 tent sites
Max RV Length: 50 feet
Facilities/Accommodations: Drinking water, dump sites, group sites, laundry, picnic tables, showers, swimming, toilets
Reservations: (435) 727-3280
Open: March 15 to October 31
Limit of Stay: Unknown
Fee Charged: Yes
Managing Agency: Private

Mitten Views
🛶 ⠿ ♿ 🚐 🚽
Location: 4 miles east of Monument Valley off Hwy. 163
Campsites: 50 RV sites, 50 tent sites
Max RV Length: 30 feet
Facilities/Accommodations: Drinking water, dump sites, group sites, handicap facilities, laundry, picnic tables, showers, toilets
Reservations: (435) 727-3287
Open: Year-round
Limit of Stay: 14 days
Fee Charged: Yes
Managing Agency: Navajo Nation

Navajo Tribal Park
🛶 🚐 🌿 🚽
Location: Monument Valley, off Hwy. 163
Campsites: 100 RV sites, tent sites
Max RV Length: Unknown

Facilities/Accommodations: Drinking water, picnic tables, showers, toilets
Reservations: (435) 727-3287
Open: Year-round
Limit of Stay: Unknown
Fee Charged: Yes
Managing Agency: Navajo Nation

NATURAL BRIDGES NATIONAL MONUMENT

Natural Bridges

Location: 1/4 mile from Visitor Center off Hwy. 95
Campsites: 13 RV sites, 13 tent sites
Max RV Length: 21 feet
Facilities/Accommodations: Drinking water, handicap facilities, picnic tables, toilets
Reservations: (435) 692-1234
Open: Year-round
Limit of Stay: 7 days
Fee Charged: Yes
Managing Agency: National Park Service

SAN RAFAEL SWELL

San Rafael Bridge

Location: 25 miles southeast of Cleveland on Buckhorn Draw Road
Campsites: 4 RV and tent sites
Max RV Length: 35 feet
Facilities/Accommodations: Nondrinkable water, picnic tables, toilets
Reservations: (435) 789-1362 or 259-6111
Open: March 15 to October 31
Limit of Stay: 14 days
Fee Charged: Yes
Managing Agency: BLM

CAMPGROUNDS: SOUTHWESTERN REGION

BEAVER MOUNTAIN

Anderson Meadow
🚰 🚐 🚽

Location: 18.2 miles east of Beaver on F.R. 137 off Hwy. 153
Campsites: 10 RV sites, 10 tent sites
Max RV Length: 24 feet
Facilities/Accommodations: Boating, drinking water, dump sites, laundry, nondrinkable water, picnic tables, swimming, toilets
Reservations: (800) 280-2267; (801) 438-2436
Open: July 15 to October 1
Limit of Stay: 14 days
Fee Charged: Yes
Managing Agency: National Forest Service (Fishlake)

Kents Lake
🚰 ♿ 🚐 🚽

Location: 15.2 miles east of Beaver on F.R. 137 off Hwy. 153
Campsites: 17 RV and tent sites
Max RV Length: 24 feet
Facilities/Accommodations: Boating, drinking water, dump sites, handicap facilities, laundry, non-drinkable water, picnic tables, swimming, toilets
Reservations: (800) 280-2267
Open: June 15 to October 1
Limit of Stay: 14 days
Fee Charged: Yes
Managing Agency: National Forest Service (Fishlake)

Little Cottonwood
🚰 🚐 🚽

Location: 6.7 miles east of Beaver off Hwy. 153
Campsites: 8 RV sites, 14 tent sites
Max RV Length: 40 feet
Facilities/Accommodations: Boating, drinking water, dump sites, nondrinkable water, picnic tables, toilets
Reservations: NA
Open: May 15 to October 15
Limit of Stay: 14 days
Fee Charged: Yes
Managing Agency: National Forest Service (Fishlake)

Little Reservoir
🚰 🚐 🚽

Location: 10.5 miles east of Beaver off Hwy. 153
Campsites: 8 RV and tent sites
Max RV Length: 40 feet
Facilities/Accommodations: Boating, drinking water, dump sites, laundry, picnic tables, swimming, toilets
Reservations: (800) 280-2267
Open: May 1 to October 1
Limit of Stay: 14 days
Fee Charged: Yes
Managing Agency: National Forest Service (Fishlake)

SYMBOL LEGEND

🚰 Drinking water   🚐 RV sites
▦ Group sites   🚽 Toilets
♿ Handicap facilities   🚿 Showers

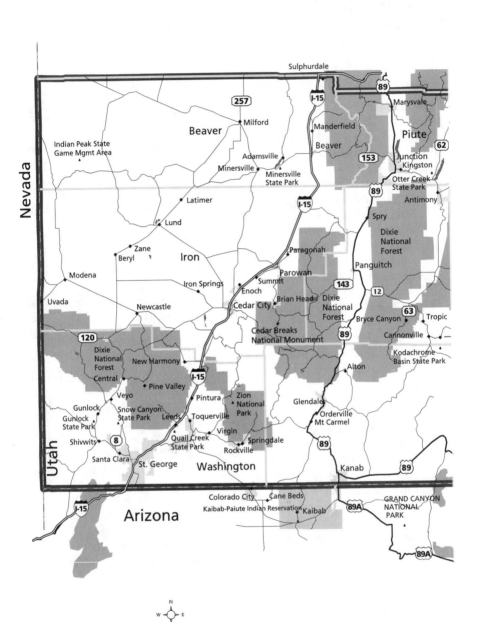

Sulphurdale

89

257

Marysvale

Milford

Beaver

Manderfield

Piute

Indian Peak State
Game Mgmt Area

Beaver

62

Adamsville

153

Junction

Minersville

Kingston

Minersville
State Park

Otter Creek
State Park

I-15

89

Antimony

Latimer

Spry

Nevada

Lund

Zane

Iron

Paragonah

Dixie
National
Forest

Beryl

Panguitch

Modena

Parowan

Iron Springs

Summit

143

12

Uvada

Enoch

Newcastle

Cedar City

Brian Head

Dixie
National
Forest

Bryce Canyon

63

Tropic

Cedar Breaks
National Monument

89

Cannonville

120

Kodachrome
Basin State Park

Dixie
National
Forest

New Harmony

Alton

Central

Pine Valley

Veyo

Pintura

I-15

Zion
National
Park

Glendale

Gunlock

Snow Canyon
State Park

Leeds

Toquerville

Orderville

Gunlock
State Park

Virgin

Mt Carmel

Shivwits

8

Quail Creek
State Park

Springdale

89

Santa Clara

Rockville

St. George

Washington

Kanab

89

Utah

I-15

Colorado City

Cane Beds

89A

GRAND CANYON
NATIONAL
PARK

Arizona

Kaibab-Paiute Indian Reservation

Kaibab

89A

N
W   E
S

20 Miles

20 KM

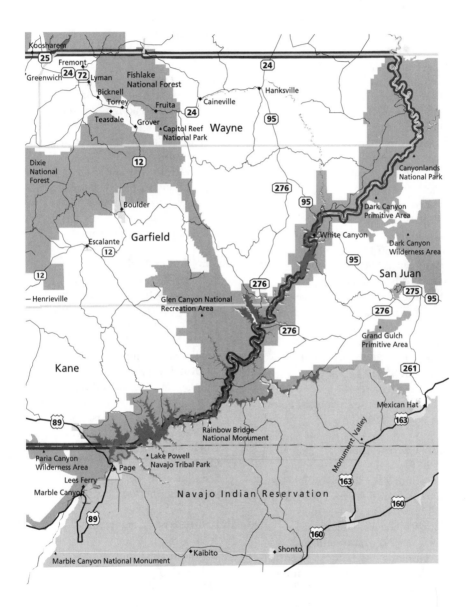

Mahogany Cove

Location: 11.2 miles east of Beaver off Hwy. 153
Campsites: 7 RV sites, 7 tent sites
Max RV Length: 24 feet
Facilities/Accommodations: Boating, drinking water, dump sites, picnic tables, toilets
Reservations: (800) 280-2267
Open: May 30 to October 15
Limit of Stay: 14 days
Fee Charged: Yes
Managing Agency: National Forest Service (Fishlake)

Ponderosa

Location: About 7 miles east of Beaver off Hwy. 153
Campsites: 5 RV and tent sites
Max RV Length: 40 feet
Facilities/Accommodations: Drinking water, fishing, group sites, picnic tables, toilets
Reservations: (800) 280-2267
Open: May 30 to October 15
Limit of Stay: 14 days
Fee Charged: Yes
Managing Agency: National Forest Service (Fishlake)

Beaver Canyon Camp

Location: 1419 E Canyon Rd., Beaver
Campsites: 55 RV sites, 31 complete RV hookups, 50 tent sites
Max RV Length: Unknown
Facilities/Accommodations: Drinking water, dump sites, fishing, handicap facilities, laundry, picnic tables, showers, toilets
Reservations: (435) 438-5654
Open: April 15 to November 10
Limit of Stay: Unknown

Fee Charged: Yes
Managing Agency: Private

Beaver KOA

Location: Manderfield Rd., Beaver
Campsites: 65 RV sites, 25 complete RV hookups, 21 tent sites
Max RV Length: Unknown
Facilities/Accommodations: Boating, drinking water, dump sites, fishing, handicap facilities, laundry, picnic tables, showers, swimming, toilets
Reservations: (435) 438-2924
Open: March 1 to October 31
Limit of Stay: Unknown
Fee Charged: Yes
Managing Agency: Private

Delano Trailer Park

Location: 480 N Main, Beaver
Campsites: 11 RV sites with complete RV hookups, 1 tent site
Max RV Length: 40 feet
Facilities/Accommodations: Drinking water, dump sites, fishing, group sites, handicap facilities, laundry, nondrinkable water, picnic tables, showers, toilets
Reservations: (435) 438-2419
Open: Year-round
Limit of Stay: Unknown
Fee Charged: Yes
Managing Agency: Private

United Beaver Camperland

Location: 1603 Campground Rd., Beaver
Campsites: 85 RV sites, 80 complete RV hookups, 30 tent sites
Max RV Length: Unknown

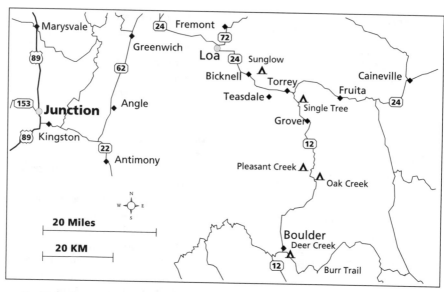

Facilities/Accommodations:
Boating, drinking water, dump sites, group sites, handicap facilities, laundry, picnic tables, showers, swimming, toilets
Reservations: (435) 438-2808
Open: Year-round
Limit of Stay: Unknown
Fee Charged: Yes
Managing Agency: Private

BOULDER MOUNTAIN / ANASAZI STATE PARK

Deer Creek

Location: 6 miles southeast of Boulder on Burr Trail
Campsites: 2 RV sites, 5 tent sites
Max RV Length: Unknown
Facilities/Accommodations:
Nondrinkable water, toilets
Reservations: (435) 586-2401
Open: March 15 to November 30
Limit of Stay: 14 days
Fee Charged: Yes
Managing Agency: BLM

Oak Creek

Location: 24 miles southeast of Teasdale on Hwy. 12
Campsites: 9 RV and tent sites
Max RV Length: Unknown
Facilities/Accommodations:
Drinking water, laundry, nondrinkable water, picnic tables, showers, toilets
Reservations: (800) 280-2267
Open: May 25 to October 25
Limit of Stay: 14 days
Fee Charged: Yes
Managing Agency: National Forest Service (Dixie)

Pleasant Creek

Location: 22 miles southeast of Teasdale on Hwy. 12
Campsites: 16 RV sites, 19 tent sites
Max RV Length: Unknown
Facilities/Accommodations:
Drinking water, fishing, nondrinkable water, picnic tables, toilets

Reservations: (800) 280-2267
Open: May 25 to September 15
Limit of Stay: 14 days
Fee Charged: No
Managing Agency: National Forest
Service (Dixie)

Single Tree

Location: 17 miles southeast of
Teasdale on Hwy. 12
Campsites: 31 RV and tent sites
Max RV Length: 24 feet
Facilities/Accommodations:
Drinking water, nondrinkable
water, picnic tables, toilets
Reservations: (800) 280-2267
Open: May 25 to September 15
Limit of Stay: 14 days
Fee Charged: No
Managing Agency: National Forest
Service (Dixie)

Sunglow

Location: 1 mile east of Bicknell off
Hwy. 24
Campsites: 7 RV and tent sites
Max RV Length: Unknown
Facilities/Accommodations:
Nondrinkable water, picnic tables,
toilets
Reservations: (800) 280-2267
Open: May 15 to October 30
Limit of Stay: 14 days
Fee Charged: Yes
Managing Agency: National Forest
Service (Fishlake)

Aquarius Mobile & RV

Location: 210 S 100 E, Bicknell
Campsites: 12 RV sites with com-
plete RV hookups
Max RV Length: 70 feet

Facilities/Accommodations:
Drinking water, dump sites
Reservations: (435) 425-3835
Open: Year-round
Limit of Stay: Unknown
Fee Charged: Yes
Managing Agency: Private

Boulder Mountain Homestead

Location: 4 miles south of Torrey on
Hwy. 12
Campsites: 10 RV sites with com-
plete RV hookups
Max RV Length: 60 feet
Facilities/Accommodations:
Boating, drinking water, dump
sites, fishing, picnic tables, toilets
Reservations: (435) 425-3374
Open: March 1 to November 30
Limit of Stay: Unknown
Fee Charged: Yes
Managing Agency: Private

Chuckwagon Campground

Location: 12 W Main, Torrey
Campsites: 12 RV sites, 6 complete
RV hookups, 10 tent sites
Max RV Length: 30 feet
Facilities/Accommodations:
Drinking water, dump sites, fish-
ing, group sites, laundry, picnic
tables, showers, toilets
Reservations: (435) 425-3843
Open: March 15 to November 1
Limit of Stay: Unknown
Fee Charged: Yes
Managing Agency: Private

Rim Rock Ranch Motel/RV Park

Location: 2523 E Hwy. 24
Campsites: 52 RV sites with complete RV hookups, 20 tent sites

Max RV Length: 52 feet
Facilities/Accommodations:
Drinking water, dump sites, fishing, group sites, laundry, picnic tables, showers, swimming, toilets
Reservations: (435) 425-3843
Open: Year-round
Limit of Stay: Unknown
Fee Charged: Yes
Managing Agency: Private

River Inn RV Park

Location: 955 E Hwy. 72, Fremont
Campsites: 18 RV sites with complete RV hookups
Max RV Length: Unknown
Facilities/Accommodations:
Boating, drinking water, dump sites, fishing, picnic tables
Reservations: (435) 836-2715

Open: Year-round
Limit of Stay: Unknown
Fee Charged: Yes
Managing Agency: Private

Thousand Lakes RV Park

Location: 1 mile west of Torrey on Hwy. 24
Campsites: 25 RV sites with complete RV hookups, 50 tent sites
Max RV Length: 65 feet
Facilities/Accommodations:
Drinking water, dump sites, fishing, group sites, laundry, picnic tables, showers, toilets
Reservations: (435) 425-3500
Open: April 1 to October 31
Limit of Stay: Unknown
Fee Charged: Yes
Managing Agency: Private

Dead trees stand out starkly against southern Utah rocks and sky.

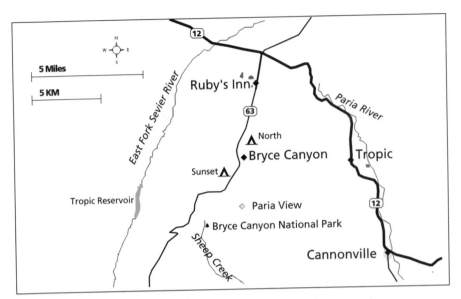

BRYCE CANYON NATIONAL PARK

Bryce Canyon National Park — North

Location: Northeast of Park Headquarters
Campsites: 55 RV and tent sites
Max RV Length: 30 feet
Facilities/Accommodations: Drinking water, picnic tables, showers, toilets
Reservations: (435) 834-5322
Open: Year-round
Limit of Stay: 14 days
Fee Charged: Yes
Managing Agency: National Park Service

Bryce Canyon National Park — Sunset

Location: 2 miles south of Park Headquarters
Campsites: 50 RV and tent sites
Max RV Length: 30 feet
Facilities/Accommodations: Drinking water, group sites, picnic tables, toilets
Reservations: (435) 834-5322
Open: May 15 to October 1
Limit of Stay: 14 days
Fee Charged: Yes
Managing Agency: National Park Service

Kings Creek

Location: At Tropic Reservoir off Hwy. 12 near Bryce Canyon
Campsites: 6 RV sites, 24 tent sites
Max RV Length: 24 feet
Facilities/Accommodations: Boating, drinking water, dump sites, laundry, nondrinkable water, picnic tables, swimming, toilets
Reservations: NA
Open: June 1 to September 15
Limit of Stay: 14 days
Fee Charged: Yes
Managing Agency: National Forest Service (Dixie)

Pine Lake
🚿 ⛺ ♿ 🚐 🚽

Location: 11 miles northeast of Bryce Canyon on F.R. 016 off Hwy. 22
Campsites: 15 RV sites, 21 tent sites
Max RV Length: 24 feet
Facilities/Accommodations:
Boating, drinking water, dump sites, group sites, handicap facilities, picnic tables, swimming, toilets
Reservations: (800) 280-2267
Open: June 1 to September 15
Limit of Stay: 14 days
Fee Charged: Yes
Managing Agency: National Forest Service (Dixie)

Red Canyon
🚿 ⛺ ♿ 🚐 🚽

Location: About 10 miles east of Panguitch on Hwy. 12
Campsites: 39 RV and tent sites
Max RV Length: Unknown
Facilities/Accommodations:
Drinking water, dump sites, group sites, handicap facilities, picnic tables, toilets
Reservations: NA
Open: May to October
Limit of Stay: 14 days
Fee Charged: Yes
Managing Agency: National Forest Service (Dixie)

Bryce Canyon Pines
🚿 🚐 🚿 🚽

Location: Milepost 10 on Hwy. 12
Campsites: 25 RV sites, 18 tent sites
Max RV Length: None
Facilities/Accommodations:
Drinking water, laundry, picnic tables, showers, toilets
Reservations: (800) 892-7923
Open: April to November

A man and his dog hike across a southern Utah landscape.

Limit of Stay: None
Fee Charged: Yes
Managing Agency: Private

Bryce Canyon Resort

Location: Bryce Canyon — Jct. Hwy.
12 & 63
Campsites: 26 RV sites with com-
plete RV hookups, tent sites
Max RV Length: 30 feet
Facilities/Accommodations:
Boating, drinking water, dump
sites, group sites, handicap facili-
ties, laundry, nondrinkable water,
picnic tables, showers, swimming,
toilets; also motel rooms
Reservations: (435) 834-5351; (800)
834-0043
Open: Year-round
Limit of Stay: None
Fee Charged: Yes
Managing Agency: Private

Ruby's Inn RV Park & Campground

Location: 1 mile north of Bryce
Canyon on Hwy. 63
Campsites: 160 RV sites, some with
complete RV hookups, 200 tent
sites
Max RV Length: None
Facilities/Accommodations:
Drinking water, group sites, hand-
icap facilities, laundry, picnic
tables, showers, swimming, toi-
lets; also hotel rooms
Reservations: (800) 468-8660; (435)
834-5341
Open: April 1 to November 1
Limit of Stay: Unknown
Fee Charged: Yes
Managing Agency: Private (Best
Western)

CAPITOL REEF NATIONAL PARK

Cathedral Valley

Location: 23 miles east of Torrey on
Hwy. 24 and 28 miles north on
Cathedral Valley Road
Campsites: 5 tent sites
Max RV Length: NA
Facilities/Accommodations: Picnic
tables, toilets
Reservations: NA
Open: Year-round
Limit of Stay: 14 days
Fee Charged: No
Managing Agency: National Park
Service

Cedar Mesa

Location: 20 miles east of Torrey on
Hwy. 24 and 23 miles south on
Notom Road
Campsites: 5 tent sites
Max RV Length: NA
Facilities/Accommodations: Picnic
tables, toilets
Reservations: NA
Open: Year-round
Limit of Stay: 14 days
Fee Charged: No
Managing Agency: National Park
Service

Fruita

Location: 1 mile from the Capitol
Reef Visitor Center (11 miles east
of Torrey on Hwy. 24), amid old
fruit orchards
Campsites: 71 RV and tent sites
Max RV Length: 30 feet
Facilities/Accommodations:
Drinking water, group sites, non-
drinkable water, toilets
Reservations: NA

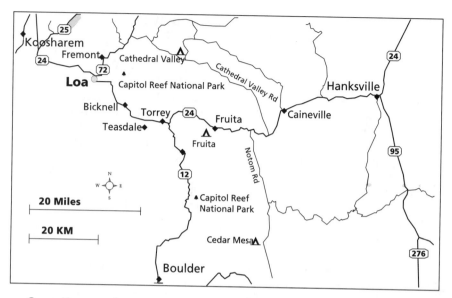

Open: Year-round
Limit of Stay: 14 days
Fee Charged: Yes
Managing Agency: National Park
Service

CEDAR BREAKS NATIONAL MONUMENT

Point Supreme

Location: 2 miles north of south
entrance to Cedar Breaks on Hwy.
148
Campsites: 30 RV and tent sites
Max RV Length: Unknown
Facilities/Accommodations:
Drinking water, picnic tables, toilets
Reservations: (435) 586-9451
Open: June 15 to October 15
Limit of Stay: 14 days
Fee Charged: Yes
Managing Agency: National Park
Service

CEDAR CITY / PAROWAN

Vermillion Castle

Location: 5.5 miles southeast of
Parowan off Hwy. 143
Campsites: 16 RV and tent sites
Max RV Length: 24 feet
Facilities/Accommodations:
Boating, drinking water, dump
sites, group sites, handicap facilities, picnic tables, toilets
Reservations: (800) 280-2267; (801)
865-3700
Open: May 15 to October 15
Limit of Stay: 14 days
Fee Charged: Yes
Managing Agency: National Forest
Service (Dixie)

Cedar City KOA

Location: 1121 N Main, Cedar City
Campsites: 96 RV sites, 57 complete
RV hookups, 36 tent sites
Max RV Length: Unknown

Facilities/Accommodations:
Boating, drinking water, handicap facilities, laundry, nondrinkable water, picnic tables, showers, toilets
Reservations: (435) 586-9872
Open: Year-round
Limit of Stay: Unknown
Fee Charged: Yes
Managing Agency: Private

Country Aire RV Park

Location: North end of Cedar City
Campsites: 40 RV and tent sites
Max RV Length: None
Facilities/Accommodations:
Drinking water , dump sites, laundry, picnic tables, showers, swimming, toilets
Reservations: (435) 586-2550
Open: Year-round, weather permitting
Limit of Stay: None
Fee Charged: Yes
Managing Agency: Private

Town and Country RV Park

Location: 50 W 200 N, Cedar City
Campsites: 10 RV sites, some with complete hookups, tent sites
Max RV Length: Unknown
Facilities/Accommodations:
Boating, drinking water, group sites, handicap facilities, laundry, picnic tables, showers, swimming, toilets
Reservations: (435) 586-9900
Open: April 1 to November 1
Limit of Stay: 30 days
Fee Charged: Yes
Managing Agency: Private

Foothills RV Park

Location: 1435 W 200 S, Parowan
Campsites: 79 RV sites with complete RV hookups
Max RV Length: 40 feet
Facilities/Accommodations:
Drinking water, handicap facilities, laundry, picnic tables, showers, toilets
Reservations: (435) 477-3535
Open: Year-round
Limit of Stay: Unknown
Fee Charged: Yes
Managing Agency: Private

Sportsmen's Country RV Park & Restaurant

Location: 492 N Main, Parowan
Campsites: 30 RV sites, 20 complete RV hookups, 8 tent sites
Max RV Length: 70 feet
Facilities/Accommodations:
Drinking water, dump sites, fishing, handicap facilities, nondrinkable water, picnic tables, showers, toilets
Reservations: (435) 477-3714
Open: Year-round
Limit of Stay: Unknown
Fee Charged: Yes
Managing Agency: Private

CEDAR MOUNTAIN / NAVAJO LAKE

Cedar Canyon

Location: 13 miles southeast of Cedar City off Hwy. 14
Campsites: 19 RV and tent sites
Max RV Length: 24 feet
Facilities/Accommodations:
Drinking water, dump sites, picnic tables, toilets

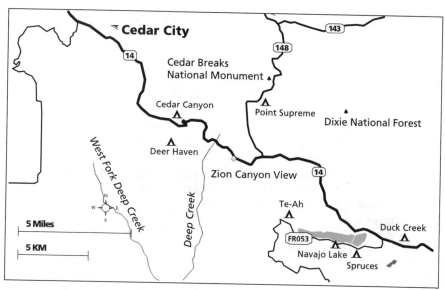

Reservations: (800) 280-2267
Open: May 15 to October 31
Limit of Stay: 14 days
Fee Charged: Yes
Managing Agency: National Forest
Service (Dixie)

Deer Haven

Location: 19 miles east of Cedar
City off Hwy. 14
Campsites: 20 RV and tent sites
Max RV Length: 24 feet
Facilities/Accommodations:
Drinking water, dump sites, hand-
icap facilities, picnic tables, toilets
Reservations: (800) 280-2267
Open: June 15 to September 1
Limit of Stay: 14 days
Fee Charged: Yes
Managing Agency: National Forest
Service (Dixie)

Duck Creek

Location: About 20 miles southeast
of Cedar City on Hwy. 14

Campsites: 96 RV and tent sites
Max RV Length: Unknown
Facilities/Accommodations:
Drinking water, fishing, group
sites, toilets
Reservations: (800) 280-2267; (877)
444-6777
Open: June to September
Limit of Stay: 14 days
Fee Charged: Yes
Managing Agency: National Forest
Service (Dixie)

Navajo Lake

Location: 25 miles east of Cedar
City off Hwy. 14
Campsites: 28 RV and tent sites
Max RV Length: 24 feet
Facilities/Accommodations:
Boating, drinking water, dump
sites, fishing, laundry, swimming,
toilets
Reservations: (800) 280-2267
Open: June 15 to September 15
Limit of Stay: 14 days

Fee Charged: Yes
Managing Agency: National Forest
Service (Dixie)

Spruces

Location: 25 miles east of Cedar
City off Hwy. 14
Campsites: 28 RV and tent sites
Max RV Length: 24 feet
Facilities/Accommodations:
Boating, drinking water, dump
sites, laundry, picnic tables, swim-
ming, toilets
Reservations: (800) 280-2267
Open: June 15 to September 15
Limit of Stay: 14 days
Fee Charged: Yes
Managing Agency: National Forest
Service (Dixie)

Te-Ah

Location: About 15 miles southeast
of Cedar City on Hwy. 14
Campsites: 42 RV and tent sites
Max RV Length: Unknown
Facilities/Accommodations:
Boating, drinking water, dump
sites, fishing, swimming, toilets
Reservations: (800) 280-2267; (877)
444-6777
Open: June to September
Limit of Stay: 14 days
Fee Charged: Yes
Managing Agency: National Forest
Service (Dixie)

CIRCLEVILLE

Double W Campground

Location: 85 S Hwy. 89, Circleville
Campsites: 30 RV sites, 6 complete
RV hookups, 10 tent sites

Max RV Length: Unknown
Facilities/Accommodations:
Drinking water, dump sites, laun-
dry, showers, toilets
Reservations: (435) 577-2557
Open: June 1 to November 1
Limit of Stay: Unknown
Fee Charged: Yes
Managing Agency: Private

CORAL PINK SAND DUNES STATE PARK

Coral Pink Sand Dunes

Location: 22 miles northwest of
Kanab off Hwy. 89
Campsites: 22 RV and tent sites
Max RV Length: 32 feet
Facilities/Accommodations:
Drinking water, dump sites, picnic
tables, showers, toilets
Reservations: (800) 322-3770
Open: Year-round
Limit of Stay: 14 days
Fee Charged: Yes
Managing Agency: Utah State Parks

ENTERPRISE

Honeycomb Rocks

Location: About 12 miles southwest
of Enterprise on F.R. 6
Campsites: 18 RV and tent sites
Max RV Length: Unknown
Facilities/Accommodations:
Boating, drinking water, fishing,
picnic tables, toilets
Reservations: NA
Open: May to October
Limit of Stay: 14 days
Fee Charged: Yes
Managing Agency: National Forest
Service (Dixie)

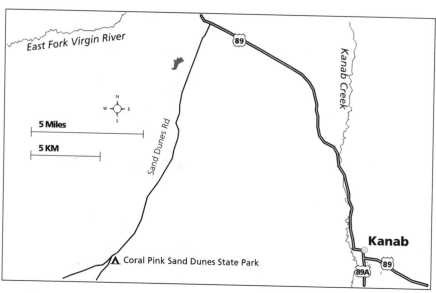

Ponderosa

🚐 🛌

Location: About 17 miles southeast
of Enterprise on F.R. 35, off Hwy.
18

Campsites: 23 RV and tent sites

Max RV Length: 45 feet

Facilities/Accommodations:
Boating, fishing, swimming, toilets

Reservations: (877) 444-6777

Open: May to October

Limit of Stay: 14 days

Fee Charged: Yes

Managing Agency: National Forest
Service (Dixie)

Upper Pines

🚶 ⁂ 🚐 🛌

Location: About 17 miles southeast
of Enterprise on F.R. 35 off Hwy.
18

Campsites: 1 RV/tent site

Max RV Length: Unknown

Facilities/Accommodations:
Drinking water, fishing, group
sites, picnic tables, toilets

Reservations: (800) 280-2267

Open: May to October

Limit of Stay: 14 days

Fee Charged: No

Managing Agency: National Forest
Service (Dixie)

GRAND STAIRCASE-ESCALANTE NATIONAL MONUMENT

Calf Creek

🚶 🚐 🛌

Location: 15.5 miles east of
Escalante off Hwy. 12

Campsites: 5 RV sites, 14 tent sites

Max RV Length: 25 feet

Facilities/Accommodations:
Drinking water, fishing, picnic
tables, toilets

Reservations: NA. Information:
(435) 826-5600, (435) 586-2401

Open: April 15 to November 30

Limit of Stay: 14 days

Fee Charged: Yes

Managing Agency: BLM

Blue Spruce

Location: About 15 miles north of Escalante on F.R. 153
Campsites: 6 RV and tent sites
Max RV Length: 18 feet
Facilities/Accommodations: Drinking water, fishing, toilets
Reservations: NA
Open: June to September
Limit of Stay: 14 days
Fee Charged: Yes
Managing Agency: National Forest Service (Dixie)

Posy Lake

Location: About 12 miles north of Escalante on F.R. 153
Campsites: 22 RV and tent sites, 1 group site
Max RV Length: 35 feet
Facilities/Accommodations: Boating, drinking water, fishing, group sites, toilets
Reservations: NA
Open: June to September
Limit of Stay: 14 days
Fee Charged: Yes
Managing Agency: National Forest Service (Dixie)

Escalante State Park

Location: 1 mile west of Escalante off Hwy. 12
Campsites: 21 RV and tent sites
Max RV Length: 50 feet
Facilities/Accommodations: Boating, drinking water, dump sites, fishing, picnic tables, showers, swimming, toilets
Reservations: (800) 322-3770
Open: Year-round
Limit of Stay: 14 days
Fee Charged: Yes
Managing Agency: Utah State Parks

Broken Bow RV Park

Location: Escalante
Campsites: 28 RV sites, 20 tent sites
Max RV Length: 47 feet
Facilities/Accommodations: Drinking water , laundry, picnic tables, showers, toilets; also cabins
Reservations: Yes
Open: Year-round
Limit of Stay: NA
Fee Charged: Yes
Managing Agency: Private

HATCH

Mountain Ridge RV Park

Location: 106 S Main, Hatch
Campsites: 18 RV sites with complete RV hookups, 10 tent sites
Max RV Length: Unknown
Facilities/Accommodations: Drinking water, dump sites, group sites, handicap facilities, laundry, picnic tables, showers, toilets
Reservations: (435) 735-4258
Open: April 1 to November 1
Limit of Stay: Unknown
Fee Charged: Yes
Managing Agency: Private

Riverside Campground

Location: Half a mile north of Hatch on Hwy. 89
Campsites: 66 RV sites, 57 complete RV hookups, 13 tent sites
Max RV Length: 43 feet

PHOTO: CHEYENNE ROUSE

A restful campsite in Escalante State Park.

Facilities/Accommodations:
Drinking water, dump sites, handicap facilities, laundry, picnic tables, showers, toilets
Reservations: (435) 735-4223
Open: Year-round
Limit of Stay: Unknown
Fee Charged: Yes
Managing Agency: Private

HURRICANE

Brentwood RV Park
Location: 150 N 3700 W, Hurricane
Campsites: 188 RV sites with complete RV hookups, 14 tent sites
Max RV Length: 40 feet
Facilities/Accommodations:
Boating, drinking water, group sites, handicap facilities, laundry, showers, swimming, toilets

Reservations: (800) 447-2239
Open: Year-round
Limit of Stay: Unknown
Fee Charged: Yes
Managing Agency: Private

Gateway Trailer Park
Location: 511 N State, La Verkin
Campsites: 5 RV sites with complete RV hookups, 5 tent sites
Max RV Length: 35 feet
Facilities/Accommodations:
Drinking water, dump sites, fishing, handicap facilities, laundry, picnic tables, showers, swimming, toilets
Reservations: (435) 635-4533
Open: Year-round
Limit of Stay: Unknown
Fee Charged: Yes
Managing Agency: Private

Kanab RV Corral

Location: Hurricane
Campsites: 40 RV sites
Max RV Length: None
Facilities/Accommodations:
Drinking water, dump sites, laundry, showers, swimming, toilets
Reservations: (888) 818-5330
Open: Year-round
Limit of Stay: None
Fee Charged: Yes
Managing Agency: Private

Pah Tempe Mineral Hot Springs Resort

Location: 825 N 800 E, Hurricane
Campsites: RV and tent sites
Max RV Length: Unknown
Facilities/Accommodations:
Drinking water, dump sites, fishing, handicap facilities, laundry, picnic tables, showers, swimming, toilets; also cabins, lodge
Reservations: (888) 726-8367; (435) 635-2879
Open: Year-round
Limit of Stay: None
Fee Charged: Yes
Managing Agency: Private

Quail Lake RV Park

Location: 4400 W State, Hurricane
Campsites: 35 RV sites, 3 complete RV hookups
Max RV Length: 40 feet
Facilities/Accommodations:
Boating, drinking water, handicap facilities, laundry, showers, swimming
Reservations: (435) 635-9960
Open: Year-round
Limit of Stay: Unknown

Fee Charged: Yes
Managing Agency: Private

Robert's Roost

Location: 113 W 400 S, Hurricane
Campsites: 13 RV sites with complete RV hookups, tent sites
Max RV Length: Unknown
Facilities/Accommodations:
Drinking water, handicap facilities, picnic tables, showers, toilets
Reservations: (435) 635-0126
Open: Year-round
Limit of Stay: None
Fee Charged: Yes
Managing Agency: Private

Silver Springs RV Resort

Location: Junction of Hwy. 9 and Hwy. 17, La Verkin
Campsites: 15 RV sites, some with complete hookups, tent sites
Max RV Length: 45 feet
Facilities/Accommodations:
Drinking water, dump sites, laundry, nondrinkable water, picnic tables, showers, swimming, toilets
Reservations: (435) 635-7700
Open: Year-round
Limit of Stay: None
Fee Charged: Yes
Managing Agency: Private

Willowind RV

Location: Hurricane
Campsites: 100 RV and tent sites
Max RV Length: None
Facilities/Accommodations:
Drinking water, dump sites, laundry, picnic tables, showers, toilets
Reservations: (888) 635-4154
Open: Year-round

Limit of Stay: 7 weeks for tents, none for RVs
Fee Charged: Yes
Managing Agency: Private

Zion RV Park
🔌 ⛺ ♿ 🚐 🚿 🚽
Location: 44 W 500 N, La Verkin
Campsites: 75 RV sites with complete RV hookups
Max RV Length: Unknown
Facilities/Accommodations: Boating, drinking water, group sites, handicap facilities, laundry, picnic tables, showers, toilets
Reservations: (800) 762-4780
Open: Year-round
Limit of Stay: Unknown
Fee Charged: Yes
Managing Agency: Private

KANAB

Ponderosa Grove
🚐 🚽
Location: 14 miles northwest of Kanab off Hwy. 89, along Hancock Road
Campsites: 7 RV sites
Max RV Length: 20 feet
Facilities/Accommodations: Group sites, picnic tables,toilets
Reservations: (435) 586-2401
Open: May 1 to November 30
Limit of Stay: 14 days
Fee Charged: Yes
Managing Agency: BLM

Coleman's Exxon & RV Park
🔌 ⛺ ♿ 🚐 🚿 🚽
Location: 355 E 300 S, Kanab
Campsites: 13 RV sites with complete RV hookups
Max RV Length: Unknown
Facilities/Accommodations: Drinking water, group sites, hand-

icap facilities, picnic tables, showers, toilets
Reservations: (435) 644-2922
Open: Year-round
Limit of Stay: Unknown
Fee Charged: Yes
Managing Agency: Private

Crazy Horse Campark
🔌 ♿ 🚐 🚿 🚽
Location: 625 E 300 S, Kanab
Campsites: 74 RV sites, 44 complete RV hookups, 10 tent sites
Max RV Length: 70 feet
Facilities/Accommodations: Boating, drinking water, handicap facilities, laundry, picnic tables, showers, swimming, toilets
Reservations: (435) 644-2782
Open: Year-round
Limit of Stay: Unknown
Fee Charged: Yes
Managing Agency: Private

Hitch'n Post RV Park
🔌 🚐 🚿 🚽
Location: 196 E 300 S, Kanab
Campsites: 20 RV sites with complete RV hookups, 15 tent sites
Max RV Length: 60 feet
Facilities/Accommodations: Drinking water, dump sites, fishing, laundry, picnic tables, showers, toilets
Reservations: (800) 458-3516
Open: Year-round
Limit of Stay: Unknown
Fee Charged: Yes
Managing Agency: Private

KANARRAVILLE

Red Ledge Campground
🔌 ♿ 🚐 🚿 🚽
Location: 15 N Main, Kanarraville

Campsites: 24 RV sites with complete RV hookups, 6 tent sites
Max RV Length: 75 feet
Facilities/Accommodations: Drinking water, handicap facilities, laundry, picnic tables, showers, toilets
Reservations: (435) 586-9872
Open: Year-round
Limit of Stay: Unknown
Fee Charged: Yes
Managing Agency: Private

KODACHROME BASIN STATE PARK

Kodachrome Basin

Location: 9 miles south of Cannonville off Hwy. 12
Campsites: 24 RV and tent sites
Max RV Length: 45 feet
Facilities/Accommodations: Dump sites, group sites, nondrinkable water, picnic tables, showers, toilets
Reservations: (800) 22-3770
Open: Year-round
Limit of Stay: 14 days
Fee Charged: Yes
Managing Agency: Utah State Parks

MINERSVILLE STATE PARK

Minersville Reservoir

Location: 12 miles southwest of Beaver on Hwy. 21
Campsites: 29 RV sites, 18 tent sites
Max RV Length: 30 feet
Facilities/Accommodations: Boating, drinking water, dump sites, fishing, group sites, nondrinkable water, picnic tables, showers, swimming, toilets
Reservations: (800) 322-3770

Open: April 1 to November 30
Limit of Stay: 14 days
Fee Charged: Yes
Managing Agency: Utah State Parks

OTTER CREEK STATE PARK

Otter Creek Reservoir

Location: 4 miles northwest of Antimony on Hwy. 22
Campsites: 24 RV sites, 6 tent sites
Max RV Length: 25 feet
Facilities/Accommodations: Boating, drinking water, dump sites, fishing, nondrinkable water, picnic tables, showers, swimming, toilets
Reservations: (800) 377-3770
Open: Year-round
Limit of Stay: 14 days
Fee Charged: Yes
Managing Agency: Utah State Parks

Koosharem Campground

Location: Koosharem
Campsites: 8 RV sites with complete RV hookups
Max RV Length: 25 feet
Facilities/Accommodations: Drinking water, dump sites, laundry, picnic tables, showers, toilets
Reservations: (435) 638-7310
Open: April 1 to November 1
Limit of Stay: Unknown
Fee Charged: Yes
Managing Agency: Private

Otter Creek Marina & Campgrounds

Location: 10 miles east of Antimony on Hwy. 22
Campsites: 24 RV sites, 6 tent sites
Max RV Length: 25 feet

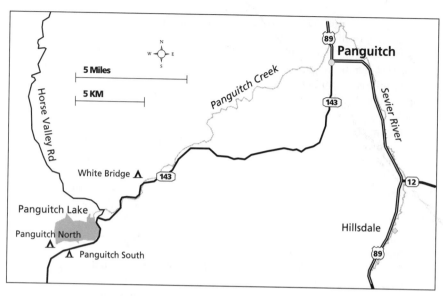

Facilities/Accommodations:
Boating, drinking water, dump sites, fishing, nondrinkable water, picnic tables, showers, swimming, toilets
Reservations: (435) 624-3292
Open: Year-round
Limit of Stay: 14 days
Fee Charged: Yes
Managing Agency: Private

PANGUITCH / PANGUITCH LAKE

Panguitch Lake North

Location: 19 miles southwest of Panguitch, near the lake
Campsites: 49 RV and tent sites
Max RV Length: 35 feet
Facilities/Accommodations:
Boating, drinking water, dump sites, fishing, handicap facilities, laundry, picnic tables, swimming, toilets
Reservations: (800) 280-2267
Open: June 1 to September 15
Limit of Stay: 14 days

Fee Charged: Yes
Managing Agency: National Forest Service (Dixie)

Panguitch Lake South

Location: 19 miles southwest of Panguitch, near the lake
Campsites: 1 RV site, 18 tent sites
Max RV Length: 35 feet
Facilities/Accommodations:
Boating, dump sites, fishing, laundry, nondrinkable water, picnic tables, swimming, toilets
Reservations: (800) 280-2267
Open: June 1 to September 15
Limit of Stay: 14 days
Fee Charged: Yes
Managing Agency: National Forest Service (Dixie)

White Bridge

Location: 10 miles southeast of Panguitch off Hwy. 143
Campsites: 29 RV and tent sites
Max RV Length: 24 feet

Facilities/Accommodations:
Boating, drinking water, dump sites, fishing, laundry, picnic tables, swimming, toilets
Reservations: (800) 280-2267
Open: June 1 to October 1
Limit of Stay: 14 days
Fee Charged: Yes
Managing Agency: National Forest Service

Bear Paw Lakeview Resort

Location: 905 S Hwy. 143, Panguitch Lake
Campsites: 20 RV sites with complete RV Hookups, 20 tent sites
Max RV Length: 35 feet
Facilities/Accommodations:
Boating, drinking water, fishing, handicap facilities, laundry, picnic tables, showers, toilets
Reservations: (435) 676-2650
Open: May 1 to October 15
Limit of Stay: Unknown
Fee Charged: Yes
Managing Agency: Private

Hitch-N-Post Campground

Location: 420 N Main, Panguitch
Campsites: 38 RV sites, 28 complete RV hookups, 10 tent sites
Max RV Length: 45 feet
Facilities/Accommodations:
Drinking water, handicap facilities, laundry, nondrinkable water, picnic tables, showers, toilets
Reservations: (800) 282-9633; (435) 676-2436
Open: Year-round
Limit of Stay: Unknown
Fee Charged: Yes
Managing Agency: Private

Panguitch KOA

Location: 555 S Main, Panguitch
Campsites: 42 RV sites, 17 complete RV hookups, 16 tent sites
Max RV Length: 60 feet
Facilities/Accommodations:
Drinking water, dump sites, handicap facilities, laundry, picnic tables, showers, swimming, toilets
Reservations: (435) 676-2225
Open: April 1 to October 15
Limit of Stay: Unknown
Fee Charged: Yes
Managing Agency: Private

Panguitch Lake Resort

Location: 791 S Resort Road, Panguitch
Campsites: 71 RV sites with complete RV hookups, tent sites
Max RV Length: 50 feet
Facilities/Accommodations:
Boating, drinking water, dump sites, fishing, handicap facilities, picnic tables, showers, toilets
Reservations: (435) 676-8326/2657
Open: May 1 to October 30
Limit of Stay: Unknown
Fee Charged: Yes
Managing Agency: Private

Red Canyons RV Park

Location: 3279 E Hwy. 12, Panguitch
Campsites: 45 RV sites with complete RV hookups, 15 tent sites
Max RV Length: Unknown
Facilities/Accommodations:
Drinking water, dump sites, handicap facilities, nondrinkable water, picnic tables, showers, toilets
Reservations: (435) 676-2690

Open: March 1 to November 1
Limit of Stay: Unknown
Fee Charged: Yes
Managing Agency: Private

Sportsman's Paradise RV Park and Campground

Location: 2153 N Hwy. 89, Panguitch
Campsites: 60 RV sites, 50 complete RV hookups, 20 tent sites
Max RV Length: 46 feet
Facilities/Accommodations: Drinking water, dump sites, fishing, handicap facilities, nondrinkable water, picnic tables, showers, toilets
Reservations: (435) 676-8348
Open: April 15 to November 15
Limit of Stay: Unknown
Fee Charged: Yes
Managing Agency: Private

PHOTO: WENDELL CHEEK

A southern Utah slot canyon.

PINE VALLEY

Blue Springs

Location: 3 miles east of Pine Valley on F.R. 035
Campsites: 16 RV sites, 20 tent sites
Max RV Length: 20 feet
Facilities/Accommodations:
   Boating, drinking water, dump sites, handicap facilities, non-drinkable water, picnic tables, toilets
Reservations: (800) 280-2267
Open: May 20 to October 31
Limit of Stay: 14 days
Fee Charged: Yes
Managing Agency: National Forest Service (Dixie)

Equestrian

Location: 2 miles east of Pine Valley on F.R. 035
Campsites: 14 RV sites
Max RV Length: Unknown
Facilities/Accommodations:
   Boating, drinking water, dump sites, toilets
Reservations: (800) 280-2267
Open: May 20 to October 31
Limit of Stay: 14 days
Fee Charged: Yes
Managing Agency: National Forest Service (Dixie)

Juniper Park

Location: 3 miles east of Pine Valley on F.R. 035
Campsites: 10 RV sites, 12 tent sites
Max RV Length: 25 feet
Facilities/Accommodations:
   Boating, drinking water, dump sites, handicap facilities, non-drinkable water, toilets

Reservations: (800) 280-2267
Open: May 20 to October 31
Limit of Stay: 14 days
Fee Charged: Yes
Managing Agency: National Forest Service (Dixie)

Pines

Location: 3 miles east of Pine Valley on F.R. 035
Campsites: 10 RV sites, 6 tent sites
Max RV Length: 20 feet
Facilities/Accommodations:
   Boating, drinking water, dump sites, group sites, handicap facilities, nondrinkable water, toilets
Reservations: (800) 280-2267
Open: May 20 to October 31
Limit of Stay: 14 days
Fee Charged: Yes
Managing Agency: National Forest Service (Dixie)

PIUTE STATE PARK / JUNCTION / MARYSVALE

City Creek

Location: 5.5 miles northwest of Junction off Hwy. 153 along City Creek
Campsites: 2 RV sites, 5 tent sites
Max RV Length: Unknown
Facilities/Accommodations:
   Drinking water, fishing, non-drinkable water, picnic tables, toilets
Reservations: (800) 280-2267
Open: May 21 to October 30
Limit of Stay: 14 days
Fee Charged: Yes
Managing Agency: National Forest Service (Fishlake)

PHOTO: WENDELL CHEEK

A rich southern Utah canyon.

Piute State Park

Location: North end of reservoir, 5 miles north of Junction off Hwy. 89

Campsites: RV and tent sites

Max RV Length: Unknown

Facilities/Accommodations: Boating, fishing, picnic tables, swimming, toilets

Reservations: NA. General information: (435) 624-3268

Open: Year-round

Limit of Stay: 14 days

Fee Charged: Yes

Managing Agency: Utah State Parks

Fat's Country RV & Tent

Location: 135 W Center, Junction

Campsites: 9 RV sites with complete RV hookups, tent sites

Max RV Length: Unknown

Facilities/Accommodations: Drinking water, dump sites, handicap facilities, nondrinkable water, picnic tables, toilets

Reservations: (435) 577-2672

Open: Year-round

Limit of Stay: Unknown

Fee Charged: Yes

Managing Agency: Private

Wildflower RV

Location: 4 miles north of Marysvale on Hwy. 89

Campsites: 30 RV sites, 12 complete RV hookups

Max RV Length: Unknown

Facilities/Accommodations: Boating, drinking water, handicap facilities, picnic tables, toilets

Reservations: (435) 326-4301

Open: April 1 to October 31

Limit of Stay: Unknown

Fee Charged: Yes

Managing Agency: Private

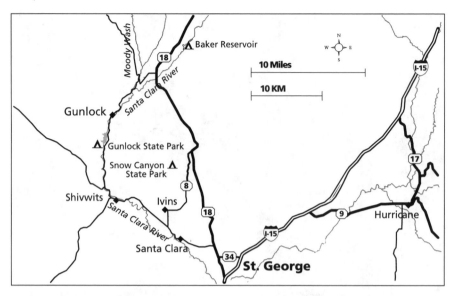

QUAIL CREEK / RED CLIFF

Quail Creek State Park

🪝 ⊞ 🚐 🚽

Location: At reservoir, 3 miles east of I-15 Exit 16

Campsites: 23 RV and tent sites

Max RV Length: 35 feet

Facilities/Accommodations: Boating, drinking water, fishing, group sites, picnic tables, swimming, toilets

Reservations: (800) 322-3770

Open: Year-round

Limit of Stay: 14 days

Fee Charged: Yes

Managing Agency: Utah State Parks

Oak Grove

🪝 🚐 🚿 🚽

Location: Northeast of Leeds on F.R. 032

Campsites: 10 RV sites, 6 tent sites

Max RV Length: 18 feet

Facilities/Accommodations: Drinking water, nondrinkable water, picnic tables, showers, toilets

Reservations: (800) 280-2267

Open: May 20-October 31

Limit of Stay: 14 days

Fee Charged: Yes

Managing Agency: National Forest Service (Dixie)

Red Cliff

🪝 ♿ 🚐 🚽

Location: 4.5 miles southwest of Leeds off I-15 at the Leeds exit, across I-15 from Quail Creek

Campsites: 10 RV and tent sites

Max RV Length: 25 feet

Facilities/Accommodations: Drinking water, handicap facilities, picnic tables, toilets

Reservations: (435) 586-2401

Open: Year-round

Limit of Stay: 14 days

Fee Charged: Yes

Managing Agency: BLM

Harrisburg Lake RV resort

Location: South of Leeds
Campsites: 120 RV and tent sites
Max RV Length: 40 feet
Facilities/Accommodations:
Boating, drinking water, dump sites, fishing, picnic tables, showers, swimming, toilets
Reservations: (435) 879-2212
Open: Year-round
Limit of Stay: 7 days
Fee Charged: Yes
Managing Agency: Private

Leeds RV Park & Motel

Location: 97 S Valley Road, Leeds
Campsites: 57 RV sites, 15 tent sites
Max RV Length: 40 feet
Facilities/Accommodations:
Drinking water, dump sites, group sites, picnic tables, showers, toilets
Reservations: (435) 879-2450
Open: Year-round
Limit of Stay: None
Fee Charged: Yes
Managing Agency: Private

ST. GEORGE

Gunlock State Park

Location: 15 miles northwest of St. George off old Hwy. 8
Campsites: Primitive tent sites
Max RV Length: NA
Facilities/Accommodations:
Boating, fishing, swimming, toilets
Reservations: NA

A beautiful, shaded site in Snow Canyon State Park.

Open: Year-round
Limit of Stay: 14 days
Fee Charged: Yes
Managing Agency: Utah State Parks

Snow Canyon State Park

Location: 5 miles northwest of St.
George off Hwy. 18
Campsites: 36 RV sites with some
hookups, 17 tent sites
Max RV Length: 35 feet
Facilities/Accommodations:
Drinking water, dump sites, picnic
tables, showers, toilets
Reservations: (800) 322-3770
Open: Year-round
Limit of Stay: 14 days
Fee Charged: Yes
Managing Agency: Utah State Parks

Baker Reservoir

Location: 25 miles north of St.
George (northeast of Veyo) off
Hwy. 18
Campsites: 10 RV and tent sites
Max RV Length: 25 feet
Facilities/Accommodations: Fishing,
picnic tables
Reservations: (435) 586-2401
Open: Year-round
Limit of Stay: 14 days
Fee Charged: Yes
Managing Agency: BLM

McArthur's Temple View RV Resort

Location: St. George
Campsites: 266 RV and tent sites
Max RV Length: 45 feet
Facilities/Accommodations: Dump
sites, laundry, showers, swim-
ming, toilets

Reservations: (435) 776-6410
Open: Year-round
Limit of Stay: None
Fee Charged: Yes
Managing Agency: Private

Redlands RV Park

Location: 650 W Telegraph, St.
George
Campsites: 200 RV sites with com-
plete RV hookups, 50 tent sites
Max RV Length: 40 feet
Facilities/Accommodations:
Boating, drinking water, fishing,
handicap facilities, laundry, non-
drinkable water, picnic tables,
showers, swimming, toilets
Reservations: (800) 553-8269; (435)
673-9700
Open: Year-round
Limit of Stay: Unknown
Fee Charged: Yes
Managing Agency: Private

THOUSAND LAKE MOUNTAIN

Elkhorn

Location: 11 miles northeast of Loa
off Hwy. 72
Campsites: 6 RV and tent sites
Max RV Length: 22 feet
Facilities/Accommodations:
Drinking water, fishing, group
sites, nondrinkable water, picnic
tables, toilets
Reservations: (800) 280-2267
Open: May 27 to September 30
Limit of Stay: 14 days
Fee Charged: Yes
Managing Agency: National Forest
Service (Fishlake)

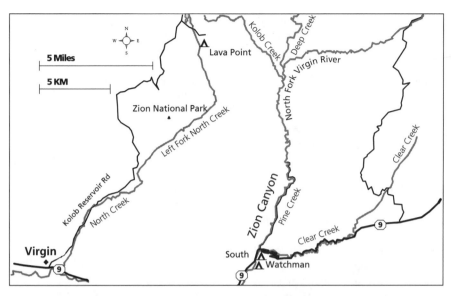

ZION NATIONAL PARK

Zion National Park — Lava Point (Kolob Area)

Location: 26 miles north of Virgin off Hwy. 9, off Kolob Reservoir Road
Campsites: 6 RV and tent sites
Max RV Length: Unknown
Facilities/Accommodations: Picnic tables, toilets
Reservations: NA
Open: June 1 to October 15
Limit of Stay: 14 days
Fee Charged: Yes
Managing Agency: National Park Service

Zion National Park — South

Location: South entrance to the park
Campsites: 140 RV and tent sites
Max RV Length: Unknown
Facilities/Accommodations: Drinking water, dump sites, handicap facilities, picnic tables, toilets

Reservations: NA
Open: April 15 to October 15
Limit of Stay: 14 days
Fee Charged: Yes
Managing Agency: National Park Service

Zion National Park — Watchman

Location: South entrance to the park
Campsites: 229 RV and tent sites
Max RV Length: Unknown
Facilities/Accommodations: Drinking water, group sites, handicap facilities, picnic tables, toilets
Reservations: NA
Open: Year-round
Limit of Stay: 14 days
Fee Charged: Yes
Managing Agency: National Park Service

Bauer's Canyon Ranch RV Park

Location: Glendale
Campsites: 20 RV and tent sites
Max RV Length: None

Facilities/Accommodations: Dump sites, drinking water, fishing, laundry, showers, toilets
Reservations: (435) 648-2564
Open: Year-round, weather permitting
Limit of Stay: None
Fee Charged: Yes
Managing Agency: Private

Bryce/Zion KOA

Location: 5 miles north of Glendale on Hwy. 89
Campsites: 59 RV sites, 19 complete RV hookups, 39 tent sites
Max RV Length: Unknown
Facilities/Accommodations: Boating, drinking water, dump sites, group sites, handicap facilities, laundry, picnic tables, showers, swimming, toilets
Reservations: (800) 648-2035
Open: May 1 to September 15
Limit of Stay: Unknown
Fee Charged: Yes
Managing Agency: Private

East Zion Trailer Park

Location: Junction of Hwy. 9 and Hwy. 89, Mount Carmel
Campsites: 20 RV sites with complete RV hookups, 1 tent site
Max RV Length: 40 feet
Facilities/Accommodations: Drinking water, handicap facilities, picnic tables, toilets
Reservations: (435) 648-2326
Open: Year-round
Limit of Stay: 10 days
Fee Charged: Yes
Managing Agency: Private

Mount Carmel Trailer Park

Location: 1 mile north of Mount Carmel Junction on Hwy. 89
Campsites: 15 RV sites, 10 complete RV hookups, 8 tent sites
Max RV Length: Unknown
Facilities/Accommodations: Drinking water, handicap facilities, picnic tables, showers, toilets
Reservations: (435) 648-2323
Open: March 15 to November 1
Limit of Stay: Unknown
Fee Charged: Yes
Managing Agency: Private

Mukuntuweep RV Park & Campground

Location: Near east entrance of Zion National Park
Campsites: 30 RV sites, 120 tent sites,
Max RV Length: 90 feet
Facilities/Accommodations: Boating, drinking water, dump sites, fishing, handicap facilities, laundry, picnic tables, nondrinkable water, showers, toilets; also cabins, teepees and Navajo hogans
Reservations: (435) 648-2154
Open: Year-round
Limit of Stay: 100 days
Fee Charged: Yes
Managing Agency: Private

Tortoise and Hare Trailer Court

Location: Orderville
Campsites: 15 RV and tent sites
Max RV Length: None
Facilities/Accommodations: Drinking water, dump sites, laundry, picnic tables, showers, toilets

Reservations: (435) 648-2312
Open: Year-round
Limit of Stay: None
Fee Charged: Yes
Managing Agency: Private

Zion Canyon Campground

Location: 479 Zion Park Blvd.,
Springdale
Campsites: 100 RV sites, 75 complete RV hookups, 75 tent sites
Max RV Length: 35 feet
Facilities/Accommodations:
Drinking water, dump sites, handicap facilities, laundry, picnic
tables, showers, toilets
Reservations: (435) 772-3237
Open: Year-round
Limit of Stay: 14 days
Fee Charged: Yes
Managing Agency: Private

Zion Ponderosa Resort

Location: Near east entrance of Zion
National Park
Campsites: 60 tent sites
Max RV Length: Unknown
Facilities/Accommodations:
Drinking water, handicap facilities, group sites, laundry, picnic
tables, showers, swimming, toilets
Reservations: (800) 293-5444
Open: April to October
Limit of Stay: None
Fee Charged: Yes
Managing Agency: Private

CAMPGROUNDS: OVER-THE-BORDER

GRAND CANYON NATIONAL PARK (ARIZONA)

Mather

🚰 ▦ ♿ 🚐 🚿 🚽

Location: In Grand Canyon Village
Campsites: 313 RV and tent sites
Max RV Length: 60 feet
Facilities/Accommodations: Drinking water, group sites, handicap facilities, nondrinkable water, showers, toilets
Reservations: (800) 365-2267 (up to five months in advance for March 31st to Dec. 1st)
Open: Year-round
Limit of Stay: 7 days
Fee Charged: Yes
Managing Agency: National Park Service

Desert View

🚰 🚐 🚽

Location: 26 miles east of Grand Canyon Village
Campsites: 75 RV and tent sites
Max RV Length: 35 feet
Facilities/Accommodations: Nondrinkable water, toilets
Reservations: NA. General information: (520) 638-7893
Open: April 15 to October 15
Limit of Stay: 7 days
Fee Charged: Yes
Managing Agency: National Park Service

North Rim

🚰 ▦ ♿ 🚐 🚽

Location: On the north rim of Grand Canyon National Park
Campsites: 75 RV and tent sites
Max RV Length: 35 feet
Facilities/Accommodations: Drinking water, group sites, handicap facilities, nondrinkable water, toilets
Reservations: (800) 365-2267
Open: Late May to late October
Limit of Stay: 7 days
Fee Charged: Yes
Managing Agency: National Park Service

Trailer Village

🚰 ▦ ♿ 🚐 🚿 🚽

Location: In Grand Canyon Village
Campsites: 80 RV and tent sites, some complete RV hookups
Max RV Length: 50 feet
Facilities/Accommodations: Drinking water, group sites, handicap facilities, nondrinkable water, showers, toilets
Reservations: (303) 297-2757
Open: Year-round
Limit of Stay: None
Fee Charged: Yes
Managing Agency: Private

SYMBOL LEGEND

🚰 Drinking water 🚐 RV sites
▦ Group sites 🚽 Toilets
♿ Handicap facilities 🚿 Showers

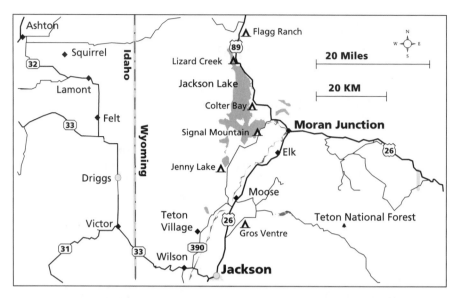

GRAND TETON NATIONAL PARK (WYOMING)

Colter Bay
🛶 ⫶⫶⫶ 🚐 🚻

Location: On Jackson Lake, 5 miles northwest of Jackson Lake Junction
Campsites: 310 RV and tent sites
Max RV Length: 35 feet
Facilities/Accommodations: Drinking water, dump sites, group sites, laundry, nondrinkable water, showers, toilets
Reservations: NA
Open: Early May to early September
Limit of Stay: 14 days
Fee Charged: Yes
Managing Agency: National Park Service

Gros Ventre
🛶 ⫶⫶⫶ 🚐 🚻

Location: 9.5 miles north of Jackson, Wyo.
Campsites: 360 RV and tent sites
Max RV Length: 35 feet
Facilities/Accommodations: Drinking water, dump sites, group sites, nondrinkable water, toilets
Reservations: NA
Open: Late April to early October
Limit of Stay: 14 days
Fee Charged: Yes
Managing Agency: National Park Service

Jenny Lake
🛶 🚻

Location: 8 miles north of Moose, Wyo.
Campsites: 49 tent sites
Max RV Length: None
Facilities/Accommodations: Drinking water, toilets
Reservations: NA
Open: Late May to late September
Limit of Stay: 7 days
Fee Charged: Yes
Managing Agency: National Park Service

Lizard Creek

Location: 46 miles north of Moose (north end of Grand Teton National Park)
Campsites: 60 RV and tent sites
Max RV Length: 35 feet
Facilities/Accommodations: Drinking water, nondrinkable water, toilets
Reservations: NA
Open: Early May to early September
Limit of Stay: 14 days
Fee Charged: Yes
Managing Agency: National Park Service

Signal Mountain

Location: 20 miles north of Moose
Campsites: 86 RV and tent sites
Max RV Length: 35 feet

Facilities/Accommodations: Drinking water, dump sites, non-drinkable water, toilets
Reservations: NA
Open: Early May to early September
Limit of Stay: 14 days
Fee Charged: Yes
Managing Agency: National Park Service

Colter Bay Village

Location: On Jackson Lake, 5 miles northwest of Jackson Lake Junction
Campsites: 60 RV sites with complete RV hookups
Max RV Length: None
Facilities/Accommodations: Drinking water, dump sites, laundry, nondrinkable water, showers, toilets; also "tent cabins"
Reservations: (800) 628-9928; (307) 543-3100/2811

A view of Teton slopes in winter.

PHOTO: WENDELL CHEEK

Open: May 26 to September 24
Limit of Stay: 14 days
Fee Charged: Yes
Managing Agency: Grand Teton
Lodge Co.

Flagg Ranch

Location: 56 miles north of Moose
(between Grand Teton National
Park and Yellowstone)
Campsites: 95 RV and tent sites,
some complete RV hookups
Max RV Length: None
Facilities/Accommodations:
Drinking water, nondrinkable
water, showers, toilets
Reservations: (800) 443-2311
Open: Closed March 15 to May 22
and Oct. 15 to Dec.15, 2000
Limit of Stay: 8 days
Fee Charged: Yes
Managing Agency: National Park
Service concessionaire

GREAT BASIN NATIONAL PARK (NEVADA)

Baker Creek

Location: On Baker Creek (2 miles
south of the park Visitor Center)
Campsites: 32 RV and tent sites
Max RV Length: Varies
Facilities/Accommodations:
Drinking water and nondrinkable
water (in summer), toilets
Reservations: NA
Open: As snow levels permit
Limit of Stay: 14 days
Fee Charged: Yes
Managing Agency: National Park
Service

Lower Lehman Creek

Location: First campground along
Lehman Creek (1 mile northeast
of Visitor Center)
Campsites: 11 RV and tent sites
Max RV Length: Varies
Facilities/Accommodations:
Drinking water and nondrinkable
water (in summer), toilets
Reservations: NA
Open: Year-round
Limit of Stay: 14 days
Fee Charged: Yes
Managing Agency: National Park
Service

Shoshone Creek

Location: 4 miles south of Baker
Creek
Campsites: Primitive tent sites
Max RV Length: Varies
Facilities/Accommodations: None
Reservations: Picnic tables, toilets
Open: As snow levels permit
Limit of Stay: 14 days
Fee Charged: Yes
Managing Agency: National Park
Service

Snake Creek

Location: 5 miles south of Baker
Creek
Campsites: Primitive tent sites
Max RV Length: Varies
Facilities/Accommodations: Picnic
tables, toilets
Reservations: NA
Open: As snow levels permit
Limit of Stay: 14 days
Fee Charged: Yes
Managing Agency: National Park
Service

Upper Lehman Creek

🔥 🚐 🚽

Location: Second campground along Lehman Creek
Campsites: 24 RV and tent sites
Max RV Length: Varies
Facilities/Accommodations: Drinking water nd nondrinkable water (in summer), toilets
Reservations: NA
Open: As snow levels permit
Limit of Stay: 14 days
Fee Charged: Yes
Managing Agency: National Park Service

Wheeler Peak

🔥 🚐 🚽

Location: At the Base of Wheeler Peak Trail (northwesternmost campground in the park)
Campsites: 37 RV and tent sites
Max RV Length: Varies
Facilities/Accommodations: Drinking water and nondrinkable water (in summer), toilets
Reservations: NA
Open: As snow levels permit
Limit of Stay: 14 days
Fee Charged: Yes
Managing Agency: National Park Service

SEMINOE STATE PARK (WYOMING)

North Red Hills

🔥 🚐 🚽

Location: 34 miles north of Sinclair, Wyo.
Campsites: 94 RV and tent sites
Max RV Length: 35 feet
Facilities/Accommodations: Boating, drinking water, dump sites, picnic tables, playgrounds, toilets

Reservations: (307) 320-3013
Open: Year-round (limited facilities in the winter)
Limit of Stay: 14 days
Fee Charged: Yes
Managing Agency: Wyoming State Parks

South Red Hills

🔥 🚐 🚽

Location: Seminoe State Park
Campsites: RV and tent sites
Max RV Length: Unknown
Facilities/Accommodations: Boating, drinking water, dump sites, fishing, nondrinkable water, toilets
Reservations: (307) 320-3013
Open: Year-round (limited facilities in the winter months)
Limit of Stay: 14 days
Fee Charged: Yes
Managing Agency: Wyoming State Parks

American Presidents Camp

🚐 🚿 🚽

Location: 2346 W Spruce, Rawlins, Wyo.
Campsites: 72 RV and tent sites, some complete RV hookups
Max RV Length: Unknown
Facilities/Accommodations: Dump sites, nondrinkable water, showers, toilets
Reservations: (307) 324-3218
Open: June 15 to October 30
Limit of Stay: Unknown
Fee Charged: Yes
Managing Agency: Private

KOA Kampground

🔥 🚐 🚿 🚽

Location: 205 E Hwy. 71 Rawlins, Wyo.

Campsites: 48 RV and 6 tent sites, some complete RV hookups

Max RV Length: Unknown

Facilities/Accommodations: Drinking water, dump sites, laundry, nondrinkable water, showers, swimming, toilets

Reservations: (307) 328-2021

Open: April 1 to October 31

Limit of Stay: Unknown

Fee Charged: Yes

Managing Agency: Private

RV World Campground

Location: 2401 Wagon Circle, Rawlins

Campsites: 100 RV sites and 5 tent sites, some complete RV hookups

Max RV Length: Unknown

Facilities/Accommodations: Drinking water, dump sites, laundry, nondrinkable water, rec room, showers, swimming, toilets

Reservations: (307) 328 1091

Open: April 1 to October 1

Limit of Stay: Unknown

Fee Charged: Yes

Managing Agency: Private

Western Hills Campground

Location: 2500 Wagon Circle, Rawlins

Campsites: 171 RV sites and 30 tent sites, some complete RV hookups

Max RV Length: Unknown

Facilities/Accommodations: Drinking water, dump sites, laundry, nondrinkable water, rec room, showers, toilets

Reservations: (307) 324-2592

Open: April 1 to November 1

Limit of Stay: Unknown

Fee Charged: Yes

Managing Agency: Private

WIND RIVER MOUNTAINS (WYOMING)

Big Sandy Reservoir

Location: 15 miles north of Farson, Wyo., off Hwy. 191

Campsites: 12 RV and tent sites

Max RV Length: Unknown

Facilities/Accommodations: Boating, fishing, toilets

Reservations: NA. General information: (801) 379-1000

Open: May 25 to September

Limit of Stay: 16 days

Fee Charged: No

Managing Agency: Bureau of Reclamations

Boulder Lake

Location: 25 miles southeast Pinedale, Wyo., off Hwy. 191

Campsites: 20 tent sites

Max RV Length: NA

Facilities/Accommodations: Boating

Reservations: NA

Open: June 1 to October 15

Limit of Stay: Unknown

Fee Charged: Yes

Managing Agency: National Forest Service (Bridger-Teton)

Fremont Lake

Location: 7 miles northeast of Pinedale along Fremont Lake Road

Campsites: 53 RV and tent sites

Max RV Length: Unknown

Facilities/Accommodations: Boating, nondrinkable water, toilets

A guide leads a group of pack horses through the Wind River Mountains.

Reservations: Yes
Open: May 25 to September 10
Limit of Stay: Unknown
Fee Charged: Yes
Managing Agency: National Forest Service (Bridger-Teton)

Green River Lake

Location: 52 miles north of Pinedale off Hwy. 352
Campsites: 39 RV and tent sites
Max RV Length: Unknown
Facilities/Accommodations: Boating, dump sites, group sites, nondrinkable water
Reservations: NA
Open: June 15 to September 10
Limit of Stay: Unknown
Fee Charged: Yes
Managing Agency: National Forest Service (Bridger-Teton)

Half Moon Lake

Location: 10 miles northeast of Pinedale off Fremont Lake Road
Campsites: 18 RV and tent sites
Max RV Length: Unknown
Facilities/Accommodations: Boating
Reservations: NA
Open: June 1 to September 10
Limit of Stay: Unknown
Fee Charged: Yes
Managing Agency: National Forest Service (Bridger-Teton)

New Fork Lake

Location: 24 miles north of Pinedale off Hwy. 352
Campsites: 15 RV and tent sites
Max RV Length: Unknown
Facilities/Accommodations: Boating, nondrinkable water, toilets
Reservations: NA

Open: June 1 to September 10
Limit of Stay: Unknown
Fee Charged: Yes
Managing Agency: National Forest
Service (Bridger-Teton)

New Fork (Group Site)

Location: 24 miles north of Pinedale
off Hwy. 352
Campsites: 3 RV and tent sites
Max RV Length: Unknown
Facilities/Accommodations: Boating
Reservations: Yes
Open: June 1 to September 10
Limit of Stay: Unknown
Fee Charged: Yes
Managing Agency: National Forest
Service (Bridger-Teton)

Upper Fremont Lake

Location: 16 miles northeast of
Pinedale along Fremont Lake
Road

Campsites: 5 tent sites
Max RV Length: NA
Facilities/Accommodations: None
Reservations: NA
Open: June 1 to September 10
Limit of Stay: Unknown
Fee Charged: Yes
Managing Agency: National Forest
Service (Bridger-Teton)

Whiskey Grove

Location: 36 miles from Pinedale
Campsites: 9 RV and tent sites
Max RV Length: Unknown
Facilities/Accommodations:
Nondrinkable water, toilets
Reservations: NA
Open: June 16 to September 10
Limit of Stay: Unknown
Fee Charged: Yes
Managing Agency: National Forest
Service (Bridger-Teton)

Pack llamas traverse a river in the Wind River Mountains.

Willow Lake
🚐 🏕

Location: 14 miles north of Pinedale off Hwy. 191
Campsites: 6 RV and tent sites
Max RV Length: Unknown
Facilities/Accommodations: Boating, nondrinkable water, toilets
Reservations: NA
Open: June 1 to October 1
Limit of Stay: Unknown
Fee Charged: Yes
Managing Agency: National Forest Service (Bridger-Teton)

Fiddlers Lake
♿ 🚐 🏕

Location: 16 miles southwest of Lander, Wyo. on Louis Lake Road off Hwy. 131 (Sinks Canyon Rd.)
Campsites: 20 RV and tent sites
Max RV Length: 24 feet
Facilities/Accommodations: Fishing, handicap facilities, nondrinkable water, picnic tables, toilets
Reservations: NA
Open: July to September 30
Limit of Stay: 16 days
Fee Charged: Yes
Managing Agency: National Forest Service (Shoshone — Washakie Ranger District)

Louis Lake
🚐 🏕

Location: 18 miles southwest of Lander on Louis Lake Road off Hwy. 131 (Sinks Canyon Rd.)
Campsites: 9 RV and tent sites
Max RV Length: 24 feet
Facilities/Accommodations: Boating, fishing, nondrinkable water, picnic tables, toilets

Reservations: NA
Open: July to September 30
Limit of Stay: 16 days
Fee Charged: Yes
Managing Agency: National Forest Service (Shoshone — Washakie Ranger District)

Popo Agie
🚐 🏕

Location: 8 miles southwest of Lander on Hwy. 131 (Sinks Canyon Rd.)
Campsites: 4 RV and tent sites
Max RV Length: 16 feet.
Facilities/Accommodations: Fishing, picnic tables, toilets
Reservations: NA
Open: July to September 30
Limit of Stay: 16 days
Fee Charged: No
Managing Agency: National Forest Service (Shoshone — Washakie Ranger District)

Sinks Canyon
🚐 🏕

Location: Six miles southwest of Lander on Hwy. 131 (Sinks Canyon Rd.)
Campsites: 9 RV and tent sites
Max RV Length: 20 feet
Facilities/Accommodations: Fishing, nondrinkable water, picnic tables, toilets
Reservations: NA
Open: May 26 to October 30
Limit of Stay: 16 days
Fee Charged: Yes
Managing Agency: National Forest Service (Shoshone — Washakie Ranger District)

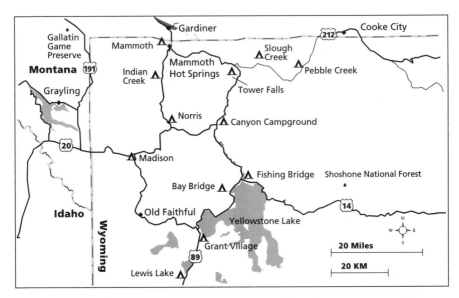

Worthen Meadow Reservoir/ Frye Lake

Location: 14 miles southwest of Lander on F.R. 302 off Hwy. 131
Campsites: 28 RV and tent sites
Max RV Length: 24 feet
Facilities/Accommodations: Boating, nondrinkable water, picnic tables, toilets
Reservations: NA
Open: July to September
Limit of Stay: Unknown
Fee Charged: Yes
Managing Agency: National Forest Service (Shoshone – Washakie Ranger District)

YELLOWSTONE NATIONAL PARK (WYOMING)

Indian Creek

Location: Indian Creek, 6 miles south of Mammoth
Campsites: 75 RV and tent sites
Max RV Length: Unknown
Facilities/Accommodations: Drinking water, nondrinkable water, toilets
Reservations: NA
Open: Early June to late October
Limit of Stay: 14 days
Fee Charged: Yes
Managing Agency: National Park Service

Lewis Lake

Location: Lewis Lake, 15 miles north of south entrance
Campsites: 85 RV and tent sites
Max RV Length: Unknown
Facilities/Accommodations: Drinking water, handicap facilities, nondrinkable water, toilets
Reservations: NA
Open: Early June to late October
Limit of Stay: 14 days
Fee Charged: Yes
Managing Agency: National Park Service

Mammoth
🛶 🚐 🛆

Location: Just north of Mammoth Hot Springs, 18 miles west of Tower, Wyo.
Campsites: 85 RV and tent sites
Max RV Length: Unknown
Facilities/Accommodations: Drinking water, nondrinkable water, toilets
Reservations: NA
Open: Year-round
Limit of Stay: 14 days
Fee Charged: Yes
Managing Agency: National Park Service

Norris
🛶 🚐 🛆

Location: Norris, just northeast of Norris Geyser Basin
Campsites: 116 RV and tent sites
Max RV Length: Unknown
Facilities/Accommodations: Drinking water, nondrinkable water, toilets
Reservations: NA
Open: Mid May to late September
Limit of Stay: 14 days
Fee Charged: Yes
Managing Agency: National Park Service

Pebble Creek
🛶 🚐 🛆

Location: Pebble Creek
Campsites: 32 RV and tent sites
Max RV Length: Unknown
Facilities/Accommodations: Drinking water, nondrinkable water, toilets
Reservations: NA
Open: Early June to end of Sept.
Limit of Stay: 14 days

Fee Charged: Yes
Managing Agency: National Park Service

Slough Creek
🛶 ♿ 🚐 🛆

Location: Slough Creek, 6 miles north and east of Tower Junction
Campsites: 29 RV and tent sites
Max RV Length: Unknown
Facilities/Accommodations: Drinking water, handicap facilities, nondrinkable water, toilets
Reservations: NA
Open: Late May to late October
Limit of Stay: 14 days
Fee Charged: Yes
Managing Agency: National Park Service

Tower Falls
🛶 🚐 🛆

Location: Tower Falls, 2 miles southeast of Tower Junction
Campsites: 32 RV and tent sites
Max RV Length: Unknown
Facilities/Accommodations: Drinking water, nondrinkable water, toilets
Reservations: NA
Open: Mid May to late September
Limit of Stay: 14 days
Fee Charged: YesManaging Agency: National Park Service

Bridge Bay
🛶 ⛺ ♿ 🚐 🛆

Location: Lower loop of road system, on Yellowstone Lake
Campsites: 400 RV and tent sites
Max RV Length: 40 feet
Facilities/Accommodations: Drinking water, group sites, handicap facilities, nondrinkable water, toilets

PHOTO: WENDELL CHEEK

Mammoth Hot Springs in Yellowstone National Park.

Reservations: (307) 344-7311
Open: Mid May to mid September
Limit of Stay: 14 days
Fee Charged: Yes
Managing Agency: AmFac Parks and
Resorts

Canyon

Location: Lower loop of road system, 1.5 miles north of Canyon JunctionCampsites: 270 RV and tent sites
Max RV Length: 40 feet
Facilities/Accommodations:
Drinking water, handicap facilities, laundry, showers, toilets
Reservations: (307) 344-7311
Open: Early June to early September
Limit of Stay: 14 days
Fee Charged: Yes
Managing Agency: AmFac Parks and
Resorts

Fishing Bridge

Location: Lower loop of road system, near Bridge Bay on Yellowstone Lake
Campsites: 400 RV and tent sites, some complete RV hookups
Max RV Length: 40 feet
Facilities/Accommodations:
Drinking water, handicap facilities, laundry, showers, toilets
Reservations: (307) 344-7311
Open: Mid May to mid Sept.
Limit of Stay: None
Fee Charged: Yes
Managing Agency: AmFac Parks and
Resorts

Grant Village

Location: Lower loop of road system, 2 miles south of West Thumb on Yellowstone Lake
Campsites: 400 RV and tent sites

Max RV Length: 50 feet
Facilities/Accommodations:
Drinking water, group sites, hand-icap facilities, laundry, showers, toilets
Reservations: (307) 344-7311
Open: Mid June to early October
Limit of Stay: 14 days
Fee Charged: Yes
Managing Agency: AmFac Parks and Resorts

Madison
🦅 ⛺ ♿ 🚐 🚻
Location: Lower loop of road sys-tem, just southwest of Madison Junction

Campsites: 270 RV and tent sites
Max RV Length: 40 feet
Facilities/Accommodations:
Drinking water, group sites, hand-icap facilities, nondrinkable water, toilets
Reservations: (307) 344-7311
Open: Early May to late October
Limit of Stay: 14 days
Fee Charged: Yes
Managing Agency: AmFac Parks and Resorts

PHOTO: WENDELL CHEEK

A creek surges over a cliff in Yellowstone.

APPENDIX

Bureau of Land Management Offices

• Utah State Office, Bureau of Land Management, P.O. Box 45155, 324 South State Street, Suite 301, Salt Lake City, Utah 84111; phone: (801) 539-4001; fax: (801) 539-4013; Office Hours: 8 a.m. - 4:30 p.m. (Mailing address: P.O. Box 45155, Salt Lake City, UT 84145-0155)

Utah Field Offices:

• Cedar City District Office, Bureau of Land Management, 176 East D.L. Sargent Drive, Cedar City, UT 84720; phone: (435) 586-2401; fax: (435) 865-3058

• Fillmore Field Office, Bureau of Land Management, 35 East 500 North, Fillmore, UT 84631; phone: (435) 743-3100; fax: (435) 743-3135

• Grand Staircase-Escalante National Monument, Kanab Headquarters, Bureau of Land Management, 180 West 300 North, Kanab, UT 84741; phone: (435) 644-4300; fax: (435) 644-4350

• Grand Staircase-Escalante National Monument, Escalante Interagency Office, Bureau of Land Management, P.O. Box 225, 755 West Main Street, Escalante, UT 84726; phone: (435) 826-5600; fax: (435) 826-5650

• Grand Staircase-Escalante National Monument, Cannonville Visitor Center, Bureau of Land Management, P.O. Box 189961, 10 Center Street, Cannonville, UT 84718; phone: Office (435) 679-8980, Visitor Center (435) 679-8981

• Henry Mountain Field Station, Bureau of Land Management, P.O. Box 99, Hanksville, UT 84734; phone: (435) 542-3461; fax: (435) 542-3461

• Kanab Field Office, Bureau of Land Management, 318 North 100 East, Kanab, UT 84741; phone: (435) 644-2672 Ext. 2694; fax: (435) 644-2694

• Moab Field Office, Bureau of Land Management, 82 East Dogwood, Moab, UT 84532; phone: (435) 259-6111; fax: (435) 259-2106

• Monticello Field Office, Bureau of Land Management, P.O. Box , 435 North Main, Monticello, UT 84535; phone: (435) 587-1500; fax: (435) 587-1518

• Price Field Office, Bureau of Land Management, 125 South 600 West, Price, UT 84501; phone: (435) 636-3600; fax: (435) 636-3657

• Richfield Field Office, Bureau of Land Management, 150 East 900 North, Richfield, UT 84701; phone: (435) 896-1500; fax: (435) 896-1550

• Salt Lake Field Office, Bureau of Land Management, 2370 South 2300 West, Salt Lake City, UT 84119; phone: (801) 977-4300; fax: (801) 977-4397

• St. George Field Office, Bureau of Land Management, 345 East Riverside Drive, St. George, UT 84790; phone: (435) 688-3200; fax: (435) 688-3235

• Vernal Field Office, Bureau of Land Management, 170 South 500 East, Vernal, UT 84078; phone: (435) 781-4400; fax: (435) 781-4400

Division of Wildlife Resources Offices

• Salt Lake Office, P.O. Box 146301, 1594 West North Temple, Suite 2110, Salt Lake City, UT 84114-6301; phone: (801) 538-4700

• Northern Region, 515 East 5300 South, Ogden, UT 84405; phone: (801) 476-2740

• Northeastern Region, 152 East 100 North, Vernal, UT 84078; phone: (435) 789-3103

• Central Region, 1115 North Main Street, Springville, UT 84663; phone: (801) 489-5678

• Southern Region, Street Address: 1470 North Airport Road, Cedar City, UT 84720; phone: (435) 865-6100 (Mailing address: P.O. Box 606, Cedar City, UT 84721-0606)

• Southeastern Region, 475 West Price River Drive, Suite C, Price, UT 84501; phone: (435) 636-0260

Hunter Education Centers

• Lee Kay Center for Hunter Education, 6000 West 2100 South, Salt Lake City, UT 84120; phone: (801) 972-1326

• Cache Valley Hunter Education Center, 2851 West Valley View Hwy., P.O. Box 454, Logan, UT 84321; phone: (435) 753-4600

National Monuments

• Cedar Breaks National Monument, 2390 West Hwy. 56, Suite 11, Cedar City, UT 84720-4151; phone: (435) 586-9451

• Dinosaur National Monument, 4545 E. Hwy. 40, Dinosaur, CO 81610-9724; phone: (970) 374-3000

• Grand Staircase-Escalante National Monument, Kanab Resource Area Office, 318 North 100 East, Kanab, UT 84741; phone: (435) 644-2672

• Grand Staircase-Escalante Interagency Visitor Center, 755 W Main, Escalante, UT 84726; phone: (435) 826-5499

• Hovenweep National Monument, McElmo Route, Cortez, CO 81321; phone: (970) 749-0510 (Cellular), (435) 459-4344 (within Utah); e-mail: HOVE_ranger_activities@nps.gov (Mailing address: Hovenweep Road-San Juan County Road 212, Montezuma Creek, UT 84534)

• Natural Bridges National Monument, P.O. Box 1, Lake Powell, UT 84533; phone: (435) 692-1234

• Rainbow Bridge National Monument, P.O. Box 1507, Page, AZ 86040; phone: (520) 608-6404; 24-Hour Emergency: (800) 582-4351; access from the Navajo Nation, (520) 871-6636 or (520) 871-6647

• Timpanogos Cave National Monument, R.R. 3, Box 200, American Fork, UT 84003; phone: Visitor Center/Information (801) 756-5238, Administrative Offices (801) 756-5239

National Parks

• Arches National Park, P.O. Box 907, Moab, UT 84532; phone: (435) 719-2299; TTY: (435) 719-2319; TDD: (435) 259-5279; e-mail: archinfo@nps.gov

• Bryce Canyon National Park, P.O. Box 170001, Bryce Canyon, Utah 84717-0001; phone: (435) 834-5322; fax: (435) 834-4102

• Canyonlands National Park, 2282 S. West Resource Blvd., Moab, UT 84532-3298; phone: (435) 719-2313

• Capitol Reef National Park, HC 70 Box 15, Torrey, UT 84775; phone: (435) 425-3791; e-mail: care_superintendent@nps.gov

• Zion National Park, P.O. Box 1099, Springdale, UT 84767; phone: (435) 772-3256 (24-hour recorded information)

National Recreation Areas

• Flaming Gorge National Recreation Area, Box 279, Manila, UT 84046; phone (435) 789-1181 or 784-3445; fax: (435) 781-5295

• Glen Canyon National Recreation Area , P. O. Box 1507, Page, AZ 86040; phone: General Information (520) 608-6404, Headquarters (520) 608-6200, 24-Hour Emergency (800) 582-4351

• Golden Spike National Historic Site, P.O. Box 897, Brigham City, UT 84302, phone: (435) 471-2341 Ext. 18 or 21; fax: (435) 471-2209

Over-the-Border Destinations

• Grand Canyon National Park, P.O. Box 129, Grand Canyon, AZ 86023; phone: (520) 638-7888

• Grand Teton National Park, P.O. Drawer 170, Moose, WY 83012-0170; phone: (307) 739-3300

• Great Basin National Park, National Park Service, Baker, NV 89311; phone: (702) 234-7331; Advance Lehman Cave ticket sales, summer only: (775) 234-7331 ext. 242

• Wind River Mountains, Wyoming: Area tourist information (800) 645-6233

• Wind River Mountains: Shoshone National Forest, USDA Forest Service, 1808 Meadow Lane, Cody, WY 82414; phone: 307-527-6241; e-mail: Information/r2_shoshone@fs.fed.us; Washakie Ranger District (307) 332-5460

• Wind River Mountains: Bridger-Teton National Forest, USDA Forest Service, P.O. Box 1888, Jackson, WY 83001; phone: (307) 739-5500; fax: (307) 739-5010

• Yellowstone National Park, National Park Service, P.O. Box 168, Yellowstone, WY 82190; phone: (307) 344-7381; TDD (307)344-2386

State of Utah Fish Hatcheries

• Brood Station, 2550 South Bicknell Circle, Bicknell, UT 84715; phone: (435) 425-3547 (Tours by appointment only)

• Fountain Green Hatchery, 700 North Big Springs Road, Fountain Green, UT 84632; phone: (435) 445-3472

• Glenwood Hatchery, 5700 East Hatchery Road, Glenwood, UT 84730; phone: (435) 896-5218

• Kamas Hatchery, 2722 East Mirror Lake Hwy., Kamas, UT 84036; phone: (435) 783-4883

• Loa Hatchery, 2100 North 300 West, Loa, UT 84747; phone: (435) 836-2858 (Tours by appointment only)

• Mammoth Creek Hatchery, 1318 South, Fish Hatchery, Hatch, UT 84735; phone: (435) 735-4200

• Mantua Hatchery, 555 East Fish Hatchery Road, Mantua, UT 84324; phone: (435) 723-6579

• Midway Hatchery, 907 South Center Street, Midway, UT 84049; phone: (435) 654-0282

• Springville Hatchery, 1000 North Main, Springville, UT 84663; phone: (801) 489-4421

• Whiterocks Hatchery, HCR 67, north of Whiterocks, UT 84085; phone: (435) 353-4855

U.S. Forest Service

INTERMOUNTAIN REGION:

• Federal Office Building, 324 25th Street, Ogden, UT 84401, 8 a.m. to 4:15 p.m. Mountain Time; visitor services phone: (801) 625-5358; fax: (801) 625-5127

ASHLEY NATIONAL FOREST

- 355 North Vernal Ave.,Vernal, UT 84078; phone: (801) 789-1181; fax: (801) 781-5142

Ranger Districts:

- Duchesne: P.O. Box 981, 85 West Main, Duchesne, UT 8402; phone: (435) 738-2482; fax: (435) 781-5215
- Roosevelt: P.O. Box 333-6, 244 West Hwy. 40, Roosevelt, UT 84066, phone: (435) 722-5018; fax: (435) 781-5237
- Vernal: 355 N. Vernal Ave., Vernal, UT 84078; phone: (435) 789-1181; fax: (435) 781-5142

DIXIE NATIONAL FOREST

- 82 North 100 East , Cedar City, UT 84720-2686; phone: (435) 865-3700; fax: (435) 865-3791

Ranger Districts:

- Cedar City: P.O. Box 627, 82 North 100 East, Cedar City, UT 84720; phone: (435) 865-3200; fax: (435) 865-3291
- Escalante: 755 West Main, Federal Building, Escalante, UT 84726; phone: (435) 826-5400; fax: (435) 826-5491
- Pine Valley: 196 East Tabernacle, Room 40, St. George, UT 84770; phone: (435) 652-3100; fax (435) 652-3191
- Powell: P.O. Box 80, 255 East Center, Panguitch, UT 84759; phone: (435) 676-8815; fax: (435) 676-8407
- Teasdale: P.O. Box 90, 138 East Main, Teasdale, UT 84773; phone: (435) 425-3775; fax (435) 425-3702

FISHLAKE NATIONAL FOREST

- 115 East 900 North , Richfield, UT 84701; phone: (435) 896-9233; fax: (435) 896-9347

Ranger Districts:

- Beaver: P.O. Box E, 575 South Main, Beaver, UT 84713, phone: (435) 438-2436; fax: (435) 438-1242
- Fillmore: P.O. Box 265, 390 South Main, Fillmore, UT 84631; phone: (435) 743-5721; fax: (435) 743-4113
- Loa: Marvin R. Turner, P.O. Box 129, 138 South Main, Loa, UT 84747, phone: (435) 836-2811; fax: (435) 836-2366
- Richfield: 115 East 900 North, Richfield, UT 84701; phone: (435) 896-9233; fax: (435) 896-9347

MANTI-LA SAL NATIONAL FOREST

• 599 West Price River Drive, Price, UT 84501; phone: (435) 637-2817; fax: (435) 637-4940

Ranger Districts:

• Ferron: P.O. Box 310, 115 West Canyon Road, Ferron, UT 84523; phone: (435) 384-2372; fax: (435) 384-3296

• Moab: P.O. Box 386, 2290 South West Resource Blvd., Moab, UT 84532; phone: (435) 259-7155; fax: (435) 259-7737

• Monticello: P.O. Box 820, 496 East Central, Monticello, UT 84535; phone: (435) 587-2041; fax: (435) 587-2637

• Price: 599 West Price River Drive, Price, UT 84501; phone: (435) 637-2817; fax: (435) 637-4940

• Sanpete: 540 North Main Street #32-14, Ephraim, UT 84627; phone: (435) 283-4151; fax: (435) 283-5616

UINTA NATIONAL FOREST

• 88 West 100 North, Provo, UT 84601; phone: (801) 342-5100; fax: (801) 342-5144

Ranger Districts:

• Heber: P.O. Box 190, 2460 South Hwy. 40, Heber, UT 84032; phone: (801) 654-0470; fax: (801) 654-5772

• Pleasant Grove: 390 North 100 East, Pleasant Grove, UT 84062; phone: (801) 342-5240; fax: (801) 342-5244

• Spanish Fork: 44 West 400 North, Spanish Fork, UT 84660; phone: (801) 342-5260; fax: (801) 342-5244

WASATCH-CACHE NATIONAL FOREST

• 8236 Federal Building,125 South State Street, Salt Lake City, UT 84138; phone: (801) 524-3900; fax: (801) 524-3172

Ranger Districts:

• Evanston: P.O. Box 1880, 1565 Hwy. 150 South, Suite A, Evanston, WY 82931-1880; phone: (307) 789-3194; fax: (307) 789-8639

• Kamas: P.O. Box 68, 50 East Center Street, Kamas, UT 84036; phone: (435) 783-4338, FTS: (801) 908-2030; fax: (435) 783-2981

• Logan: 1500 East, Hwy. 89, Logan, UT 8432; phone: (435) 755-3620; fax: (435) 755-3639

- Mountain View: P.O. Box 129, Lone Tree Road, Hwy.. 44, Mountain View, WY 82939; phone: (307) 782-6555; fax: (307) 782-7152

- Ogden: 507 25th Street, Suite 103, Ogden, UT 84402; phone: (801) 625-5112; fax: (801) 625-5914

- Salt Lake: 6944 South 3000 East, Salt Lake City, UT 84121; phone: (801) 733-2660; fax: (801) 733-2699

Utah State Parks and Recreation

- Boating information: (800) 743-3792

- OHV/ATV information: (800) 648-7433

- Salt Lake Office, P.O. Box 146001, 1594 West North Temple, Suite 116, Salt Lake City, UT 84114-6001; phone: (801) 538-7220

- Northwest Region, 1084 North Redwood Road, Salt Lake City, UT 84116; phone: (801) 533-5127

- Northeast Region, SR 319, 777 West Box 3, Heber, UT 84032; phone: (435) 649-9109

- Southeast Region, 1165 South Hwy. 191, Suite 7, Moab, UT 84532; phone: (435) 259-3750

- Southwest Region, 585 North Main, Cedar City, UT 84720; (435) 586-4497

World Wide Web Resources

Internet sites for more information on recreational opportunities, destinations and facilities:

- Amazing Outdoors (comprehensive outdoors information about Utah and neighboring areas): www.AmazingOutdoors.com

- Bureau of Land Management, national site: www.blm.gov/nhp/index.htm

- Bureau of Land Management, Utah: www.ut.blm.gov

- National Forest Service: www.fs.fed.us

- National Park Service: www.nps.gov;

- National Weather Service: www.nws.noaa.gov/,

- Recreation.gov — Information about recreational activities on federal lands (including National Park Service, BLM, Bureau of Reclamation and U.S. Fish & Wildlife land): www.recreation.gov

- River Digest - Utah: www.river-management.org/digest/utahdigest.html

- *Utah Outdoors* magazine: www.UtahOutdoors.com
- Utah State Parks: parks.state.ut.us (no "www")
- Utah Wildlife Resources: www.nr.state.ut.us/dwr/dwr.htm
- Utah Department of Natural Resources: www.nr.state.ut.us/default.htm
- Utah Travel Council — Can assist with trip planning, but lists primarily private campgrounds: utah.com/ (no "www")

INDEX

General information and locations

(Cities, forests, monuments, parks, recreation areas)

CAMPGROUNDS / RV PARKS – BY REGION

Northern Region

Over-the-Border Destinations

About the senior writer

Gaylen Webb is an avid outdoors enthusiast and native Utahn living in northern Utah.

After developing claustrophobia while living in Texas and Missouri, where "public land" does not exist, he returned to Utah, where he and his family enjoy the wide open spaces and the freedom to wander without trespassing.

Gaylen has a degree in journalism from Brigham Young University, and is currently working on a "Schlepper's Guide to the Uintas."